The Red Flags of a Narcissist

The Red Flags of a Narcissist

A Comprehensive Guide to Help You Avoid Narcissists and Other Types of Manipulative, Controlling, or Abusive People

by
Dana Morningstar

Other Books by the Author

Start Here: A Crash Course in Understanding, Navigating, and Healing from Narcissistic Abuse

Out of the Fog: Moving from Confusion to Clarity After Narcissistic Abuse

The Narcissist's Playbook: How to Identify, Disarm, and Protect Yourself from Narcissists, Sociopaths, Psychopaths, and Other Types of Manipulative and Abusive People

Dear Dana: FAQs About Dating After Narcissistic Abuse

Insight Journal: A Three-Year Journal

The Five-Minute Gratitude Journal: A One-Year Journal

Dedication

To my mother and brother, whose unwavering love and support gave me the strength to rebuild my life and find my voice again. You never stopped believing in me, even when I had. Your patience during my healing process and your gentle guidance helped me remember who I was before I lost myself.

To Marisol, my dear friend and editor, whose patience, insight, and encouragement helped shape these words into something that might help others. You are the best sounding board a writer could hope to have. Your thoughtful feedback and careful attention to every detail made this book immeasurably better, and your friendship made the entire process less lonely.

To Darren, one of the best friends a person could have. Thank you for all of your encouragement over the years, for listening without judgment, and for reminding me of my worth when I had forgotten it myself. Your friendship has been a constant source of light during the darkest times.

And to everyone who has experienced the confusion and pain of loving someone incapable of loving them back: may you find the clarity and courage to choose yourself.

COPYRIGHT

Disclaimer

This book is intended for educational and informational purposes only and is not intended to diagnose, treat, cure, or prevent any medical or psychological condition.

All names, identifying details, and personal examples have been changed to protect the privacy and confidentiality of individuals involved, unless they are matters of public record or my own experiences. Any resemblance to actual persons, living or deceased, or to actual events is purely coincidental.

If you are in immediate danger or experiencing thoughts of self-harm, please contact emergency services or call the National Suicide Prevention Lifeline at 988, or the National Domestic Violence Hotline at 1-800-799-7233.

Table of Contents

Part 3: Putting it All Together 296

Part 4: Moving Forward 322

Introduction

Narcissism. It's a word we hear so often nowadays, yet few are aware of its destructive nature anymore. That is, unless they've had dealings with a narcissist in some way, then they'll be all too familiar with the devastation they can cause and how bleak a relationship with one is.

Fortunately, with the spread of social media, there has also been greater social awareness for the understanding of narcissism. One of the positives of this is that discussions of abuse have moved away from physical abuse as the singular "real" form of abuse, to the recognition of how the more insidious forms of abuse—like emotional and psychological abuse—can be equally as destructive and potentially lethal.

If you've opened this book, you're likely looking for answers. Maybe you've been trapped in a relationship that made you feel lost, depleted, and doubting your own sanity. Or perhaps you're attempting to make sense of the behavior of someone in your life—a partner, family member, friend, or colleague—whose actions have left you feeling confused and hurt. The progression of narcissistic abuse is typically a lonely one, filled with self-doubt and isolation. The intent of this book is to shed light on this complex and harmful dynamic, to allow you to understand the indicators and, most importantly, to navigate your way towards healing.

It is a gut-wrenching experience to love or live with someone who has narcissistic leanings. You will constantly be walking on eggshells, never knowing when you will annoy them and trigger one of their tantrums or get rejected by them. The emotional roller coaster of their volatile moods—from warm to cold, from supportive to demeaning—constantly keeps you off balance. Targets frequently state they feel like they're losing their minds, asking themselves if they're going crazy due to the constant gaslighting and manipulation.

The isolation that accompanies narcissistic abuse is perhaps one of its most devastating aspects. You may have noticed your support system slowly eroding as the narcissist in your life worked to separate you from friends and family. When you finally gather the courage to speak up, you're often met with disbelief: "But they seem so charming and caring." This stark disconnect between the narcissist's public persona and private behavior uniquely compounds trauma, leaving you not only isolated but questioning your own perceptions.

If you're reading this because you have a "problematic person" in your life, you are most likely feeling physically exhausted and emotionally depleted. Having a narcissist in your life creates a state of chronic hypervigilance. Your nervous system is constantly on alert as you observe their moods, anticipate their needs, and try to prevent their next eruption. This chronic stress response manifests both psychologically and physiologically. Along with depression and anxiety, you may also experience insomnia, gastrointestinal issues, chronic pain, and a host of other symptoms that mainstream medicine can't seem to figure out. What most don't realize is that these physical symptoms of trauma persist long after the relationship ends, leaving many survivors feeling traumatized and confused as to why.

There may also be financial or career consequences—which many survivors are ashamed to share—and these financial hardships can be severe. Perhaps you've found yourself financially dependent on the narcissist after they pressured you to quit your job, undermined your career prospects, or even insisted or guilted you into giving them a large portion of your money.

Perhaps your work performance has suffered due to the constant emotional turmoil at home, or you've missed opportunities for advancement because the narcissist in your life couldn't tolerate your success. The economic impact of these relationships can leave targets feeling, or actually being, financially trapped and with limited options for escape.

If any of this describes you or your situation, please know that you aren't alone. In the following chapters, we'll explore the nature of narcissism, the insidious progression of narcissistic abuse, and most importantly, practical strategies for recovery. Whether you're still in the relationship or have already left, whether the narcissist in your life is a romantic partner, family member, or colleague, this book offers a roadmap to understanding, healing, and moving forward. You are not alone on this path, and with each page, I hope you'll find not only insight but also the reassurance that a healthier, more peaceful life awaits you on the other side of this experience.

Disclaimer

While this book primarily explores the red flags of a narcissist in intimate relationships, it's crucial to understand that narcissistic abuse can occur in any dynamic between two people. Abusive people exist in every gender, sexuality, nationality, profession, socioeconomic status, education level, race, and religion. They can be family members, friends, colleagues, neighbors, classmates, or anyone else.

To make these shared experiences more inclusive, I've used quite a few gender-neutral names and made sure to present both men and women in the role of abuser and target. I did this because abusive relationships are inherently confusing, and the traditional narrative of abuse—a man abusing a woman—can make it harder for those outside this dynamic to recognize their experience. For example, men may struggle to acknowledge abuse from women or the other men in their lives, just as women may have difficulty recognizing abuse from other women. Similarly, people might not readily identify abuse from parents, friends, coworkers, or others outside the intimate partner context.

The fundamental truth is this: while the gender of the abuser and their role in our lives may vary, the patterns of manipulative and abusive behavior remain remarkably consistent. I encourage you to focus on these behavioral patterns rather than the specific characters or relationships in these stories.

For transparency, the personal narratives in this book are based on actual events. However, when the story is neither my own nor public knowledge, I have altered identifying details to protect privacy.

Part 1: Understanding Narcissism and Recognizing Danger

CHAPTER 1

What is a Narcissist?

The word "narcissist" comes from the Greek myth of Narcissus. Narcissus was a stunningly handsome young man who fell in love with his reflection in a pool of water. Indifferent to the affections of others, Narcissus became so captivated by his image that he could not look away. Consumed by desire for the reflection he cannot possess, he ultimately wastes away. Depending on which version of the myth you read, he either dies beside the pool or transforms into the narcissus flower. Either way, things don't end well for him. The myth of Narcissus serves as a cautionary tale about the dangers of self-absorption. At first glance, we can see why narcissists are named after Narcissus. However, the word "narcissist," and even the Greek myth from which it originates, doesn't begin to capture the damage that a narcissist's level of self-absorption does to others.

Narcissistic Personality Disorder (NPD)

Narcissistic Personality Disorder is defined in the Diagnostic and Statistical Manual of Mental Disorders, Fifth Edition (DSM-5) as a pervasive pattern of grandiosity (in fantasy or behavior), need for admiration, and lack of empathy, with onset by early adulthood and present in a variety of contexts. For a diagnosis to be made, an individual must meet at least 5 of the following 9 criteria:

1. **Grandiose sense of self-importance** – Exaggerating achievements and talents, expecting to be recognized as superior without commensurate achievements

2. **Preoccupation with fantasies** of unlimited success, power, brilliance, beauty, or ideal love

3. **Belief in being "special" and unique** - Should only associate with other special or high-status people or institutions

4. **Need for excessive admiration** - Constantly seeking praise, validation, and attention from others

5. **Sense of entitlement** - Unreasonable expectations of especially favorable treatment or automatic compliance with their expectations

6. **Interpersonally exploitative behavior** - Taking advantage of others to achieve their own ends

7. **Lack of empathy** - Unwilling to recognize or identify with the feelings and needs of others

8. **Envy of others** - Either feeling envious of what others have or believing that others are envious of them

9. **Arrogant, haughty behaviors or attitudes** - Displaying condescending, superior, or dismissive behavior toward others

NPD is found in 1%–2% of the general population and is more common among males than females. The disorder has highly variable presentations, with individuals potentially being grandiose or self-loathing, extraverted or socially isolated.

Antisocial Personality Disorder (ASPD)

Antisocial Personality Disorder is characterized by a pervasive pattern of disregard for and violation of the rights of others, with this behavior beginning by age 15 and present in various contexts. For diagnosis, an individual must be at least 18 years old and show three or more of the following behaviors:

1. **Failure to conform to social norms** concerning lawful behaviors, such as performing acts that are grounds for arrest

2. **Deceitfulness** - Repeated lying, use of aliases, or conning others for personal profit or pleasure

3. **Impulsivity** or failure to plan ahead

4. **Irritability and aggressiveness** - Repeated physical fights or assaults

5. **Reckless disregard for safety** of self or others

6. **Consistent irresponsibility** - Repeated failure to sustain consistent work behavior or honor financial obligations

7. **Lack of remorse** - Being indifferent to or rationalizing having hurt, mistreated, or stolen from another person

Additionally, there must be evidence of conduct disorder with onset before age 15, and the antisocial behavior cannot occur exclusively during episodes of schizophrenia or bipolar disorder.

ASPD affects an estimated 2-5% of the population and is more common among males than females (3:1 ratio). About half of those with substance use disorders meet criteria for ASPD, and the disorder often co-occurs with other mental health conditions.

Important Distinctions

While both disorders involve problematic interpersonal behavior, there are key differences:

- **NPD** is primarily characterized by grandiosity, need for admiration, and lack of empathy, with behavior often driven by maintaining a superior self-image

- **ASPD** is characterized by consistent disregard for others' rights and social norms, with behavior often involving exploitation, aggression, and criminal activity

How and Where Psychopathy Fits In

It's worth noting that psychopathy, while related to ASPD, is not a clinical diagnosis in psychiatric settings but rather is assessed using specialized tools like the Psychopathy Checklist-Revised (PCL-R). About 75% of those incarcerated may meet ASPD criteria, but only about 15% meet criteria for psychopathy.

It's also worth noting that mental health professionals outside and inside of the prison system don't use this checklist on a regular basis, if at all. There are several reasons for this:

First, it's not a formal diagnosis, which is often needed for treatment and billing purposes. Second, there is significant overlap with ASPD. Third, because there is significant overlap, the subtle distinctions, while interesting, aren't really relevant when it comes to treatment, especially in jail, as the mental health services are limited and often inadequate due to the challenges of the prison system.

And even if there was a bounty of individual therapy available, those with ASPD or psychopathy would most likely be uninterested in attending. That is, of course, unless it benefited them in some way such as helping get them an early release.

Unfortunately, the focus of the jail/prison system in the US is to be punitive and not restorative. Meaning, the focus is on punishment, not providing the tools (mental health or otherwise) to help prisoners reform their lives in any meaningful way. Frankly, the fact that any prisoner who serves their time and then is released into society has been able to become a productive member of society says a lot more about their determination than it does about the mental health system.

Both conditions can involve manipulation and lack of empathy, but the underlying motivations and presentations differ significantly.

Diagnostic Framework

- **ASPD** is an official clinical diagnosis in the DSM-5 that can be made by mental health professionals

- **Psychopathy** is not a formal medical diagnosis but rather is assessed using specialized research tools, primarily the Psychopathy Checklist-Revised (PCL-R) created by Dr. Robert Hare

ASPD focuses on observable behaviors:

- Failure to conform to social norms, deceitfulness, impulsivity, aggression, reckless disregard for safety, irresponsibility, and lack of remorse

- Emphasis on antisocial conduct and rule-breaking behaviors

- Must have evidence of conduct disorder before age 15

Psychopathy emphasizes personality traits and emotional deficits:

- Inability to experience emotions as others do and engagement in antisocial behaviors

- Includes traits like superficial charm, grandiose self-worth, pathological lying, cunning/manipulative behavior

- Shallow emotions, lack of empathy, failure to accept responsibility

- More focus on the emotional and interpersonal dysfunction

Emotional Capacity

- **ASPD** individuals may still have some capacity for genuine emotions and attachments, though impaired

- **Psychopathy** involves more profound emotional deficits, including shallow emotions and an inability to form genuine emotional connections. Psychopathy is generally considered much more treatment-resistant due to the deeper personality and emotional deficits

In essence, you can think of psychopathy as a more severe and specific subset that includes both the behavioral problems of ASPD plus significant emotional and interpersonal deficits. The concept of psychopathy was in part introduced because ASPD was of limited use in correctional settings, as ASPD was too broad and didn't capture the most dangerous individuals who showed the deeper personality disturbances that psychopathy measures.

Additionally, while all those with Antisocial Personality Disorder and Psychopathy are, at the core, narcissists, not all narcissists would be considered to have ASPD or Psychopathy. And because there is significant overlap between all three of these personality disorders, the red flags in this book aim to cover a wide range of problematic behavior that is found among all of them. The key takeaway is that whether someone meets the criteria for NPD, ASPD, psychopathy, or simply displays narcissistic traits, the fundamental problem remains the same: their mistreatment of others.

So, while many focus on the narcissist's ego and arrogance, it's more important to recognize the consequences of their selfishness: their inability to feel genuine remorse or empathy for the pain they cause others. However, the challenge in assessing whether someone actually has genuine empathy and remorse is crazymaking within itself. The reason being, a highly manipulative narcissist can fake empathy and remorse when it benefits them. They often do this to avoid trouble or to further their agenda, while simultaneously getting better at hiding what they are up to. Additionally, emotional traits like empathy are complex to measure, and outside of catching them again in bad behavior, there's no way to tell if their remorse is genuine or just another manipulation tactic.

At first glance, narcissists may appear confident, charming, and charismatic; all traits that draw us in. Yet beneath these traits lies a darker reality: a person wracked by an insatiable hunger for praise, power, and validation at the expense of others. Beneath this personable exterior is a profoundly and pathologically self-centered person whose conduct wears on relationships, destroys careers, and causes extreme harm to the mental health of those around them. However, unlike the myth, it's those around the narcissist who suffer. And that's the sad reality of narcissism: the people around the narcissist get hurt the worst while the narcissist does not care and is not bothered by the damage they cause. The impact is usually devastating, with the victims left to question what occurred, doubting their perception of reality and feeling partially or wholly to blame.

A Note About Terminology and Language

When discussing abusive relationship patterns and destructiveness, "narcissist" is frequently used to describe a specific collection of abusive behaviors. My use of the term "narcissist" refers more to narcissistic behavior than it does to a clinical diagnosis. I use the word "narcissist" for two reasons: first, it describes the self-serving, manipulative, entitled, and abusive behavior pattern we are to explore. And second, it's much easier to read than "the individual showing narcissistic or otherwise problematic behavior."

Recognizing the Harm

The focus of this book isn't for you to try and figure out if the problematic person in your life has NPD, ASPD, or psychopathy. My goal is for you to spot problematic behavior regardless of whether there is a diagnosis involved, because many times, and for a variety of reasons, there won't be. In other words, the diagnosis of NPD or ASPD is only a pointer to certain problematic behaviors. Those behaviors can and do exist outside of a diagnosis.

So, whether someone fits the criteria for NPD, ASPD, or not, the focus should always be on the impact their actions have and how to protect your well-being in the face of abusive behavior. I say this because an abusive relationship is a confusing relationship, and frankly, I'd go so far as to say that most, if not all, "confusing" relationships have elements of manipulation and abuse in them. During the manipulation and abuse, so much confusion can be present that the target might think that they, not the manipulator, are the problem. Or, the target may see the problematic behavior for what it is, but think that given enough love, understanding, therapy, rehab, or religion that this person can change. This is dangerous thinking, and it keeps people stuck. The reality is that when it comes to manipulative and abusive people, their behavior tends to get worse with time, not better.

I think most anyone who has ever been in a relationship with a narcissist or other type of manipulative person understands why so many people stay. After all, most narcissists don't show their true colors immediately; and even when those red flags surface, they can be easy to dismiss. And when the cracks in their mask do start to show, the target has the same thought process that most people have which is to want to get their loved one help. And they might even see positive changes happen...but nothing that lasts. When the narcissist is on their best behavior, it can seem like proof that change is possible. Targets often mistake these moments for real progress, believing the relationship is, or can be, fixed. After all, if narcissists can be decent sometimes, surely, they have the capacity to have a moral compass or appropriate behavior on a consistent basis, right? Unfortunately, narcissists are experts at manipulation, and any positive behavior is usually meant to set the stage for future manipulation. Recognizing problematic behavior is crucial for protecting yourself.

CHAPTER 2

How Red Flags Feel

Understanding the Nature of Red Flags

Before we can heed the warning of a red flag, we must first understand what a red flag is and how they come across. When we hear the term "red flag," we typically imagine something obvious: a clear, unmistakable warning sign of danger. However, the reality is that most red flags are felt rather than seen.

Instead of dramatic revelations, red flags often come across as subtle sensations: a slight uneasiness in your stomach, a whisper of doubt in your mind, or that inexplicable feeling that something doesn't feel quite right. These feelings might seem insignificant in the moment, so they are easily dismissed as paranoia or oversensitivity.

Our intuition, however, is far more sophisticated than we give it credit for. Your subconscious mind processes millions of pieces of data per second, picking up on subtle behavioral cues and inconsistencies that your conscious mind hasn't yet registered. When something feels "off," your subconscious has often noticed patterns that your logical mind is still trying to piece together.

The Five Stages of the Progression of a Red Flag

Understanding how warning signs progress can help you recognize and respond to them before they become entrenched patterns. Like a slowly heating pot of water, the progression from mild concern to serious problem often happens so gradually that we don't realize we're in trouble until we're immersed in it.

Stage 1: Confusion.

The first warning signs are often so subtle they're easy to dismiss. Confusion is always the first sign. It's that moment when something doesn't quite add up and you find yourself thinking **"Huh, that's weird"** or **"Wow, what the hell?!"**

This initial confusion manifests as that slight pause where you're trying to process what just happened. It's the mental equivalent of a record scratch—a brief moment where the flow of normal interaction stops because something feels off. You might think "Huh, that's strange" or "Huh, I didn't expect that response" or simply "Huh..." as your brain tries to make sense of an inconsistency.

Recognizing Subtle Warning Signs

These can manifest as a flash of intense anger over seemingly nothing—like when you mention working late with a colleague and a flash of anger crosses over your partner's face. A person sending you a text or meme that is off-putting or concerning, for example sending a video clip of a con artist and saying that person is their spirit animal (that they aspire to be like that person). Or a jealous or controlling comment disguised as concern, such as "I don't like you going out with your friends; they are a bad influence on you." Sometimes it's catching a look of pure disgust or contempt directed at someone when the person thinks no one is watching, only to see them immediately switch back to a normal expression when they realize they've been seen.

Other warning signs include someone disregarding your boundaries and pressuring you to do something you're uncomfortable with—continuing to push after you've said no, making you feel guilty for having limits, accusing you of doing things you aren't doing, or acting like your boundaries are unreasonable. Or, perhaps, it's the adult who goes above and beyond for your child, taking an almost excessive interest in them—offering special treats, one-on-one time, or gifts that seem disproportionate to their relationship with your family. Even something as mundane as a car accident can be a red flag if it feels intentional, which is a tactic predators sometimes use as a way to get unsuspecting targets out of their cars in isolated areas.

And sometimes, a red flag manifests as a person giving you the creeps for a reason you can't pinpoint. For example, in 1978, Cheryl Bradshaw chose Rodney Alcala as her date on the TV show "The Dating Game." Despite his charming performance that won him the date, Bradshaw later said, "I started to feel ill. He was acting really creepy. I turned down his offer. I didn't want to see him again." She told the show's producer, "There's weird vibes that are coming off of him. He's very strange. I am not comfortable." Her instincts were right. Alcala was in the middle of a murder spree and was later convicted of seven murders, though investigators believe he may have killed as many as 130 people. Bradshaw's willingness to trust her gut feeling likely saved her life.

These moments often happen so quickly that you might convince yourself you imagined them or that you're being too sensitive. But your subconscious picked up on something important. Trust that initial "Huh..." feeling—it's your internal warning system working exactly as it should.

However, sometimes the mask slips dramatically, and you get an immediate "Wow, what the hell?!" moment. These might include someone violently slamming a door when they've never shown anger like that before; someone who slaps you when the relationship has previously been good; a person who suddenly screams at you over something trivial; someone who punches a wall during what seemed like a normal disagreement; a friend who suddenly makes a cruel, cutting remark which is completely out of character for them; or someone who abruptly threatens you when you've never seen this side of them before. These explosive moments are your psyche's alarm bells going off at full volume.

Regardless of how the red flag comes across, it's not uncommon for people to override their intuition with thoughts like "I'm being too sensitive" or "They didn't mean to come across that way." We dismiss our concerns because things aren't always bad, or because we hope we're wrong about this being a problem. But that initial "Huh..." moment is your subconscious picking up on something important—don't dismiss it too quickly. And those "What the hell?!" moments should never be minimized or excused away, no matter how much someone apologizes afterward.

Stage 2: Growing Unease

If you minimize your concerns, feelings of discomfort begin to accumulate. This stage is characterized by an increasing sense of "cognitive dissonance," which is the psychological discomfort that occurs when we want a situation to be different than it is.

You might find yourself keeping a mental list of odd moments you can't quite explain, experiencing frequent confusion about their behavior, feeling a persistent sense that something is "off," feeling anxious before or after interactions, or feeling you need to explain or justify their behavior to others.

During this phase, the problematic behavior may increase in frequency but might not necessarily increase in intensity. While the picture isn't yet clear, the fact that there's a problem is starting to come into focus, and it's becoming harder to ignore that something feels wrong.

Stage 3: The Fog of Self-Doubt

This stage marks a critical turning point where you begin to question your grasp of reality. The manipulation has started to erode your ability to trust your judgment or perception of events.

You question your memory of events, wonder if your standards are unreasonable, feel responsible for other people's behavior, start to doubt your judgment in different areas of life, experience increasing anxiety and depression, find yourself making excuses for the narcissist's behavior, and feel persistent guilt for having negative thoughts about the person.

This stage is particularly problematic because it often coincides with the manipulator's escalation of problematic behavior. As your self-doubt increases, and their problematic behavior starts to become their new normal, your acceptance of them pushing your boundaries grows stronger.

Stage 4: The Search for Clarity

Driven by mounting confusion and anxiety, you enter an active phase of seeking understanding. You extensively research toxic relationships, gaslighting, pathological lying, and other terms that fit your situation. You frequently talk with friends about what's going on and may begin journaling or seek professional counseling.

Some even grasp at autism as an explanation for the "unusual" behavior such as a lack of empathy or remorse—but that diagnosis doesn't begin capture your experience. Paradoxically, this search for clarity often leads to more confusion as you encounter conflicting advice and perspectives. Even if people tell you that your experiences are problematic, you may find yourself defending the problematic person by minimizing or justifying their behavior.

Stage 5: Walking on Eggshells

By this stage, the relationship has become a psychological minefield. You have developed an elaborate system of monitoring and modifying your behavior in an attempt to prevent problems. Daily life becomes an exhausting exercise in hypervigilance. You carefully choose words and actions to avoid triggering negative responses, maintain constant awareness of mood changes in the other person, find yourself rehashing conversations or arguments trying to figure out where things went wrong, feel exhausted from constantly thinking about this situation, experience physical symptoms of chronic stress, and stop reaching out to your support system because you feel ashamed that it's gone on for as long as it has.

Reactions and Sensations to Red Flags

Red flags manifest in your body long before your mind fully processes them. Learning to recognize these physical signals can serve as an early warning system:

- **Rehashing conversations: Wondering who has the problem—them or you**

- **Asking others about your situation in an attempt to understand it: Confusion abounds**

- **Stomach sensations:** Tightening, uneasiness, knots, nausea,

- **Heart rate changes:** Racing heart, skipped beats, or pounding

- **Breathing patterns:** Shallow breathing, holding your breath, or hyperventilation

- **Muscle tension:** Tightness in shoulders, jaw clenching, or overall rigidity

- **Energy shifts:** Sudden fatigue, restlessness, or feeling drained

- **Sleep disruption:** Difficulty falling asleep, staying asleep, or sleeping too much

- **Temperature changes:** Feeling hot, cold flashes, or sweating

But What if Everything Feels Like a Red Flag?

When you have an anxiety disorder or previous trauma, your internal warning system can get stuck on high alert, always looking for danger even when you're actually safe. This means your body might react just as strongly to something harmless as it would to a real threat. The feelings are exactly the same - your heart races, your chest gets tight, or you get that sick feeling in your stomach. This can make it really difficult to tell the difference between anxiety and your gut instinct actually warning you about something genuinely concerning. For people with anxiety, telling them to follow their gut instincts might mean that they'd never leave the house!

When trauma has changed how you detect threats, your gut might tell you that your new coworker is dangerous because they remind you of someone who hurt you before, that going to a party will be a disaster because past social events went badly, or that something bad is about to happen but you don't know what. The same system that's supposed to keep you safe can end up keeping you away from good opportunities, relationships, and experiences. So, what do you do?

The key lies in spotting important differences between anxiety-driven panic and real intuitive warnings. This takes practice, and doesn't always help, but you can develop this skill by paying close attention. *When anxiety takes over, it usually feels urgent and certain.* There's no doubt or hesitation, just a clear command like "don't do this," "stay away from that situation," or "you're in danger." These anxiety signals often focus on the same kinds of things over and over, and they want you to react right away for no particular reason you can pinpoint, or if you can pinpoint it, the reason is often disproportion to the feeling.

When Mental Health Episodes Affect Perception

Some other mental health challenges that can give a person a false positive when it comes to gut instincts would be Obsessive Compulsive Disorder (OCD) or psychosis. With OCD, there is chronic anxiety in certain areas of their life. It's the feeling of "if I don't act now, then something bad will happen." The differentiator is that the "act now" part usually means doing something repetitive and unrelated to the event.

For people who have experienced psychosis, mania, or other episodes that affect perception and thinking, distinguishing between genuine red flags and confusion created by mental health symptoms provides a different set of challenges. During these episodes, the confusion a person might feel isn't so much the "huh, that's odd" that comes from real intuition, but rather the feeling of disorienting confusion that comes from the brain processing information differently. Disorienting confusion tends to lead to the question of "what on Earth is happening?!" Reality starts to shift into something bizarre and possibly terrifying. You might feel certain that someone is dangerous or that a situation is threatening when that certainty is actually coming from paranoid thoughts, delusions, or altered perception rather than actual intuitive warnings.

The key difference is often in the type of the confusion (disorienting vs confusion that gives you pause) and what other symptoms are present. Mental health-related confusion typically comes with other signs you might recognize from past episodes, such as racing thoughts, usually elevated mood, reduced need (or lack of) sleep, feeling disconnected from reality, unusual coincidences seeming extremely meaningful, or thoughts that feel urgent and all-consuming but don't quite make sense when you try to explain them to someone else.

In contrast, genuine intuitive confusion tends to be more grounded. When we experience intuitive confusion and are able to be honest with ourselves, we can usually explain why something feels off, even if we can't pinpoint exactly what it is.

If you have a history of mental health episodes that affect your thinking, it can be helpful to have trusted friends or mental health professionals who can help you reality-check your perceptions when you're feeling uncertain about whether what you're sensing is real or related to your mental health.

Any of these added challenges can create a frustrating cycle where you question every uncomfortable feeling, wondering if you're being smart and careful or just letting fear control your choices. You might ignore real warning signs because you're used to your anxiety giving you a false alarm, or you might avoid anything that makes you uncomfortable at all, even when that discomfort doesn't actually mean danger.

Learning to tell the difference between trauma responses and mental health disorders and genuine gut warnings takes time. Often there is a need for professional help, and the practice of noticing the different qualities of these internal signals, such as the urgency versus the pause and the certainty versus the questioning. Doing this can help you figure out what these feelings are really telling you about a situation versus what they're telling you about how your nervous system is doing right now.

When Bias Masquerades as Intuition

Another layer that complicates trusting our gut feelings is recognizing when racism, prejudice, or unconscious bias might be influencing what we think are instinctive responses. Sometimes what feels like a "gut reaction" to avoid someone, or something is actually learned bias from our culture, family, or media consumption rather than genuine intuition about danger. This is especially important to examine when our discomfort centers around people who look different from us, come from different backgrounds, or belong to groups we've been taught to fear or distrust.

These biased reactions can feel very much like real intuition - they create the same physical sensations and sense of certainty. The difference is that bias-driven reactions tend to focus on someone's identity (their race, religion, appearance, accent, or social class) rather than their actual behavior or the specific situation. They often come with ready-made stories or assumptions about what "those people" are like, and they usually kick in immediately upon seeing someone rather than developing based on how the person actually acts.

To work through this, it helps to pause and ask yourself some honest questions when you have a strong negative gut reaction to someone: What specifically am I reacting to? Is it something they've actually done or said, or is it how they look or sound? Would I have the same reaction to someone who was the same skin color, religion, or socio-economic status as me who was acting the same way? Am I normally suspicious of people with differences like this? And, if so, why? Ask yourself, "Where did I learn to suspicious of people with differences like this?" Taking time to examine these reactions doesn't mean ignoring legitimate safety concerns. It means making sure your safety decisions are based on actual behavior and circumstances rather than stereotypes or prejudice.

Keep in mind that real gut feelings, on the other hand, *start with confusion and a moment where you pause.* True intuition stops you in your tracks; if only even for a few seconds, instead of demanding you react immediately. It feels more like "something doesn't feel right here," followed by "let me figure out what's going on" or "nah, I bet it's nothing" followed by a rationalization rather than no confusion, no pause, and, instead, an immediate and/or repetitive feeling of "danger, get out now."

Why Physical Responses Matter

Your body's warning system operates on multiple levels, from subtle physiological changes to more obvious emotional responses. Scientific research has shown that our brains can identify threats and make decisions before we're consciously aware of them. Studies using brain imaging technology have revealed that our neural circuits respond to danger signals milliseconds before we have conscious awareness of any threat.

The challenge is that modern life has trained many of us to override these natural warning systems in favor of politeness or social conformity. We ignore our discomfort to avoid appearing rude or judgmental, often to our detriment.

Learning to Honor Your Feelings

The good news is that you don't need to spend years cultivating self-esteem or assertiveness skills to keep yourself safe. Feeling anxiety and uneasiness is enough of a problem in itself for you to slow things down or stop them altogether. You don't need to know someone's intentions or whether their behavior will escalate. The fact that you have a "gut feeling" that something is off—that you feel anxious, unsettled, and at times afraid—is enough reason to take protective action.

CHAPTER 3

Spotting Problematic People

The Best Hiding Place for Evil is Behind Good

When Kerri Rawson discovered that her father, Dennis Rader, was the BTK killer (an acronym for "Bind, Torture, Kill" which was a name he gave himself), her world fell into shambles. How could the man who had shown her how to ride a bicycle, who was an active member of his church congregation, and who, by all accounts, was a good father, husband, and person have been responsible for a 30-year killing spree?

Her attempt to reconcile these two worlds (the loving father and the cold-blooded murderer) demonstrates one of life's most uncomfortable truths: the best hiding place for evil is behind good.

The discovery of these two very different sides to her father compelled her to question every childhood memory, every family photograph, and every moment of seeming tenderness. Trying to reconcile her father's actions was confusing and terrifying. While he assisted her with homework or went to her school functions, he was more than likely also planning his next killing, carefully documenting his crimes, and teasing the police with anonymous letters. The dual nature of his life (loving family man and vicious killer) illustrates how adept predators are at compartmentalizing their lives. This compartmentalization allows them to craft a veneer of respectability, enabling them to remain above suspicion, even in the eyes of those who know them best.

It's worth noting that Kerri is an absolutely amazing woman. She has gone on to transform her pain into her purpose, being an outspoken advocate for victims of abuse, crime, and trauma; and uses her experience to help others heal from violence and betrayal.

Beyond the Wolf in Sheep's Clothing: Understanding the Four Types of People

Here's the text broken into several paragraphs for better readability:

Most of us go through life operating on a fundamental assumption that people are who they appear to be. We trust the friendly neighbor, feel wary of the person with an unconventional appearance, and generally believe that someone's outward presentation reflects their true character. But this assumption can be one of the most dangerous mistakes we make.

The truth is that there's often a significant gap between how people present themselves and who they actually are beneath the surface. Understanding the reality that appearance and character can align or completely contradict each other is one of the most important protective skills you can develop.

When you learn to recognize these patterns, you'll be better equipped to identify genuine threats hiding behind friendly faces, appreciate good people who might look intimidating, and navigate relationships with greater wisdom and safety.

It's also worth noting that you don't owe anyone access to your life simply because they seem nice or because society tells you not to judge. If someone gives you an uncomfortable feeling or their appearance genuinely puts you off, it's perfectly acceptable to trust that instinct and keep your distance.

This isn't about being unfairly judgmental; it's about knowing what works for you and honoring your comfort levels. Your peace of mind and sense of safety matter more than being polite to everyone you encounter.

Wolf in Sheep's Clothing

These are the most dangerous individuals: people who are genuinely harmful but work meticulously to appear trustworthy, helpful, or charming. They understand that a benevolent facade is their most effective weapon for gaining access to victims. Think of the beloved neighbor everyone trusts who's secretly abusing their family, the respected coach exploiting young athletes, or figures like Ted Bundy, who volunteered at suicide hotlines while conducting murder sprees, or Bill Cosby, who spent decades as "America's Dad" while preying on women.

These predators actively cultivate positive personas, knowing that trustworthiness is their best camouflage. They're often described as "charismatic," "helpful," or "the last person you'd suspect"—precisely because they've invested enormous energy in appearing that way.

Sometimes people transition into this category through major life changes. A person might start as a sheep in sheep's clothing— genuinely good and appearing good—but develop a serious addiction that fundamentally alters their behavior and moral compass. They may begin lying, stealing, or manipulating loved ones to feed their addiction while maintaining their previously established reputation as trustworthy. Their friends and family continue to see them as the person they used to be, making it easier for them to exploit that trust. Similarly, someone might experience trauma, mental health crises, or other life circumstances that gradually shift their character while they work to maintain their positive public image.

Wolf in Wolf's Clothing

These are the obviously problematic people who look exactly like what they are. The aggressive person yelling at strangers, someone displaying threatening behavior, or individuals with clearly visible signs of instability fall into this category. They might have tattoos of serial killers or gang signs, or display other visual markers that signal genuine questionable behavior, danger or instability. While they can certainly be dangerous, they're actually less likely to cause widespread harm because most people instinctively know to maintain distance from them.

Sheep in Wolf's Clothing

These are fundamentally decent people who happen to look intimidating, unconventional, or threatening according to societal standards. The heavily tattooed person who rescues stray animals, the goth teenager who's incredibly kind and sensitive, or the person whose appearance defies conventional norms but whose character is solid. Society often unfairly judges these individuals as dangerous when they're completely harmless.

Sheep in Sheep's Clothing

These are genuinely good people who appear genuinely good. They represent the majority of humanity—regular folks whose outward appearance accurately reflects their character. The challenge is that from the outside, they can look remarkably similar to wolves in sheep's clothing until you get to know them better.

The Problem with First Impressions

This categorization reveals why first impressions can be so misleading and potentially dangerous. The person who triggers all your alarm bells might be completely harmless, while the person who seems absolutely wonderful could be someone you should avoid at all costs.

We're essentially trained to spot the snake in the street (obvious danger we can see coming) but miss the snake in the grass (hidden danger that's perfectly camouflaged). The snake in the street is aggressive, visibly threatening, and clearly dangerous. But the snake in the grass blends seamlessly into its surroundings, appearing harmless until it strikes.

The Importance of Graduated Trust and Continual Reevaluation

Given this reality, the concept of graduated trust becomes crucial. Rather than operating in binary mode—either fully trusting or completely distrusting someone—we need to develop a more nuanced approach that allows trust to build gradually over time and through consistent actions.

Graduated trust means:

• Starting with appropriate caution regardless of someone's appearance

• Allowing trust to develop based on consistent behavior patterns

• Paying attention to actions rather than just words

• Maintaining healthy boundaries until someone has proven themselves reliable

• Understanding that trust is earned through time and consistency, not granted based on charm or first impressions

This concept aligns with Brené Brown's "marble jar" metaphor for trust. The story of the marble jar comes from Brown's personal experience when her daughter, Ellen, was in the third grade. Ellen came home devastated after sharing something deeply personal with friends at school, only to have those friends betray her confidence. By the end of recess, the entire class knew her secret and was laughing and pointing at her. Ellen declared she would "never trust anyone again."

To help her daughter understand trust, Brown used the marble jar her teacher had in her classroom as a metaphor. The marble jar is where her teacher would add marbles when the kids made good choices together and removed them for poor choices. When filled, the class would get a pizza party. Brown explained to her daughter that trust is like a marble jar. We share personal things with others marble by marble. Over time, they've done thing after thing after thing where you realize, "I know I can share this with this person."

Like a marble jar that gets filled one marble at a time through small acts of trustworthiness and reliability, healthy relationships build trust gradually through consistent positive behaviors. However, it's crucial to understand that while trust is built marble by marble, it doesn't always get broken the same way. When someone engages in behavior that is problematic enough—betrayal, manipulation, or harm—we would be wise to dump out the entire jar, not empty it one marble at a time. Sometimes the behavior is so egregious that we don't just dump the jar out—we walk away from the relationship entirely. This isn't being unforgiving; it's recognizing that certain actions fundamentally violate the foundation of trust and require starting completely over, if at all.

Equally important is the ongoing process of reevaluation. Since people can move between categories throughout their lives, we must remain observant and willing to adjust our assessment of individuals based on new information and changing behaviors. If we are paying attention, we are continually reevaluating who is in our lives based on the information we have. This doesn't mean being paranoid or constantly suspicious, but rather staying alert to significant changes in people's behavior patterns, especially when those changes involve increased secrecy, manipulation, or harm to others. Someone who has been trustworthy for years might begin exhibiting concerning behaviors that signal a shift in their character or circumstances.

The Right to Be Discerning

It's important to understand that you don't owe everyone a chance to prove themselves. There's a significant difference between being judgmental and being discerning:

Being judgmental means judging a person or situation with a sense of moral superiority. The focus is on whether you determine them to be either good or bad.

Being discerning means making decisions about a person or situation based on your own safety, comfort level, and life experience. The focus is on what is in alignment with your wants and needs. There is no sense of moral superiority, and it's not about making the other person bad or wrong.

For example, you might encounter someone who could be a lovely person but has tattoos of serial killers, or looks a certain way that makes you uncomfortable. You don't need to judge them as bad or wrong. When you are discerning, you might determine that you aren't comfortable getting to know a person with these kinds of interests. Choosing not to invest time in finding out whether they're problematic isn't being unfairly judgmental—it's being appropriately discerning about your personal boundaries.

Your time, energy, and emotional safety are valuable resources. You have every right to be selective about how and with whom you share them. This doesn't mean being cruel or dismissive, but it does mean trusting your instincts and making choices that align with your comfort level and values.

Breaking Free from Dangerous Conditioning

The most dangerous aspect of our cultural conditioning is that the more someone defies our stereotype of what a threat looks like, the less likely we are to notice genuine warning signs. A child warned about "creepy men in vans offering candy" might not recognize danger when it comes from a friendly woman in a nice car asking them to look at a puppy.

To protect ourselves and our loved ones, we need to:

- Recognize that character and appearance don't always align

- Develop better instincts based on behavior patterns rather than surface presentation

- Practice graduated trust with everyone, regardless of how they appear

- Accept that being discerning about who we allow into our lives is not only acceptable but necessary

- Understand that some of the most dangerous people in society have invested heavily in appearing trustworthy

Your safety and peace of mind are more important than avoiding the possibility of hurting someone's feelings by being cautious. The goal isn't to become paranoid or closed off, but to develop a more sophisticated understanding of human nature that keeps you safe, while still allowing for meaningful connections with genuinely good people.

The Continuum of Narcissistic Behavior

Narcissistic behavior exists on a continuum ranging from obnoxious to dangerous and destructive to deadly. This continuum is fundamentally about self-orientation—how much someone prioritizes themselves over others.

Obnoxious narcissism is problematic but not necessarily dangerous. This might include the coworker who constantly steers conversations back to themselves, the friend who can't celebrate your achievements without making it about them, or the family member who turns every gathering into their personal stage.

Dangerous and destructive narcissism involves manipulation, emotional abuse, and systematic harm to others. These individuals don't just seek attention; they actively work to control, diminish, and emotionally or psychologically destroy others to maintain their sense of superiority.

Deadly narcissism represents the most extreme end, where individuals may engage in physical violence, stalking, or even murder due to a need for power and control.

Cultural Conditioning That Blinds Us

Even though we are taught at a young age not to take candy from strangers or not to open the door for someone we don't know, we are also taught to have manners, respect our elders, and not to judge others. These are essential skills for getting along well in society; however, outside of being told to avoid strangers when we are young, we aren't really taught how to protect ourselves when we are older.

Women's Conditioning Conflicts. Women are usually conditioned to be on the lookout for dangerous situations: we carry mace; we avoid dark parking lots and alleyways; if we're going on a date, we meet in a public place. However, we are also socialized to be accommodating and non-confrontational. The result is that if we encounter a potential threat, we often second-guess ourselves and hope we are making a big deal out of nothing because we don't want to cause a scene or come across as dramatic or difficult.

Men's False Confidence. Men have their own set of challenges regarding problematic people and situations. Men are conditioned to think that because women and children are the primary targets of violent acts, bad things won't happen to them. And even if they were to become a target, they'd be able to fight them off or somehow get away unharmed. This is especially the case for tall, muscular men, whose experience has consistently shown them that others are afraid of them. Society teaches men to be tough and to put on a brave face. These messages are dangerous because men tend to unnecessarily put themselves in harm's way, thinking they could or should be able to handle whatever problem there might be.

The Psychology of Denial

One of the more confounding aspects of human nature is how we manage to rationalize away warning signals, particularly when they involve people we care about. This isn't a personal failing; it's a deeply ingrained psychological mechanism that serves to protect our existing worldview and emotional investments.

When confronted with evidence that someone we trust or care for might be dangerous, our minds often go to extraordinary lengths to maintain our original perception of them. We make excuses, find alternative explanations, or refuse to acknowledge what's right in front of us. This is why family members of convicted killers often maintain their loved one's innocence even in the face of overwhelming evidence.

This resistance to acknowledging duality in human nature: that someone can be both kind and cruel, caring and dangerous, reflects our deep-seated need for a simpler, more manageable world. It's easier to believe in clear-cut heroes and villains than to accept that danger often comes wearing a mask of kindness.

When Hope Becomes Dangerous

Listening to the warnings of our intuition is increasingly harder the more emotionally or financially invested we are in something. Suppose the red flag comes from a parent, friend, co-worker, or lover, and we want to continue a relationship with them. If this is the case, then the more likely it is we will minimize and rationalize our concern. That is, until enough red flags come up, our discomfort with the situation becomes so strong, that we feel like doing something.

I saw a YouTube video a while back that illustrates this point well. The YouTuber had been out of work for quite some time and was desperate for a job. When she replied to a help-wanted ad for a nanny position, she arrived at an address that turned out to be a storefront in a large, vacant strip mall. The storefront had no legitimate-looking sign, only a piece of paper taped to the front door saying it was a caregiver agency. The YouTuber said her gut instinct told her everything was wrong, but she rationalized what she'd experienced so far because she needed the job. She told herself there could be a logical explanation for these odd things— perhaps they'd just moved in, explaining the lack of a professional sign and sparce furniture in the waiting room. Maybe the gruff looking receptionist was a family member of the owner.

Things got stranger when she was led down a hallway to an "interview room" containing only two folding chairs. The interviewer seemed confused about which position she was applying for. When she clarified she was there for the nanny position, he appeared disinterested in her answers about work experience. At one point, the man left to use the bathroom, and during this time, she called her boyfriend, expressing her fear that she might be in danger as this place was possibly a front for a sex trafficking operation. Whether it was hearing herself voice these concerns aloud or her boyfriend's encouragement to leave, something finally pushed her to act.

She rushed out of the room, encountering both the interviewer and the receptionist. She turned the corner just as she reached the hallway. Before they could react, she made an excuse about feeling ill and fled to her car, locking the doors immediately. She managed to drive a block away before having to pull over, her body shaking from the surge of adrenaline.

So what happened here?

Why did this woman ignore so many glaring red flags? Why didn't she leave the moment she pulled into the parking lot and saw the suspicious storefront? Why did she rationalize away the makeshift office setup? Why did she follow a stranger who gave her bad vibes down a hallway despite every internal alarm bell ringing? Why did she continue with the interview even as her gut screamed that this was a front for something sinister? The answer lies in a powerful force that can override our survival instincts: desperation. Her urgent need for employment and the mounting pressure of overdue bills led her to cling to the hope that this opportunity was legitimate. She kept suppressing the intuition until the inner warning signs became so intense that she had to take immediate action.

Learning to Recognize the Patterns

The key to protecting ourselves lies not in relying on obvious signs of danger keep us safe but in learning to recognize and trust our intuition when something feels off. We don't need to wait until a wolf looks like a wolf before we take action, as doing so means we've waited too long.

It's crucial to note that missing these subtle signs doesn't make someone responsible for what happens to them. Predators are expert manipulators who prey upon our vulnerabilities and specifically target and work to override our natural warning systems. All we can do is pay attention to red flags when they surface and err on the side of caution.

CHAPTER 4

Understanding Your Gut Instinct

Your Ancient Warning System

That moment of "huh, that's weird" is our ancient warning system; the same system that kept our ancestors alive for millions of years. Yet, we often ignore these warning signals, dismissing them as paranoia or overthinking. *In short, we don't miss red flags, we dismiss them.* And this dismissal usually happens because we don't want to overreact.

What we casually call intuition or gut instinct is actually a sophisticated neural network processing vast amounts of information. Your brain takes in over one million bits of data per second, but your conscious mind can only process about 40 bits. This means your subconscious constantly analyzes patterns, behaviors, and subtle cues you aren't consciously aware of.

The Science Behind Your Sixth Sense

Whenever I talk about the importance of honoring our gut instinct, I get pushback. And I understand why—encouraging people to listen to their sixth sense sounds like a bunch of hippy woo woo, but it's not.

The human brain consists of three distinct systems working together: the reptilian brain (handling survival), the mammalian brain (processing emotions), and the prefrontal cortex (managing rational thought). When you get a "gut feeling," your reptilian brain detects a threat before your conscious mind can understand why.

The Three-Brain Response

When we encounter a potential threat, our reptilian brain is immediately activated, such as when we hear a noise in the middle of the night. This activation happens before you're consciously aware of any danger, triggering physical responses like increased heart rate or muscle tension.

The mammalian brain then processes this information through your emotional filters, connecting current experiences with memories and learned responses. This is why you might feel anxious in a similar situation where you've previously experienced danger.

Your prefrontal cortex attempts to make logical sense of these signals, often trying to fit them into your existing worldview. However, trying to logically understand red flags can lead to rationalizing them, especially when the potential threat doesn't match our expectations of what danger looks like.

When Logic Overrides Safety

The challenge with this system is that our prefrontal cortex uses logic and reason to filter information, and oftentimes, the signs that we are in danger are barely detectable. It might be a look someone gave us, something they said, or how they said it. Logically, our brains go to what is most likely, or what we hope is most likely: that we are probably not in danger.

Why? Because 99 out of 100 times, a concerning behavior turns out to be no big deal. The person walking behind us in the parking lot is in a hurry, not trying to abduct us. The off-putting look or comment from someone is unsettling but doesn't necessarily mean they are a threat.

However, *danger is best assessed situationally rather than statistically.* While the odds of something concerning being harmless are higher than something actually being a threat, the potential for a threat is still very possible.

How Your Body Warns You

When we say we have a "gut feeling," we're describing a very real physiological response: a visceral response, which is literally our organs reacting to perceived danger. This warning system connects to our entire body through the vagus nerve, stretching from our brainstem to our abdomen.

These three systems work together to create what we experience as intuition: a complex interplay of physical sensations, emotional responses, and cognitive processing. The challenge lies in learning to respect all three systems rather than allowing our rational mind to override the essential warning signals from our more primitive brain structures.

Learning to Trust Your Instincts

The first step in trusting your instincts is accepting that you don't need concrete proof to take protective action. The feeling of "something doesn't feel quite right" is enough reason to create distance or set boundaries, including leaving the situation or person entirely.

Safety focuses on prevention rather than certainty. You don't need to prove there's danger to take protective action. The goal is to avoid potentially dangerous situations before they escalate.

Tips to Get in Tune with Your Instincts

Pay Attention to Physical Sensations Start noticing what happens in your body when your gut feelings activate. Notice when your heart rate increases, your stomach tightens, or your breathing changes in response to specific people or situations.

Honor Initial Reactions Practice honoring your initial reactions before your rational mind starts making excuses. That first "huh, that's weird" moment is often your most authentic response to a situation.

Keep a Gut Feeling Journal Document times when you experienced gut feelings and what happened when you listened to or ignored them. This can help you identify patterns and build confidence in your intuition.

Create Distance When Needed When you feel something is off, create physical or emotional distance to give yourself time to think clearly. This distance might mean removing yourself from a situation, ending a conversation, or taking a break from a relationship.

Use the "Best Friend Test" Ask yourself what advice you'd give a loved one in your situation. We're often better at recognizing danger when we're not directly emotionally involved.

Trust Your Discomfort Trust that your discomfort is valid, even if others don't understand or support your decisions. Your primary responsibility is to your safety and well-being.

Risk Looking Foolish Remember that it's better to risk looking foolish than to ignore a warning signal that could protect you from harm. You don't owe anyone an explanation for maintaining your safety and boundaries.

The Challenge with Emotional Investment

Heeding the warnings of our gut instinct becomes more challenging the more emotionally or financially invested we are in a situation. If the person displaying red flags is a parent, friend, coworker, or intimate partner, and we want to maintain a relationship with them, we will be more inclined to quiet our internal warning system—until enough red flags surface and our anxiety about the situation becomes so great that we must take action.

Moving from Recognition to Action

I speak from both personal and professional experience when I say this: removing yourself from a situation that causes mental distress is never an overreaction. Life presents enough challenges on its own—there's no reason to add unnecessary stress to the mix.

Consider the risk-reward calculation: if you're wrong about potential danger, the worst outcome is typically temporary awkwardness or inconvenience. But if you ignore your instincts and they prove correct, the consequences could be devastating.

When I share this perspective, I often hear pushback like, "But what if missing out has bigger consequences? What if I feel uneasy about meeting someone for a date and cancel, and I miss out on finding "the one?" Or what if I miss out on a business investment because I was too scared to invest?"

My response is straightforward: if a person or situation is truly right for you, it won't arrive wrapped in suspicion, anxiety, and self-doubt. When someone or something is genuinely meant for you, it comes with a sense of calm and comfort—or at minimum, a deep knowing that feels right. If you have no peace, it's not for you.

I was going to say that in terms of a business decision, feeling like something is off might simply mean that you need more information before you decide. However, that's not true. There's a difference in the feeling of confusion in terms of "I don't get it" versus the feeling of confusion being "huh, that seems off."

The challenge is that if you listen to your gut instinct, you'll avoid potential harm. So, you'll have to get comfortable taking the risk that you are "making a big deal out of nothing," or that others will think you are being dramatic or difficult. It's okay. People are going to think whatever they are going to think. You don't need to stand there and argue about your boundaries, and you for sure don't need them to agree with your decisions.

If you're worried about missing out on a person or opportunity because red flags are making you hesitant, remember this: there is no single "opportunity of a lifetime"—there are only "opportunities in your lifetime." Another will come along. And when something is truly meant for you, you'll know it not by the anxiety it creates, but by the peace it brings. So, trust your instincts. They exist for a reason and honoring them is one of the most valuable forms of self-care you can practice.

CHAPTER 5

The Number of Red Flags for it to be a Dealbreaker

When Enough is Enough

Sarah stared at her phone for the tenth time that day, debating whether to block James, a guy she'd been seeing for the past few months. Just that morning, he'd cancelled their plans at the last-minute yet again, which was the third time this month. Then he got upset when she said she didn't appreciate such short notice and accused her of being "needy" and "controlling." The night before, he'd shown up an hour late to dinner without apologizing, then spent most of the evening on his phone texting someone he claimed was "just a friend." When Sarah mentioned feeling ignored, he rolled his eyes and said she was being "dramatic." "Come on Sarah, you don't need this in your life," she said to herself. "How much more does he have to do before you dump him?" A better question Sarah could ask would be, "Why am I staying in something that causes this much stress and frustration?"

The Myth of Multiple Red Flags

When it comes to spotting red flags in a relationship, it can be easy to fall into the trap of believing we need to spot multiple red flags before deciding to leave. We keep a mental tally, waiting for enough evidence to justify our exit. However, this approach fundamentally misunderstands the nature of red flags: one serious warning sign can be as damaging as fifty seemingly mild ones.

The goal should be recognizing when a relationship or situation doesn't work for you. You don't need to wait until things become toxic to your well-being. It's not about keeping score but recognizing when a situation isn't working for you.

This mental scorecard approach often stems from a deep fear of making the "wrong" decision. We worry that we're being too hasty, too judgmental, or too quick to give up on someone who might just be going through a rough patch. So, we rationalize: "Maybe if I just see a few more concerning behaviors, then I'll know for sure." But this logic assumes that more evidence will somehow make the decision easier or more justified, when in reality, it often just prolongs our discomfort and confusion.

Think about it this way: if someone consistently makes you feel anxious, unheard, or unsafe, does it really matter whether they do it through one major incident or ten smaller ones? The impact on your well-being is the same. Your nervous system doesn't distinguish between different types of mistreatment—it just knows when something feels wrong. Waiting for additional confirmation often means enduring more harm while hoping things will somehow become clearer.

The truth is that healthy relationships shouldn't require you to build a case for why you deserve better treatment. In good relationships, you don't find yourself mentally cataloging incidents or wondering if you're overreacting to concerning behavior. When someone is right for you, their actions consistently make you feel valued and respected, not like you're walking on eggshells waiting for the next shoe to drop.

Where These Ideas Come From

Society constantly tells us we should stick it out in relationships no matter what. We hear that love takes work, that we should fight for what we want, and that giving up too easily means we don't really care. While good relationships do take effort, there's a huge difference between *working through* problems and *putting up with* someone who treats you badly. The idea that "real love conquers all" can keep us stuck in situations where we confuse putting up with bad behavior for being loyal.

These messages are everywhere. Movies show us characters who keep chasing someone even after being told "no" multiple times. Romance books make the unpredictable, moody guy seem romantic once the woman proves she'll never leave. Social media is full of quotes about "fighting for love" and "never giving up on someone you think about every day." Even people who care about us often say "just work it out" or "give them one more chance" without really understanding what's going on.

Here's the problem with all this advice: it doesn't help us tell the difference between healthy effort and just enabling bad behavior. Working on a relationship might mean having tough talks about how you communicate differently, figuring out disagreements about your future, or learning how to support each other when life gets stressful. These things take patience and effort from both people. What shouldn't take endless work is getting someone to treat you with basic respect, listen to your boundaries, or take your feelings seriously.

When we buy into these messages, we start thinking our standards are too high. We tell ourselves that wanting consistency is asking too much, that expecting honesty is being demanding, or that wanting to feel safe in a relationship is unrealistic. We start believing that if we just love harder, communicate better, or become more understanding, we can somehow fix a relationship that's just not working.

This way of thinking is dangerous because it makes everything our responsibility. If the relationship isn't working, it must be because we haven't tried hard enough, been patient enough, or loved enough. It makes leaving feel like we've failed instead of recognizing it as taking care of ourselves. It turns walking away into "giving up" instead of "choosing what's best for you."

The truth is that some behaviors aren't meant to be fixed with more love. Things like manipulation, constantly dismissing your feelings, lying all the time, or making you question what's real aren't relationship problems to solve—they're signs that you need to protect yourself. Real love shouldn't cost you your peace of mind or make you feel like you're losing yourself altogether.

The Dangerous Urge to "Fix" Red Flags

One of the most common traps we fall into is believing we can help someone change their problematic behavior. We tell ourselves, "They just need someone who understands them," or "Once they see how much I care, they'll want to be better." This thinking is especially seductive when someone shows glimpses of the person they could be—those moments when they're charming, vulnerable, or seemingly committed to change.

But here's what we often miss: you can't love someone into treating you well. You can't communicate your way out of being disrespected. You can't be patient enough, understanding enough, or supportive enough to fundamentally alter someone's character or their willingness to treat you with basic consideration.

When we focus on fixing or changing someone, we're essentially saying that our well-being is less important than their potential. We're choosing to endure present harm for the possibility of future improvement. This isn't love. It's self-abandonment disguised as compassion.

The Stories We Tell Ourselves

It's amazing the excuses we can make for red flag behavior, often without even realizing we're doing it. Some of the most common rationalizations include:

"They're just stressed right now." Stress doesn't create character—it reveals it. How someone treats you when they're under pressure shows you who they really are, not who they are despite the pressure.

"Their ex really hurt them, so they have trust issues." While past trauma is real and deserves compassion, it's not your job, nor is it possible to heal someone else's wounds, especially at the expense of your own well-being.

"They're not usually like this." If someone shows you a pattern of concerning behavior, believe the pattern, not the exceptions to it.

"Everyone has flaws." There's a difference between normal human imperfections and behaviors that consistently harm your mental health or sense of safety.

These excuses keep us trapped because they shift our focus from our own experience to their circumstances. Your feelings about how you're being treated matter more than the reasons behind their mistreatment of you.

Trusting Your Inner Voice

"How bad does it have to get before I leave?"

If you're asking yourself this question, you're already past the point where you should have walked away. Yet so many of us stay, ignoring the quiet voice inside that whispers, "Something doesn't feel right here."

Your emotional compass is reliable, even when concrete evidence seems elusive. If someone's behavior consistently leaves you emotionally drained, confused about reality, constantly on edge, or questioning your judgment, these feelings alone constitute valid reasons to leave. You don't need documented proof of lies or manipulation to justify protecting your mental health.

Consider how you feel after spending time with this person versus how you feel with friends or family who genuinely care about you. Healthy relationships, even during difficult conversations, should generally leave you feeling heard, respected, and valued.

If you consistently walk away feeling smaller, more anxious, or questioning your own perceptions, pay attention to that pattern. Your nervous system is giving you information that's worth taking seriously, even if you can't articulate exactly what's wrong.

Deciding what to do is not about the number of red flags, but about the impact they have on your well-being. One red flag can be just as significant as multiple ones.

The fear of being seen as "too sensitive" or "overreacting" keeps many people trapped in harmful dynamics. *But sensitivity to mistreatment isn't a character flaw—it's emotional intelligence.* Your standards aren't too high simply because someone else can't meet them. The right person for you won't make you feel like you're asking for too much when you expect basic respect and consideration. Remember that choosing to leave doesn't require you to prove your case to anyone else; it only requires you to honor what you know to be true about your own experience.

When Others Disagree With Your Decision

One of the hardest parts of following your instincts is dealing with people who don't understand your choice to leave. Friends and family members might say things like "But they seem so nice when I talk to them," or "Everyone has flaws," or "You're being too picky." These comments can make you second-guess yourself, especially when they come from people you trust.

Keep in mind that other people only see what you or others choose to show them. They don't live your daily reality. They don't feel the anxiety you feel before seeing this person or the relief you feel when they leave. They don't experience the constant walking on eggshells or the way your self-confidence has slowly eroded.

It's also worth noting that some people are invested in you staying in relationships, even unhealthy ones, because your unhappiness makes them examine their situations, and potentially their dissatisfaction with their relationships. Sometimes the advice to "work it out" says more about their fear of change than it does about what's best for you.

You don't need anyone else's permission to prioritize your well-being. You don't need to convince others that your standards are reasonable or that your feelings are valid. Trust that you know your own experience better than anyone else possibly could.

The Bottom Line

The question isn't "How many red flags constitute a dealbreaker?" The question is "How long will I allow myself to feel frustrated, disappointed, upset, depressed, or anxious?"

Part 2: The Red Flags of a Narcissist

Before diving into the red flags of a narcissist, I need to mention three points:

1. There is considerable overlap among these warning signs as well as the experiences presented for each of the red flags. You may notice some redundancy as we explore different aspects of narcissistic patterns—this is intentional, as these behaviors often connect and reinforce each other in complex ways.

2. The following red flags are signs of problematic behavior. I want to make it clear that while the behavior listed in the subsequent chapters is typical for those with NPD or ASPD, this doesn't mean that everyone who has these behaviors has NPD or ASPD. As a reminder, the goal of this book is to help you see problematic behavior for what it is, independent from a diagnosis a person may or may not have.

3. Problematic people are still people and, as such, their behavior manifests in ways that are unique to them. I say this because it's common for people to think, "if you've met one narcissist, you've met them all." However, it's more accurate to say that if you've met one narcissist, you've met one narcissist. Not every person with narcissistic traits will display every red flag discussed here, and the intensity and expression of these behaviors vary significantly from person to person.

Here are some examples:

- A narcissistic ex who never attempted to control your physical presence or social life, but was controlling and critical in other aspects, such as your career or family relationships.

- A mother who habitually displayed cruelty to you and your siblings in public or private spaces without any care of her public image, contradicting the common notion that narcissists are concerned about maintaining a perfect public image.

- An ex who never once used love bombing or hoovering tactics. Instead, the dynamic of the relationship was reversed—you were the one who was constantly praising them and seeking reconciliation after the breakup.

- A father with very evident narcissistic traits like arrogance and grandiosity, but who also showed remarkable skill at giving *seemingly* genuine compliments and *seemingly* genuine apologies.

- A partner who initially seemed "normal" and capable of having a healthy relationship and presented none of the usual red flags. The relationship was relaxed and enjoyable until you stumbled across their double life. It was only at this point did their entitlement and lack of empathy shine through.

- An ex who was arrogant, entitled, and grandiose, but was never manipulative—at least not in ways that you are aware of.

These examples are part of why it's so valuable to learn about narcissistic behavior in terms of an overview of this behavior. In short, it's vital that you see narcissistic behavior as a spectrum, rather than as a checklist. While it's useful to be aware of common patterns, not having rigid expectations of how narcissism "should" look allows you to trust your experience even when it doesn't exactly match textbook descriptions. In the following sections, we'll be talking about specific red flags, but be sure to keep this individuality in mind.

Early Warning Signs (The Idealize Phase)

The beginning of a relationship with a narcissist rarely feels dangerous. In fact, it often feels like the opposite—intoxicating, magical, almost too good to be true. This is the idealize phase, where you're showered with attention, affection, and promises that seem to fulfill your deepest hopes for connection. The red flags during this period are subtle, often disguised as romantic gestures or signs of intense passion.

These early warning signs are easy to miss because they're wrapped in what feels like love. The excessive flattery feels wonderful after past disappointments. The rapid pace of the relationship seems like evidence of a deep connection. The way they seem to know exactly what you need feels like destiny rather than calculation. Your friends and family might even comment on how happy you seem, how much this person appears to adore you.

But underneath the surface of this seemingly perfect romance, patterns are already forming. The foundation being laid isn't one of mutual respect and genuine intimacy—it's one of control disguised as devotion. Learning to recognize these early red flags can help you see the difference between healthy enthusiasm and manipulative love-bombing. The signs in this section may feel subtle now, but they're the seeds of the chaos that will follow. Trust your instincts when something feels too intense, too fast, or too perfect. Real love doesn't need to overwhelm you to convince you of its authenticity.

Red Flag #1: Love Bombing

Shannon's Story

I was so desperate for someone to show me they loved me that when I experienced love bombing (although I didn't know what that meant at the time) I felt intoxicated. I thought that when someone loves you, you're supposed to be their whole world, so nothing registered as feeling off. I was completely sucked in by all the attention and affection and couldn't get enough of it. When the love bombing disappeared and was replaced by thoughtless and rude behavior—or even ghosting me for days on end, I couldn't figure out what I had done wrong. All I knew is that I would do anything needed to change so things could go back to normal. I now know this unbridled passion wasn't normal—it was love bombing, and it would never last—but my former self didn't know that.

It took me ten years to finally leave this relationship, and when I did, I was a shell of who I once was. And when I did start dating again, every relationship felt flat because I kept comparing it to the over-the-top behavior my now ex showered me with. Somehow, I ended up coming across the term "love bombing" online, and that was a significant turning point in my healing. I realized that love bombing wasn't romantic. It was problematic. And when my ex stopped love bombing and began emotionally abusing me, it wasn't because there was something wrong with me; it was because there was something wrong with him.

How This Red Flag Feels

Though all love bombing is manipulative, some are more skilled at it than others. Being targeted by a skilled love bomber can be exhilarating, even if it seems like everything is happening too quickly. When you're targeted by an unskilled love bomber, it's going to feel like something is off, but you might not be able to quite figure out what. Here are two examples:

A Less Skilled Love Bomber

Cybil had gone on a few dates with Mark. From the moment they met, Mark seemed certain she was the one for him. Cybil, on the other hand, thought Mark was a nice enough guy but that he was moving way too fast. His compliments were sickly sweet and one after another, each slightly off-key as though he was reading from a script of what love would be. Additionally, he would make these over-the-top gestures, but mainly when other people were looking. It's like he wanted the attention for being the best boyfriend ever—which is what everyone else thought he was. However, to Cybil, everything he did felt too performative and like he had some sort of ulterior motive, whether it was attention or something else, she wasn't sure.

Skilled Love Bombers

The first few months of Riley's relationship with Jayden felt magical—it was like being wrapped in sunlight. Every morning Jayden texted her with thoughtfully crafted messages about how she'd changed his world and how lucky he was to have met her. He remembered tiny details from their conversations weeks ago, surprising her with her favorite coffee order or leaving sticky notes with inside jokes on her car.

When she mentioned missing her grandmother's cooking, he spent a weekend learning to make some of her grandmother's recipes. His attentiveness made her feel seen in a way she'd never experienced, as if someone had recognized every beautiful thing she didn't realize she'd possessed because nobody had ever treated her like this before.

Since this behavior and these types of feelings can also be found at the start of a healthy relationship, it can be difficult to tell the difference. However, a difference tends to be how each love bomber responds to your boundaries.

When the relationship is healthy, boundaries are respected. If you feel things are moving too fast and express a desire to slow down, a sincere partner will adjust their behavior to where you feel comfortable and not pressured. This differs from a love bomber who, if you mention any concerns or reservations and want things to slow down, will pressure you in various ways to keep the fast pace going. Some ways they might pressure you could be through giving the silent treatment, threatening to leave, making the issue yours, telling you that you don't know what love is, or that you have problems with relationships and trust, given your past.

Understanding Love Bombing

Love bombing manifests as an overwhelming flood of attention and affection early in a relationship, carefully designed to create emotional dependency. While it masquerades as a passionate romance, this behavior is a calculated manipulation tactic. The love bomber's excessive displays of devotion aren't genuine expressions of care but strategic moves in a larger game of control.

The addictive quality of love bombing comes from the fact that it can induce a strong chemical reaction in the brain. Under the barrage of constant attention and adoration, the victim gets a rush of dopamine and other feel-good hormones. This emotional high is especially intense for individuals who have been emotionally neglected or have long-standing self-esteem problems, which makes them more vulnerable to this kind of manipulation.

The Strategic Web of Love Bombing

At its core, love bombing serves four distinct purposes for the manipulator. First, it establishes control by creating emotional dependence through overwhelming affection. Second, it provides ego gratification, feeding the love bomber's narcissistic need for admiration and validation. Third, it helps secure various emotional, financial, or social resources. Finally, it fast-tracks attachment, making it harder for the target to leave, even as the manipulation becomes clear.

The effect of love bombing leaves targets on a paralyzing emotional rollercoaster. When the excessive attention inevitably dies down, targets are left confused, upset, fearful that they did something to cause the withdrawal of affection, and in desperate need to get it back. The majority become emotionally reliant on their abuser's validation, and it becomes ever harder to discern and extract themselves from the manipulation involved.

Those who have experienced previous abusive relationships that involved coldness or cruelty, the love bomber's warmth and attention can seem like a dream come true. However, as with any abusive person, they promise a dream and deliver a nightmare.

Key Takeaways:

1. **Build a life you love before you start dating.** A full, rich life with multiple sources of emotional fulfillment creates resilience against manipulation. This means developing various interests, maintaining healthy friendships, pursuing career goals, and cultivating your sense of purpose. When you have a fulfilling life, you're less likely to tolerate poor treatment or rush into relationships out of loneliness. Focus on becoming the person you want to be, independent of any romantic relationship. Creating a life you love is, perhaps, your strongest shield against manipulation.

2. **Take things slowly.** When I first started speaking about manipulative people and love bombing, I'd encourage people to move at a pace that was comfortable for them; not a pace that was comfortable for the other person. The challenge with this is that sometimes moving full speed ahead can feel so "right" that moving fast seems like the right thing to do. It's not. Getting to know someone involves seeing how they respond to a variety of situations over time.

3. **You might fall in love with personality, *you live with character*.** Additionally, spending hours upon hours early on in a relationship can cause you to feel like you know this

person. You don't. You won't start to get an idea of who they really are until you see them at their worst. You need to know how they handle not getting their way, being told no; others setting a boundary with them, and how their morals surface in different situations.

4. **Remember that authentic love develops gradually and respectfully - it doesn't need to overwhelm you to prove its worth.** A genuine person will respect your pace and boundaries, while manipulators often push for rapid commitment and attachment. Watch especially for signs of pushiness or guilt-tripping when you express a need for space or independence.

Red Flag #2: Rushing Intimacy

Parker's Story

Joe and I hit it off right away. Looking back on things, I'm embarrassed about how fast we moved. He seemed like the perfect guy, and I felt like a teenager in love. He seemed so sure that I was the one for him, and, at the time, I thought it was nice that he wasn't into playing games. He seemed to feel as intensely about me as I did about him.

What struck me as odd was that he wanted to move full speed ahead after the second date. I remember thinking that things were moving way too fast. Whenever I brought up my concerns with him, he'd keep reminding me of how great things were between us and not to overthink things. I was recently out of a bad marriage, and I guess I was scared that I was overthinking things. I wondered if my hesitation to move fast was because I had an issue with commitment or was being paranoid. I didn't want to lose him or the relationship, so I glossed over my concerns, and he moved in with me after dating for only three months.

At first, things were great. But once we combined our bank accounts, and lives overall, he started to change. He began yelling, calling me names, and getting upset over seemingly nothing. It was like he was on his best behavior until he secured a place in my life and then he got comfortable enough show who he really was. I guess he thought I wouldn't or couldn't leave him since my life was so intertwined with his. I broke up with him about six months into our relationship, but then he wouldn't move out!

The whole situation was an absolute nightmare. The police said since he'd been there for more than 30 days that I'd need to formally evict him. I tried that route, but then found out that the courts move slow, and it could take over a year for him to be evicted. I couldn't handle the stress of coming home and seeing him with his smug attitude, eating my food, sitting on my couch, and making himself comfortable as though there was nothing wrong with what he was doing. In fact, I think he enjoyed making the situation as uncomfortable as possible for me. It finally got to the point where I decided to move out. My relationship with Joe cost me thousands of dollars to get out of and took a major toll on my mental and physical health. I will never move that fast with anyone again.

The Whirlwind

Manipulators often create a whirlwind romance or friendship with their target. This whirlwind involves rushing intimacy or moving fast, and it is done in part by dangling some promise of an ideal future or something that the target wants, coupled with pressuring them to "act now," or else it will be gone. The target gets knocked off balance emotionally and may feel compelled to jump into a relationship with them in fear they might miss this "opportunity."

Tragically, most of the society doesn't see a whirlwind romance as the red flag that it is. Watch any TV show, fairytale, or romantic comedy, and the characters fall in love before they know the person. They quickly combine their lives, and, ultimately, we are given the idea that doing so leads to the perfect, romantic, happily-ever-after.

Even in real life, you'll hear about couples who got married within the first few weeks of knowing each other, and they've been happily married for the past 40 years. These couples are the exception, not the norm. There's a term for this. It's called "survivorship bias." Survivorship bias is a logical fallacy, or error in thinking, where the focus is on certain groups of people (or objects) who "survived" a situation while overlooking those who didn't. The result is an incorrect conclusion.

For example, if you focus only on successful entrepreneurs who dropped out of college to start a business, the erroneous conclusion could be made that dropping out of college contributes to having a successful business. It does not. To avoid survivorship bias, we must look at a large enough sample size and accurately determine the statistical probability of success or failure. In terms of a relationship, the vast majority of people who rush into getting married within a few months of knowing the other person doesn't end well.

Moving fast rarely ends well. More often than not, relationships like this reveal themselves to be controlling, exploitative, and abusive. Those with a more balanced and grounded perspective do not move at this pace. They understand, and value, the necessity of having peace in their life. They keep their friends and hobbies. They are selective about who comes into their inner circle and aren't in a rush to have someone else "complete them" or make their lives "whole" because they already live a life they love. For these reasons, a new love interest feels like the frosting on the cake, not the entire cake itself.

There are nine main ways that a manipulator rushes intimacy:

1. **False Flattery.** Manipulators use excessive compliments and charm to gain time and attention, making their target feel special, chosen, and appreciated. This strategic flattery is designed to lower defenses and create a quick emotional attachment.

2. **Premature Pet Names.** They use intimate terms like "baby" or "honey" far too early, often signing messages with kisses or hearts. When questioned, they'll claim this is their natural way of showing affection. However, this casual use of intimate language reveals how meaningless these terms are to them.

3. **Sex as a Weapon.** Many targets may confuse great sex with having a great connection, but don't be fooled. Manipulators can do a fantastic job of making their target feel like there is a deep connection when, in fact, none is present.

4. **Sharing Deeply Personal Stories About Themselves.** Developing a deep relationship requires sharing personal parts of our lives, such as our past relationships or our current hopes, dreams, or fears. A manipulator will often push for premature emotional intimacy, using their own (potentially fabricated) disclosures to make you feel obligated to share deeply personal information before trust is established. True intimacy and trust develop gradually over time and are earned through consistent, respectful behavior, not rapid or pressured disclosures. Setting and maintaining appropriate boundaries around self-disclosure is not being cold or closed off; its a crucial form of self-respect.

5. **Wanting to Spend Hours on the Phone Talking or Texting with You.** They attempt to consume their target's time through constant calls and texts. Consuming your time serves two purposes: creating false intimacy through intense communication, which makes it harder for the target to walk away due to the time invested; and isolating the target from other relationships.

6. **Quick Cohabitation.** They push, early on, to move in together, often for practical advantages like financial support, access to children, or increased control over their target's daily life. This significant step is proposed long before a genuine foundation of trust has been built.

7. **Future Faking.** They discuss marriage, home buying, or having children within weeks of meeting. This "future faking" hooks targets with an idealized vision of life together. Once targets are invested in this fantasy, they're more likely to ignore red flags as the manipulator's true nature emerges.

8. **Financial Entanglement.** Manipulators may suggest combining finances, credit, or bills early in the relationship. Each shared account or financial commitment is another way to bind the target, making it more difficult to leave once the manipulation becomes clear.

9. **Claiming a Soulmate Connection.** Manipulators constantly reinforce the idea of an intense, special connection through phrases like "we're soulmates," "we have a connection you can't deny," "think with your heart and not your head," "we must have known each other in a past life," or "this is meant to be." This romantic pressure helps override the target's hesitation about the relationship's pace.

Key Takeaways:

1. **You are in control of the pace.** Trust your instincts if things are happening too fast. You do have the right and the obligation to control the pace of any relationship. If someone else is making you feel guilty or anxious about needing to slow down, then this is a red flag. If you're concerned that moving slowly will kill the relationship, then that doesn't mean there's something wrong with you, and you should speed up. It simply means this isn't the relationship for you.

2. **Everything is easier to get into than it is to get out of.** Getting entangled in someone's life is much easier than disentangling later. Each layer of commitment— emotional, financial, or practical - creates another bond that will be difficult and painful to undo. This is precisely why manipulators push for quick entanglement on multiple fronts. Take time to evaluate each step of increasing commitment.

3. **Time reveals the truth.** Nothing beats observing how a person behaves in various situations and circumstances over a period of time. No degree of intense connection, chemistry, or professed commitment can substitute for the test of time. Observe how they deal with stress, disappointment, and not getting their own way. Observe how they treat others, not only you.

4. **Trust must be earned.** Healthy relationships unfold gradually, in a way that permits trust to grow through steady,

dependable behavior over time. It's normal and reasonable not to fully trust someone you don't know.

5. **Love bombing isn't love.** Intense attention, flattery, and declarations of love early on may feel intoxicating, but they're not signs of genuine love. Real intimacy develops through shared experiences, mutual understanding, and demonstrated trustworthiness over time.

Red Flag #3: Claims of a Soulmate Connection

Alex's Story

From the very beginning, she spoke about our relationship like it was written in the stars. She'd look into my eyes and tell me I was "her person." The one she'd been searching for her entire life. She said we had a connection that transcended the physical world, that we were twin flames meant to find each other across lifetimes. When we first kissed, she whispered that she could feel our souls recognizing each other, that this was bigger than just attraction or chemistry. She'd text me things like "I can sense your energy even when we're miles apart" and "the universe conspired to bring us together." At first, this felt incredibly romantic and special. I'd never had someone speak about me with such conviction, like I was some kind of missing piece she'd finally found. The way she described our bond made me feel chosen, like I was part of something magical and rare.

But gradually, I realized these beautiful words had become chains. Whenever I tried to set boundaries or questioned her behavior, she'd remind me that soulmates don't abandon each other, that our connection was too sacred to throw away over something trivial. If I wanted space or time with friends, she'd become devastated, saying things like "but we're supposed to be each other's home" or "twin flames don't need anyone else." The same spiritual language that once made me feel special now made me feel trapped. She'd cycle between showering me with these cosmic declarations of love and then withdrawing completely when I didn't live up to her impossible standards. During the silent treatments, I'd question everything; had I imagined our connection? Was I throwing away something truly magical? Then she'd return with tears, talking about how we were destined to be together, how she'd never felt a love this pure before, and I'd get pulled back in. I knew I needed to leave but felt like I couldn't.

The Seduction of the Soulmate Connection

What renders toxic relationships harder to exit than good ones is the intensity that often accompanies them. When manipulators create a soulmate connection, they offer something far more tempting than love. They create the illusion of perfect understanding, complete acceptance, and a bond that transcends ordinary relationships.

This intensity is carefully designed from the start. Manipulators are skillful architects of emotion. They come on strong and confident that you are the one for them. The bonding is immediate and consuming, it's as though you knew each other in a past life.

Understanding Emotional Addiction

In the early stages, you're not just loved; you're worshipped. You're showered with attention, affection, and understanding that feels almost telepathic. They seem to know exactly what you need before you express it, creating an intoxicating sense of being truly seen and understood.

They transform themselves into a perfect reflection of your deepest desires. Every hope you've ever had for a relationship seems to materialize. They're not just compatible; they're the perfect person for you—and they want you to feel the same about them. To achieve this, they study your dreams, fears, and unmet needs and become the solution.

This level of mirroring creates a powerful psychological hook. The relationship becomes your everything. Beyond love, you also feel a sense of destiny, completion, and transcendent connection. When these relationships turn volatile, the thought of leaving can feel soul crushing.

Key Takeaways

1. **Be wary of anyone claiming that you are somehow destined to be together—especially if you've only known them for a few months.** Best case scenario, both

of you have rose-colored glasses on and have fallen in love with the idea of who each of you thinks the other is. Worst case, their professions of a soul mate connection are part of their manipulation.

2. **Love bombing, rushing intimacy, and claiming you are "the one" for them when they don't know you, are all signs to slow down.** If you notice any single one of these red flags, watch for the others since they tend to operate together and not in isolation.

Red Flag #4 Charming

Elizabeth's Story

Elizabeth believed she knew what love looked like. Her boyfriend Ted was thoughtful, well-spoken, and had a gift of making everyone feel important, especially her three-year-old daughter, Molly. Despite her deep feelings for Ted and how great he was to her and her daughter; Elizabeth couldn't ignore the unsettling coincidences between Ted and descriptions of an unknown serial killer on the news. There was a pattern of women disappearing on nights when Ted was mysteriously absent. The same make and model Volkswagen that Ted drove was spotted before and after several of the murders. The crutches in Ted's apartment matched witness descriptions of props used by a suspect in an attempted kidnapping. This attacker also went by "Ted." And the perhaps the most damning of all was that the police sketch that bore a striking resemblance to her boyfriend.

The first similarity between her boyfriend and this killer could be brushed off as a coincidence. The second similarity could also be a coincidence, although her suspicions and concerns were mounting. After all, her boyfriend was so good to her and her daughter. How could he possibly be a vicious killer? As the additional red flags piled on, Elizabeth knew there were too many coincidences to deny: she had to call the police.

Despite calling the King County Police Department at least three times, her warnings initially gained little traction. Elizabeth's boyfriend, Ted Bundy, didn't fit the profile investigators had constructed. They were looking for someone with a violent criminal history, not a charming law student with a clean record. This oversight cost law enforcement precious time as Bundy continued his killing spree while hiding behind his carefully crafted façade of normalcy.

The most haunting aspect of Elizabeth's story is that even after reporting her suspicions, she remained entangled in her relationship with Bundy. His extraordinary ability to manipulate and explain away her concerns kept her doubting her judgment, even as evidence mounted. She later described in her memoir how his charm acted like a powerful drug, making her question her instincts despite the growing pile of red flags and despite her gnawing concern that he was, in fact, a brutal killer responsible for the deaths of at least 28 women.

Looking back, Elizabeth's experience vividly illustrates how even someone who recognized signs of danger could remain under a skilled manipulator's influence. While her initial reports helped put Bundy on law enforcement's radar, it would take years, and many more victims, before he was finally brought to justice, leaving Elizabeth to grapple with the terrifying reality that she had shared her life, and exposed her young daughter, to one of America's most vicious serial killers.

Her story serves as a chilling reminder: *Charm, one of humanity's most appealing traits, can also be its most dangerous weapon.*

When Magnetism Masks Malice

One of the definitions of charm is that it is the ability or quality for one person to delight another. Another definition for charm is the ability to control or achieve by magic, as in charming a cobra. Charming behavior is disarming. It makes others feel at ease.

However, when this charm is manipulative, it's desire is to gain control over others for the charmers self-serving interests. The most dangerous manipulators tend to be the ones who are the most charming. Master manipulators, such as narcissists and sociopaths, often possess a chameleon-like ability to adapt to any situation. They become what others want them to be, and they do so with an ease of confidence that draws people in. Their ability to smooth talk their way and say exactly what is needed at exactly the right time gives them an aura of profound understanding and rapport that can be irresistible to those whom they target.

Beneath this pleasant exterior is a purely strategic approach to relationships. Though they might be the life of any party and rapidly build up extensive social networks, their relationships are always essentially superficial and transactional. They see people not as persons deserving of respect and concern but as means to achieve their ends, whether that be power, money, or prestige.

How the Red Flag of Charm Feels

Narcissistic charm has a manufactured sheen, like a sales pitch wrapped in a smile. The person's attention feels calculated, their laughter a beat too quick, their comfort level around strangers a bit too relaxed, and their compliments slightly too polished. You might feel they're performing on a stage rather than truly connecting. However, it's essential to remember that manipulative charm sometimes comes across as quite sincere; it can take a while to realize that someone's charming personality is actually a manipulation tactic.

Key Takeaways:

1. **Charming behavior is disarming.** After all, the phrase "con artist" derives from "confidence artist" for a reason: people don't entrust their lives to those they distrust. When someone is funny and likable, it's easy to let our guard down.

2. **While you might fall in love with someone's personality, you live with their character.** While charm can create an immediate positive impression, only time reveals the true nature of a person's character through their consistent actions, respect for boundaries, and genuine concern for the well-being of others.

While a narcissist's charm might initially draw you in, it isn't sufficient to establish the powerful connection they require to keep you in their grasp to manipulate you further. That is where the second strategy enters the picture: their uncanny skill at reflecting precisely what you're seeking.

Red Flag #5: Mirroring

Anna's Story

I met Justin on a dating app, and from the moment we began chatting, it was clear we had a lot in common. He was saying all the right things; it's like he could read my mind. We both shared a passion for foreign films and had the mutual dream of opening a beachside cafe in Costa Rica. When I mentioned I volunteered weekly at the animal shelter, Justin enthusiastically shared stories about his rescue pets. Even our childhood experiences eerily aligned—we had each lost a parent young and found healing through art therapy. The connection felt so genuine and deep that I didn't hesitate to invite him back to my place when we finally met in person. But after our passionate night together, Justin's endless stream of texts suddenly stopped. My messages went unanswered, and his dating profile disappeared. I was devastated and confused.

It would take months of therapy for me to understand that what felt like amazing chemistry was actually mirroring. Basically, he was reflecting back everything that was near and dear to me just so he could get me in bed. I learned that mirroring is so effective because we all have an instinctive trust to feel comfortable with people who are like us. I felt, and still feel, so incredibly violated.

Understanding the Science of Similarity

We're naturally drawn to people who seem similar to us - it's hardwired into our brains. When we meet someone who shares our interests, mannerisms, or beliefs, our brains release feel-good chemicals that signal "this person is safe." This biological response made perfect sense for our ancestors as recognizing others that were like us meant identifying potential allies and community members who wouldn't pose a threat.

In healthy relationships, this mirroring happens naturally over time. Friends might unconsciously pick up each other's phrases, coworkers sync up their communication styles., couples develop shared interests, and a similar sense of style. When done naturally and authentically, this gradual merging helps build genuine connections.

However, narcissists have learned to weaponize this natural tendency. They've figured out that by quickly creating a sense that you're remarkably similar, they can bypass your usual caution and fast-track their way to your trust. In authentic relationships, mirroring is about two people becoming in sync to the point they mirror each other's similarities. With manipulators, mirroring is just about copying you to gain control.

The Perfect Reflection: Tactics of Manipulation

When manipulators employ mirroring tactics, they create an uncanny replica of their target that goes beyond surface resemblance. Whatever you happen to be interested in becomes your mirroring manipulator's passion—from your love of foreign films to your passion for environmental causes. Not only do they agree with you, but they express the same intensity and often in the same-sounding words.

This mirroring extends beyond superficial interests to encompass deeper aspects of identity. They might adopt your spiritual beliefs, mirror your emotional wounds, or claim to share your most profound life experiences. A manipulator might discover you lost a parent young and suddenly reveal they, too, experienced similar childhood trauma, what may be completely fabricated.

The deception can become incredibly detailed and sophisticated. Some manipulators research their targets extensively through social media, carefully crafting their persona to match their targets' interests and values. They might even alter their appearance, change their style of dress, or adopt new mannerisms to create what feels like perfect compatibility.

The Dark Side of Perfect Compatibility

The most insidious aspect of pathological mirroring is the way it takes advantage of our deepest desire to be understood and connected. Targets usually comment that they feel as though they've at last found their "soulmate" or "twin flame," unaware that they are in love with a brilliantly devised mirror image of themselves.

As time goes on, this false connection makes it difficult to trust your instincts when things begin to feel off. The validation and approval are so strong that targets overlook huge red flags, brushing them aside as minor flaws in an otherwise ideal match.

Breaking Free from the Mirror

Recognizing pathological mirroring requires developing an awareness of what an authentic connection really looks like. Healthy relationships don't need perfect compatibility; they allow for differences, disagreements, and individual growth. They develop gradually, with both parties maintaining their unique identities while building genuine points of connection.

As you get into new relationships, look for warning signs of too much similarity, particularly at the beginning of a relationship. Beware of individuals who appear to have your hobbies, opinions, and life experiences in common.

If you are dating someone and they ask you what you are looking for, be wary about giving specifics early on. It's common for a person who is interested—even one with the best of intentions— to want to reflect back to you what you are looking for.

What I tend to see with online dating is someone will put on their profile that they don't want someone who will play games, someone who puts their family first, as well as knows how to treat them right. On the surface, these preferences seem reasonable enough, and they are.

However, to a manipulator, they can tell right off the bat that this person has been burned a few times in relationships, because it should be a given that another person doesn't want to play games, understands that you would make your family a priority, and that they'd know how to treat you.

This goes back to there being a problem if you must teach another adult the basics of adult behavior. So, if a person has to spell this out it's because they've been involved with a problematic person before. All this information gives a manipulator enough to reel them in.

Perfect compatibility, especially in the early stages of a relationship, is natural, but it's not lasting. Meaning, both people are usually on their best behavior when they meet someone they like. It takes time for differences to surface. Let me give you an example. Back in the 1990's there was a show that was on MTV called "The Real World." The premise was that seven strangers lived together and agreed to have their lives filmed for TV. The catch phrase for the show was, "The Real World: When People Stop Being Polite and Start Being Real." That catch phrase is the most accurate and succinct way to describe how we all are when it comes to who we are initially and, with time, who we reveal ourselves to be—because just like with the show, everyone is on their best behavior at first.

Key Takeaways

1. **Excessive similarity, especially early in a relationship, is a red flag.** This instant perfect compatibility might feel magical, but it's more likely to be a manipulation tactic rather than a genuine bond.

2. **Healthy relationships maintain space for individual identity and growth; they don't   require perfect alignment of interests, values, or experiences.** Real connections thrive on the genuine exchange of different perspectives, experiences, and ways of seeing the world.

3. **The more chemistry you feel with someone, the slower you need to go.** Having intense chemistry with someone can make you want to move full-speed ahead. The reality is that the two of you don't know each other as well as you might feel that you do.

Red Flag #6: Intensity

Tina's Story

I first noticed Cameron's intensity during a dinner with friends. While everyone else was engaged in casual conversation, his eyes would lock on mine in a way that made me uncomfortable.

He'd stare so long and hard that our mutual friend Sarah pulled me aside later to ask if anything was going on between us because he seemed entranced by me. I must admit I was flattered and felt special, like I was chosen, but I didn't know why or what it was about me that he found so alluring. Even though I was uncomfortable with how Cameron would look at me, I couldn't help but start feeling attracted to him because I'd never felt like such an object of desire. After all, isn't that what we're taught to want: someone who looks at us like we're the only person in the room?

His intensity only escalated from there. Within a few days, Cameron liked and commented on my old social media posts from years ago. He knew about my trip to Spain in 2019, my old job at the cafe, and had even seen my college graduation pictures. He'd send multiple texts throughout the day analyzing things I'd posted or mentioned online in passing: "I noticed you love Thai food. There's this amazing place downtown," or "That quote you shared about healing really speaks to your journey after your parents' divorce." What I initially interpreted as thoughtful attention to detail now feels more like research, like he was studying me and gathering information about what he learned. Cameron and I dated briefly, just long enough for his intensity to turn into jealousy, possessiveness, and control. When that began to happen, I knew I needed to leave. I had dated an abusive guy before and saw a lot of the same behaviors with Cameron. I now realize that his intensity wasn't passion or connection; it was predatory and nothing I'll find romantic or sexy ever again.

The Cultural Romanticization of Intensity

In 2005, the young adult coming-of-age romance novel *Twilight* was released. It quickly captivated readers with the story of Bella Swan, a 17-year-old girl who falls in love with Edward Cullen, a 104-year-old vampire.

In one pivotal scene, Edward confesses his dangerous nature to Bella:

"I'm a killer," Edward warns.

"I don't believe that," Bella responds.

"That's because you believe the lie—the camouflage," he explains. "I'm the world's most dangerous predator. Everything about me invites you in."

Bella's reply is simple but revealing: "I don't care."

"I've killed people before," he continues.

"It doesn't matter," she insists.

His voice grows more intense. "I wanted to kill you. I've never wanted a human's blood so much in my life."

"I trust you," Bella says.

Edward's response is ominous: "Don't."

This scene epitomizes the concerning romantic dynamic between them: he presents himself as a lethal threat, yet she places her complete trust in him despite—or perhaps because of—the danger he represents.

Many readers interpreted Edward's behavior throughout the series—watching Bella sleep and attempting to control her decisions—as protective rather than concerning, reinforcing the story's portrayal of love and desire.

While some were swept up in the allure of vampire lore and the idea of a love so intense and consuming, others were alarmed by Edward's controlling and predatory behavior. Despite the concerns, *Twilight* became a massive cultural phenomenon and bestseller, forever reshaping (for better or worse) vampire fiction.

In 2011, *Fifty Shades of Grey* exploded onto the bestseller list with a strikingly similar premise. This time, the imbalanced power dynamic was a between an older and sexually dominant billionaire, Christian Grey, and Anastasia Steele, a college student. What many may not realize is that *Fifty Shades* took shape in a *Twilight* fanfiction group. Readers of *Twilight* wanted to hear more about the romance between Edward and Bella, a theme that the author of *Twilight*, Stephanie Meyer, wasn't keen on, given her Mormon roots and subsequent desire to keep *Twilight* free of premarital sex. E.L. James, the author of *Fifty Shades of Grey*, gave many *Twilight* fans what they were looking for. Though, to make the story her own, she removed the fantasy element of vampires and werewolves but kept the dynamic between the two characters and dialed up the sexual intensity.

The Allure of Being Chosen

Neither *Twilight* nor *Fifty Shades of Grey* are one-off successes. In fact, it's the opposite. It's the same story told in different ways. So, what is it about these kinds of narratives that readers, especially women, find so alluring? Intensity. Initially, this level of intensity can seem romantic: the idea that a powerful man could find someone like us, an everyday average woman, so captivating, so vital to their existence, that they would stop at nothing to be with them. And again, through a romanticized lens, a dominant love interest who wants to shield the vulnerable object of their desire from the world, can create a sense of safety within the reader, as though we too could be loved and cared for in such a protective, albeit all-consuming, way.

The Dark Reality Behind Romantic Intensity

When viewed through a more critical lens, this level of intensity is far from romantic. Instead, it is more like a predator-prey dynamic where the victimizer overpowers the victim's sense of self. It's not a love story but a dangerous power play that, in the real world, rarely, if ever, ends well. Usually, the dominant person retains a perpetual state of control, and, in time, the object of their affection becomes stripped of their individuality and autonomy; their wants, needs, thoughts, and feelings, become reduced to little more than that of an object.

Unfortunately, confusing intensity and control with care and concern is commonplace within society, not just literature and film. Friends, family, and even the police, therapists, and religious leaders can confuse intensity for sincerity, believing that obsessive actions taken by the controlling person shows how much they care. *True care and concern are never obsessive, and they don't raise any hint of a red flag.* If someone's interest in you feels like too much too soon, or presents to an uncomfortable degree, then it's time to slow things down or get as much distance as you need from this person, even if that means ending things with them.

Understanding Intense Behavior

In relationships with narcissists, intensity manifests through a carefully orchestrated series of tactics. It often begins with love bombing.

This intensity is typically followed by a whirlwind romance, where the manipulator moves quickly to establish what they claim is a "soulmate" connection. They employ obsessive attention, controlling behaviors, and persistent pursuit to maintain their hold over their target.

Perhaps most insidiously, they often mirror the target's interests and desires, creating an illusion of perfect compatibility. This mirroring makes the intense connection feel natural and meant-to-be, rather than the calculated manipulation it is.

The Escalation of Control

When faced with resistance or attempts to establish boundaries, manipulators often escalate their tactics dramatically. Their responses can range from desperate pleading to emotional outbursts, from threats of self-harm to grandiose promises of change.

They might vow to attend therapy, enter rehabilitation, or embrace religion—whatever they believe will most effectively maintain or regain control over their target. These promises are rarely genuine and typically serve only to extend their influence. The escalation can be terrifying and exhausting for the target, who often feels responsible for the manipulator's emotional state and behavior.

Breaking Free from Toxic Intensity

The end of a relationship with a narcissist often leaves survivors in a complex emotional state. Many find themselves confused by the contrast between healthy and unhealthy relationships, struggling to find satisfaction in balanced connections.

There's often a lingering fear that they'll never experience such passionate love again, combined with anxiety about entering new romantic relationships. The intensity of the experience can make future relationships feel lacking, even when those relationships are healthier.

However, it's crucial to recognize that what felt like passionate love was a calculated form of control and domination. True healing begins with the understanding that genuine love doesn't require this level of intensity to be meaningful. So, while healthy relationships may not provide the same emotional highs, they offer something far more valuable: genuine connection, mutual respect, consistency, and the space for both partners to grow and thrive as individuals.

Key Takeaways

1. **Relentless intensity isn't romantic; it's predatory.** Just because our culture romanticizes obsessive intensity in relationships doesn't mean it's healthy. If someone's interest in you feels overwhelming or makes you uncomfortable— even if others find it romantic—trust your instincts.

2. **When someone claims they're just "passionate" or "care too much," they're often justifying their problematic behavior.** A healthy relationship develops at a comfortable pace and respects your boundaries. Whereas manipulators use whirlwind romance and overwhelming attention to bypass your normal defenses.

3. **Real love doesn't need intensity to be meaningful.** While toxic relationships offer dramatic emotional highs and lows, accompanied by makeups and breakups, healthy connections provide something far more valuable: genuine respect, consistent support and stability, a sense of deep calm, and room for both people to maintain their individuality. Don't let the appeal of intensity keep you from recognizing and appreciating authentic connection.

Red Flag #7: Persistent

Jamie's Story

I thought blocking Amber's number would finally give me peace, but she found endless new ways to reach me. Despite our brief five-month relationship, I found myself walking on eggshells, dealing with her extreme emotional swings from loving to combative over seemingly nothing: issues so small that if I had them with someone else, they'd be resolved within a few minutes. She'd accuse me of being distant or uncommunicative, even though we saw each other as much as our schedules would allow.

When I'd point this out and even offered to rearrange my schedule during the week so that I could see her more, she would be unsatisfied with any solution I came up with and then shift to another topic—usually one that involved finding fault with me. It was as though she was looking for a fight, although she claimed I was the one who was being difficult. I began to question if I was the problem, and in an attempt to get clarity, I showed screenshots of our text messages to my therapist. I made sure to give as much context and detail as possible because I didn't want to inadvertently paint an inaccurate picture of what was happening. If I was the problem, I wanted to know. When my therapist saw our text exchanges, she shook her head, told me that Amber was abusive, and encouraged me to leave.

After I ended things, the real nightmare began. Amber sent an onslaught of messages from new email addresses and phone numbers. In some of these messages she claimed to want "closure"; in others she referenced our good memories; and in others she'd turn vicious, weaponizing every insecurity I'd shared with her about my weight and bouts of erectile dysfunction. Her attacks weren't just mean, they were cruel.

Even a year later, while I'm in a healthy new relationship, she periodically emails me claiming she'll never give up unless I confirm it's really over. While I am tempted to fire off an email letting her know that, yes, things are really over, I know that what she's really after is for me to reopen communication with her. One friend summed up her persistence and attempts at communication perfectly. He said our situation reminds him of vampire lore, in that a vampire can't come in unless you invite them. He said she's like a vampire knocking at the door, changing her voice and approach in hopes she could fool me into inviting her in.

Understanding Pathological Persistence

Narcissists and problematic people, in general, see boundaries not as stop signs but as mere suggestions. And, because narcissists feel entitled to get their way, they see no problem with steamrolling over the boundaries of others. This is the world of pathological persistence: behavior so relentless and calculated that it can overwhelm even the most resilient individuals. Narcissists are known for their persistent behavior, which stems from their deeply ingrained need for control and lack of empathy. This persistent behavior often revolves around manipulation, deceit, and self-centeredness, and it rarely changes, even in the face of consequences.

Examples of how a narcissist can be persistent:

1. ### Constant Pursuit Despite Rejection:

   Even when I told him I wasn't interested or needed space, he wouldn't stop contacting me. He'd send texts, call, and even show up at my door or workplace, always insisting that he was 'just checking in.' No matter how often I asked him to leave me alone, he would act like I didn't mean it and keep pushing for my attention or approval.

2. ### Pushing Boundaries Repeatedly:

   I'd set a clear boundary, like asking him not to call me at work, but he'd constantly ignore it. He'd call anyway, sometimes multiple times a day, saying things like, 'I just wanted to hear your voice,' or 'I thought you might change your mind.' It felt like he didn't respect my boundaries at all, and no matter how firm I was, he wouldn't let up.

3. **Refusing to Let Go After a Breakup:**

After we broke up, he kept showing up at my house, sending me gifts, and even sending long, emotional messages saying that we were 'meant to be together.' He refused to accept my decision and acted like it was just a phase. Whenever I told him to stop, he'd claim he couldn't live without me or that I was making a huge mistake.

4. **Repeatedly Criticizing and Pressuring for Change:**

He would constantly point out everything he thought was wrong with me, no matter how many times I asked him to stop. If I changed one thing to try to make him happy, he'd find something else to criticize. It felt like he was never satisfied and always pushed me to be someone I wasn't, no matter how hard I tried.

5. **Refusing to Take "No" For an Answer:**

I remember telling him I wasn't ready to commit, but he would keep hounding me about it. He'd say things like, 'But why not? We'd be perfect together,' or 'I just don't understand why you're resisting.' Even after saying 'no' multiple times, he returned with more reasons why I should change my mind.

6. **Trying to Control Your Social Interactions:**

When I started spending time with friends or making plans without her, she would make passive-aggressive comments or insist that I should prioritize her over everyone else. Even though I'd explain that I needed my time, she'd keep asking, 'When will you be home? When can we hang out?' and would make me feel guilty for having a life outside of her.

7. **Repeatedly Trying to Manipulate and Guilt You:**

Whenever I disagreed with him or stood my ground, he would argue relentlessly, claiming I was unreasonable. He'd keep bringing up past instances when he did things for me. Or he'd find some other situations he could use to guilt trip me. No matter how often I told him I wasn't changing my mind, he would keep pushing until I gave in just to end the argument.

8. Using Others to Pressure You:

If I ever stood up for myself, he'd involve mutual friends or family members, asking them to convince me to change my mind or see things from his perspective. Even if I asked them to stay out of it, they would keep coming to me, saying things like, 'He's really upset. Don't you think you should reconsider?' He was persistent in using others to wear me down.

9. Attempting to Rekindle the Relationship:

Even after a long period of no contact, he would find ways to reach out, whether through mutual friends, social media, or even accidentally 'bumping into me.' He would always try to re-establish contact, claiming that things would be different or that he had changed, no matter how many times I told him I had moved on.

Key Takeaways:

1. **Don't mistake their persistence as a sign that they care or that things will be different and better this time.** Remember, this level of pathological persistence isn't about caring; it's about control. When someone repeatedly tries to force their way back into your life after you've set boundaries, they're demonstrating a fundamental disregard for your autonomy and wishes.

2. **If someone doesn't respect your boundaries, they don't respect you.** Even if this persistence masquerades as devotion or remorse, it's a form of emotional manipulation designed to wear down your resistance. Genuine care and respect mean accepting when someone needs space or wants to end a relationship, not launching repeated campaigns to override their decisions.

3. **Please know that if the problematic person in your life *isn't* persistent, this doesn't mean that you *aren't* important or lovable.** Many people struggling with toxic relationships torture themselves with thoughts like "If I mattered to them, they would fight harder to keep me," but this belief system comes from stories and media that romanticize unhealthy pursuits. *Your value as a person exists independently of how others treat you.* To do otherwise is to let your self-esteem rise and fall based on how others treat you, placing the keys to your happiness in someone else's hands. You have value and are worthy of love and being treated with respect. Don't let anyone, let alone an abusive person, determine your value.

Red Flag #8: They Are Always the Victim

Leah's Story

In my first few conversations with Jake, I remember thinking he seemed so wounded yet resilient. The way he told it, his ex-wife had destroyed him financially, cleaning out their joint accounts and maxing out their credit cards before leaving him for another man. He spoke about it with such raw hurt, explaining how he'd tried to save their marriage by suggesting couples therapy, but she refused to go. She just kept spending and lying about it until he was nearly bankrupt. I could relate to this as I went through something similar with my ex. It took me a year to discover the truth: Jake's ex had taken what little money remained and run because he'd been secretly gambling away their savings and retirement for years. His story about her spending and cheating? Well, according to his ex, he was the one who cheated. And based upon all his other lies, I believe her. Hell, I'm sure he's telling his new girlfriend some completely fabricated story about me.

The Art of Victim Narratives

Professional victims are masterful storytellers. They weave tales of past relationships where they're either the hero who tried everything, or the victim who was used or abused. Some are obvious, painting their former partners as "crazy" or "unstable." Some are more covert in their approach: they'll say nice things about their ex while carefully weaving in false, exaggerated, or true but misleading details that make you see the ex as the problem.

These stories often follow a predictable pattern: the ex was troubled, but they tried to help; they gave everything to make it work, but in the end, nothing was ever enough. This narrative accomplishes two things at once: it earns your sympathy while explaining away their failed relationships.

These stories are compelling because they often contain just enough truth to be believable. They might acknowledge small faults of their own, carefully chosen to make their overall victim narrative more convincing. "I wasn't perfect," they'll admit, "but I tried everything I could." It's only with time that more of the truth comes out. Usually, the reality is that they were using, abusing, or cheating on their former partner. The narcissist wasn't this Prince (or Princess) Charming that they seemed to be. The narcissist was the problem but, of course, they never see themselves that way. Even if they do admit to lying, cheating, stealing, using, or abusing others, they always have some excuse for their bad behavior, often blaming everyone else but themselves. This mentality is the typical mentality of an abusive person. It's the "look at what you made me do" narrative that they cling to so that they can avoid accountability.

Ramona's Story

I remember sitting in one of my many therapy sessions, utterly confused about who the real problem was: me or Liem. I'd never been in a relationship like this before, where things were so damn difficult most of the time and conversations would suddenly derail into accusations and hurt feelings over what seemed like nothing.

I found myself speaking to my therapist at length about our relationship problems, desperately trying to figure out how to smooth things over and keep them that way. But Liem was so convinced that I was the difficult and manipulative one—the one who wasn't truly invested in making our relationship work—while from my perspective, he was the one being difficult and manipulative.

We were each seeing our own individual therapists, which only made things worse. My therapist saw him as the problem, and I was pretty sure his therapist thought the same of me. The competing narratives felt like dueling realities, and I was caught in the middle, questioning everything I thought I knew about myself.

For about a year, I made myself nuts trying to figure out if I was, in fact, the manipulative one who was somehow inadvertently pushing him to the breaking point on a regular basis. I didn't think

I was doing this—I'd never had this issue with anyone else in my life—so I was genuinely confused and scared.

I wondered if I had some deep-seated pathology that had somehow laid dormant all these years and was, for whatever reason, activated specifically by my relationship with Liem. I don't know if I'd call Liem a narcissist, as he wasn't particularly self-absorbed or grandiose, but he did lack empathy and seemed incapable of understanding my side of things.

What I do know for sure is that there was a big part of me that felt relieved when our relationship finally ended. I was exhausted from all the fighting over seemingly trivial matters and constantly feeling like I was somehow abusing him just by existing.

Even though my therapist tried repeatedly to get me to see that he was the manipulative and abusive one, I couldn't fully believe her. I was so concerned that she was only hearing my skewed version of events.

To this day, Liem feels like he is the victim of me. I heard from mutual friends that he's started a social media account dedicated to narcissism and documenting the things I supposedly did to him. His retelling of events is somewhat accurate—it's not like he fabricated entire scenarios—but his recollection is, in my opinion, heavily skewed and leaves out crucial context that would frame everything in a completely different light.

The Hidden Pattern

Behind every expertly crafted victim's story lies a pattern visible only with time and distance. They tend to have a long list of people who no longer speak to them—not just exes but former friends, estranged family members, and old colleagues who've cut ties.

These broken relationships aren't random bad luck. They result from a consistent pattern of behavior: creating chaos, manipulating situations, and refusing to take responsibility. When confronted with evidence of their misconduct, they expertly shift blame, rewrite history, and position themselves as the victim of others' unreasonable behavior. Of course, they won't tell you any of this. If you get a rough outline of events from them, they'll leave out pertinent details about their behavior that radically change the story.

The most disturbing aspect is how genuinely they believe their revised versions of events. Their ability to blur reality with fantasy can be so complete that they might pass a lie detector test because they've convinced even themselves that their distortions are truth.

The Savior Trap

These victim narratives are particularly compelling for empathetic people, especially those who have experienced similar past hurts. There's something appealing about feeling like you are the one who finally understands and supports them after all they've been through.

This dynamic creates a powerful hook: you begin to feel special, chosen to be the one who will love them properly, heal their wounds, and prove that not everyone will hurt them. This role feels noble, important, and deeply meaningful until you realize it's a role countless others have played before you.

The savior position also serves another purpose: it makes it harder to hold them accountable for their behavior. After all, you want to avoid the narcissist saying, "You are just like all the others," who'd hurt them. So, when you try to prove to the narcissist that you're different, not like the others, you are actually being emotionally manipulated.

When someone consistently portrays themselves as the victim in every situation, the odds are that the next chapter of their story will feature you as the latest person who hurt them. Notice what they say about others and the pattern these stories reveal. Professional victims collect grievances and leave a trail of people who, they say, "took advantage of them."

Key Takeaways

1. **When someone has a long list of people who no longer speak to them, notice how they talk about these events.** If they're never at fault, or their responsibility is always minimized, you're likely dealing with somebody who isn't living in reality.

2. **The most dangerous victim stories are the subtle ones.** Persistent trash-talking of exes is a clear red flag. However, also be wary of those who appear to take partial blame, or speak with surface-level sympathy about their exes, while still positioning themselves as the wronged party. This sophisticated manipulation is designed to make their victim narrative more believable.

3. **Being cast as the special person who finally understands them is a trap, not an honor.** This role feels meaningful, but it's a well-rehearsed dynamic designed to keep you trying to prove you're different from "all the others." When you finally set boundaries or hold them accountable, you'll become the next character in their victim narrative.

Warning Signs in Yourself

Sometimes the most important red flags aren't found in someone else's behavior; they're found in the quiet corners of your own mind. These internal warning signs are your psyche's way of trying to protect you, even when you're not ready to listen. They emerge as persistent doubts, growing unease, and questions that won't go away no matter how hard you try to rationalize them.

The signs in this section represent your intuition working overtime, desperately trying to break through the fog of manipulation and confusion. When you find yourself wondering if you're the problem, when nothing shocks you anymore, or when you start questioning someone's basic humanity, these aren't signs of your weakness or paranoia—they're signs of your survival instincts kicking in. Your mind is trying to wake you up to what your heart may not be ready to accept.

Pay attention to these internal red flags. They often appear before the external situation becomes undeniably dangerous. When trusted friends try to warn you, when you feel a creeping sense of physical danger, or when you're no longer surprised by cruel behavior, your subconscious has already recognized what your conscious mind is still processing. These warning signs within yourself are not evidence that you're overreacting. They're evidence that you're finally starting to see clearly.

Red Flag #9: You Wonder if You're the Problem

Harper's Story

When my mother was diagnosed with terminal cancer, my world became a haze of medical appointments, heart-wrenching conversations, and constant caregiving. Her small one-bedroom apartment became our entire world—I slept on the living room couch, friends and family members took turns to help and offer comfort, and healthcare professionals came and went at strange hours. With each passing day, I felt a mix of utter exhaustion and complete overwhelm.

I could barely find the strength to get through the day, and the small amount of energy that I did have, I feared, would bring on a panic attack.

Amidst all this physical and mental fatigue, my boyfriend Ethan would text me, complaining that I "never made time for him."

"I've never felt so alone right now," Ethan's message read. "You've been completely absent from our relationship. I need you to make time for me, to call me, to be present for me. I miss you."

When I tried to explain the overwhelming circumstances—my mother's declining health, my lack of sleep, the constant medical care, how challenging it was for me to carve out time to make a phone call (let alone a private one) the emotional toll of watching a parent die—Ethan would respond with statements that made me feel selfish.

"Other people manage to balance their personal lives during tough times," he would say. "You can't step outside for just ten minutes to call me?" I could understand why Ethan was feeling hurt and unimportant, and I felt terrible about not being able to be more present for him, but I just didn't have the energy to be there for him emotionally too. I needed a shoulder to lean on, and didn't have the strength for him to lean on me too. It was all too much for me, and Ethan didn't seem to understand no matter how many times or how many ways I tried to express this to him. He always spin the focus back on himself and his need for my time and attention.

I was left feeling so confused and drained. On one hand, I could empathize with why Ethan felt the way he did. But on the other, I couldn't understand why he was incapable of extending empathy and understanding to me for my situation and emotional state. When other friends or family called, they were empathetic and supportive. There was such a difference in how I felt when they called—they were my support system and they were there to help take the weight off my shoulders, whereas my time with Ethan felt like he was piling it on.

I didn't dream of bringing this up to Ethan, because, in part, he felt how he felt—his feelings were as valid as mine. Also, I certainly did not have enough energy for a fight, which is what any conversation we had about my time inevitably devolved into. But secretly, I was growing angrier and more resentful towards him. Here I was, in the most painful time in my life, where I needed him the most, and instead of offering help, or at least being merely understanding, Ethan couldn't be there for me.

I was so stressed out that I began seeing a therapist twice a week. One session focused on the stress and sadness surrounding my mother, and the other session focused on my stress, sadness, and anger surrounding Ethan's behavior. I truly felt as though I was going to have a nervous breakdown. I loved Ethan, but at the same time his behavior, his lack of empathy, was breaking my heart and I didn't know how to reconcile these two feelings.

The Anatomy of Confusion

There are a handful of reasons confusion is present when dealing with a narcissist. It could be due to their entitlement, level of self-absorption, or lack of empathy, as is the case with Harper's boyfriend Ethan. In Harper's situation, she's confused because, on one hand, Ethan's request for more of her time is somewhat understandable—after all, they are in a relationship.

However, Harper is confused by how Ethan doesn't seem to understand why she isn't able to communicate more, and, worse, why he is adding to her stress by pushing her to give more of herself than she can. For Harper, and for most people who are empathetic, they wouldn't dream of adding more work to someone who is clearly at their limit.

So, while Ethan is feeling alone and unsupported, so is Harper. Harper has clearly maxed out her emotional bandwidth and has nothing left to give. An empathetic partner would be understanding and supportive of Harper during this time and, ideally, ask how they could help. At a minimum, a partner like Ethan who is feeling unsupported would realize they need to turn to their friends, family, or therapist to discuss their feelings instead of putting more expectation on an already-taxed partner.

Confusion and a Narcissist

For many narcissists, confusion serves a dual purpose in maintaining control, although the mindset and level of awareness can be different.

The first type of narcissist is one who is intentional about getting and keeping control. They often use confusion as a calculated weapon. These types of narcissists deliberately create an environment where nothing is clear, where truth becomes slippery, and where the victim's perception is constantly challenged. This isn't accidental; it's a strategic approach. When you step out of line and act in a way they disagree with, they intentionally bombard you with their perspective, creating confusion to disorient you until you return to where they believe you belong. This deliberate confusion causes extreme self-doubt which keeps you off-balance, making it easier for them to maintain control.

The second type of narcissist may create confusion unintentionally, yet it serves the same purpose. Much like a child, everything in their world revolves around their wants and needs, and when you fail to meet their expectations, they genuinely feel victimized. Their confused, emotional reactions, such as dramatic shifts in mood, inconsistent messages, and unpredictable responses, stem from a genuine belief that you've wronged them. However, with either type of narcissist, their intentions are the same: they want you to make them your top priority. At whatever cost.

The Self-Doubt Spiral

For Harper, the situation with her mother and Ethan's lack of understanding wasn't isolated. There were numerous occasions through their three-year relationship where she wondered who had the problem: was Ethan the one being demanding, difficult, and lacking empathy or was it her?

She often felt she was letting Ethan down, even though that was never her intention. There was the time he'd got upset when she'd expressed anxiety about meeting his college friends, and he got upset with her, dismissing her feelings as "looking for an excuse not to go." Even small moments, like when she'd forgotten to pick up his dry cleaning and he'd remarked, "You really need to write things down, because I can't even count on you for the simple things." Comments like these left her feeling like she was difficult to be with, but at the same time wondering of Ethan was being unnecessarily "harsh" with her. Each time, Harper found herself apologizing, trying harder, and wondering why she couldn't just be the partner Ethan seemed to want.

Recognizing the Red Flags

Harper first noticed something was wrong when she realized that asserting herself with Ethan somehow always ended with her apologizing. Somewhere along the line, the conversation would get twisted, and the focus would fall on her. With time, Harper learned that whenever she had an issue or concern with Ethan, that she was better off staying quiet. If she didn't, she knew she was in for an hours-long, exhausting, and one-sided conversation where Ethan would justify his behavior and point out why she was the problem.

Manipulative and controlling dynamics include:

- Constant confusion about relationship dynamics

- Feeling like you're always explaining or defending yourself

- Second-guessing your perceptions and memories

- Walking on eggshells avoiding certain conversations to keep the peace

- Feeling guilty, bad, or unreasonable for having wants and needs that differ from theirs

- Feeling emotionally exhausted after interactions

These aren't just relationship challenges—they're a series of manipulations (either intentionally or unintentionally) designed to erode your boundaries and for the other person to get their way.

Breaking the Cycle of Confusion

Harper's turning point came after she came across some information about abusive relationships. She identified with some of what she was reading and got involved with an online support group. In there, she was able to read hundreds of experiences that were like hers. Seeing her situation reflected back to her through the experiences of others allowed her to see her situation more clearly. One comment on her post read, "Ask yourself if you feel this confused, and like you are the problem, when you are with your close friends. Odds are you don't."

Harper was taken aback by what she just read. The commenter was right: she didn't normally feel so confused and full of self-doubt, wondering who had the problem or how to make things better. Things with them went smoothly. When she was around her friends, things were just…easy. They rarely fought, and when they did, things got ironed out and back on track in a short amount of time. She, for sure, wasn't questioning herself, wondering if she was the abusive, manipulative, or difficult one.

Harper realized that she'd felt this level of confusion and anxiety two other times in her life. Once, she had a "friend" in high school who was domineering and controlling, and, at times, made her life hell. The second time was with a boss who ran hot and cold. She never knew what she was walking into or what she'd be blamed for when she came to work. The common themes between these three relationships were that she felt anxious, uneasy, full of self-doubt, and like no matter what she did, things never ran smoothly for long— she kept "getting in trouble" despite her best efforts to go with the flow and be as accommodating, friendly, and solutions-oriented as possible.

After a few weeks in the support group, Harper realized that while she still had a lot of confusion about whether it was her or Ethan that had the issue, she concluded that it didn't matter. What she did know for certain, was that she couldn't live with this stress anymore. If, despite her best efforts, things kept going off track and were causing her a lot of anxiety and untold amounts of tears, then this relationship wasn't healthy, wasn't working, and wasn't worth her sanity and peace of mind. And like many people in the group continually pointed out, the path to healing begins with recognizing that the confusion was never about her—even though it felt like it. The constant confusion, crazy-making, and exhausting conversations, were always about Ethan's need for control.

Key Takeaways

1. **Trust your baseline reality.** Compare how you feel in this "concerning" dynamic with how you feel around others. If you're constantly confused, anxious, on guard, and second-guessing yourself with this person, but feel confident, clear-headed, and relaxed around others, then there is a

problem. Healthy relationships don't feel draining; they feel nourishing.

2. **It doesn't matter if a person is intentionally or unintentionally manipulative and controlling, as the result is the same.** When another person feels that they are right and entitled to get their way, they will often accuse you of being difficult, demanding, controlling, or being selfish and lacking empathy. Sometimes this can be projection on their end, however, some people truly have a skewed perspective of events to where they see any of your wants and needs that aren't in alignment with theirs as you being the problem. You don't need to stay and figure out if their behavior is intentional or not. All you need to look at is whether this relationship is nourishing or draining.

3. **Your feelings are valid.** If you have a problem with how someone is treating you, this doesn't make you too sensitive. It means the other person has crossed one of your boundaries. If they spin your concerns back onto you to make it seem like your issue, then they aren't being accountable for their actions and, instead, dismissing how you feel. The fact that you're questioning yourself is proof of your empathy and self-reflection—qualities a narcissist fundamentally lacks. And if someone lacks the ability to self-reflect and to be accountable, then no sincere relationship is possible with them.

Red Flag #10: Nothing They Do Surprises You Anymore

Melissa's Story

I don't know exactly when I stopped being shocked by my husband Nathan's behavior. Maybe it was after I discovered he'd been stealing money from his elderly mother's account while pretending to "help manage her finances." Or perhaps it was when I found out he'd been living a double life with another woman for the past three years, even attending her family holidays while telling me he was away on business trips. His lies had become so routine, so expected, that finding evidence of new ones barely registered anymore. My friends would gasp in horror at his latest betrayal, while I felt nothing.

When I discovered he'd been badmouthing me to our mutual friends, painting me as unstable and abusive while positioning himself as the long-suffering victim, I didn't even have the energy to get angry or cry. When I learned he'd been using my social security number to open credit cards, I just added it to my mental list of his betrayals.

The man who once seemed like my soulmate I now viewed more as a sociopath, yet I found myself feeling oddly calm - like finally seeing clearly after years of fog. The pain was still there, but it had transformed into something different: a quiet acceptance that this was who he had always been, and who he would always be. For the past fifteen years, I'd held onto hope that he'd change, or that the last outrageously selfish thing he did would be the last. But that was never the case. I know I need to leave, but I feel stuck. I can't afford to move out, let alone start over.

The Mechanics of Manipulation

Staying in a relationship with a narcissist after you've tolerated numerous forms of unacceptable behavior for whatever reason:

you hoped they'd change; you believed their excuses and lies; you thought this time was the last, and so, leads to what's known as a "managing down of expectations." The result is that their unacceptable behavior becomes normalized.

At first, the red flags are so subtle that they're almost invisible. A cutting comment about your appearance might be disguised as a joke. A grip that's just a little too tight could be passed off as passion or playfulness. An insistence that you cancel your plans to accommodate them might seem like intense care or love. Moments like this are (intentional or unintentional) boundary pushes. How you respond tells them how much they can get away with.

Human beings have a remarkable capacity for adaptation. What would have been unacceptable at the beginning of the relationship gradually becomes tolerable, even expected. Like the proverbial frog in the pot of water, the water gets warmer, and you don't even realize you're being cooked.

This adaptation happens through a process of continuous normalization. Each small transgression recalibrates your understanding of acceptable behavior. A slight criticism becomes an acceptable form of communication. A controlling behavior becomes a sign that you need to be micromanaged. Emotional withdrawal transforms into something you must work to prevent.

The Brutal Reality

What makes this process truly horrifying is the narcissist's calculated indifference. They no longer even bother to promise change. Why? Because they know, with absolute certainty, that their target will stay—and if the target does leave, that the target will, eventually, come back.

Over time, the target's expectations have been managed down to virtually nothing. Communication breaks down not because of loud arguments, but because the target has been conditioned to stay quiet to keep the peace. An apology becomes irrelevant, and, yet the target clings to these empty words thinking that maybe this time things will be different. Basic respect seems like an impossible luxury. Hope becomes the strategy and maintaining the relationship becomes the only goal.

Please don't ever let another person get comfortable with disrespecting you. Don't wait for them to change. Hold onto your power and get clear with where your dealbreakers are. And most critically, be prepared to walk away when those dealbreakers happen.

Key Takeaways

1. **Examine your boundaries, standards, and dealbreakers.** Tolerating the intolerable doesn't happen overnight. It starts by minimizing and justifying bad behavior. Once someone shows you they have no regard for you or others, you better believe that the behavior you see now will continue to get worse.

2. **Your expectations matter.** The moment you start accepting less than you deserve is the moment you begin to lose yourself. Expectations are the guardrails of healthy relationships, protecting your dignity, emotional well-being, and personal boundaries. When you systematically lower these guardrails, you create a dangerous emotional landscape where abuse can flourish unchecked. Your standards don't need to be negotiable; they are the fundamental markers of your self-respect.

3. **Hope is not a strategy.** Waiting and hoping someone will change when their behavior continues to stay the same is a recipe for continued abuse. Manipulators are masters at exploiting hope, offering just enough intermittent kindness to keep their targets believing in the possibility of change. Staying in a toxic situation is a slow descent into emotional destruction. If you can't leave now, consider working towards a plan to leave. You can contact your local domestic violence shelter for help in how to do this.

Red Flag #11: Others Have Tried to Warn You

Zoe's Story

I can still hear the tremor in my mother-in-law's voice from that night at our engagement party. When Jacob was off chatting with his friends, his mother pulled me aside. "There's something wrong with Jacob," she said; her eyes darting around to make sure he couldn't hear. "He can't love…not really…not fully." I remember how I'd smiled politely, surprised by what she said, but chalking it up to some complicated mother-son dynamic I didn't understand. Hindsight being what is it, I now realize that several people had warned me about Jacob over the years, but I dismissed their concerns for various reasons. I glossed over my brother's concern after he saw Jacob fly into road rage while the three of us were on our way to go bowling, telling myself that he was stressed from work.

Four years later, I stood helpless in our half-renovated kitchen, as Jacob berated me over a miscommunication with a contractor that led to yet another delay. I didn't realize anyone else heard what he was saying. However, the next day, while Jacob was at work, a contractor pulled me aside and told me he was concerned about how Jacob treated me. I was horrified, embarrassed, and had no response—just the heavy weight of shame as I realized these strangers could see what I'd spent years trying to deny.

The horrible truth became clearer every day. His mother knew. My brother knew. The contractor knew. Everyone seemed to know but me, but now I saw things clearly. I found myself looking back at our relationship with a fresh set of us and what I saw was deeply concerning, but the most troubling was how long all so much of his problematic behavior flew under my radar.

The Voices of Concern

Our closest relationships are often our most powerful early warning systems. Friends and family possess a unique vantage point. They see the subtle shifts in our behavior, the gradual erosion of our self-esteem and spirit that we might be too close to recognize.

At first, the changes might seem minor. You start declining invitations, making excuses. Social gatherings become complicated negotiations. Your partner's mood becomes the invisible force controlling your decisions. Dinner with friends requires careful planning, a delicate dance of potential triggers, and unspoken tensions. Your loved ones watch, concerned, as you become a smaller version of yourself. You find yourself apologizing for your partner's behavior.

These warning signs often emerge in seemingly innocent conversations. A friend might casually mention how your partner seems "intense" or "controlling." A family member expresses concern about the way your partner talks to you or others. These are not random comments but observed red flags. Most critically, these warnings come from people who have nothing to gain, unlike a manipulator who benefits from controlling you.

Eventually, the weight of evidence becomes impossible to ignore. The warnings, once dismissed, transform into a painful reality. This moment of recognition is both devastating and liberating. The puzzle pieces snap into place. The seemingly random comments, the concerned looks, the whispered warnings—they all make sense now. You realize that those who tried to warn you saw what you couldn't or wouldn't.

Key Takeaways

1. **Trust the collective wisdom.** When multiple people express concern about your relationship, it's not a coincidence. These warnings come from a place of observation, offering perspectives you might be too close to see.

2. **Listen to your intuition.** The fact that others are voicing concerns, often means your own intuition has been whispering similar doubts. Pay attention to that inner voice. If you feel confused about your relationship, journaling

about what's going on can help. While journaling can be cathartic, the largest benefit tends to come with time. As with time comes emotional distance, allowing you to re-read past situations with a fresh perspective.

Red Flag #12: You Question Their Humanity

My Story

Shortly before my father's death, he gathered my brother, our stepmother, and me to discuss that upon his passing there would be a trust set up for our stepmother. My father said the reason for the trust was that he was concerned about "certain members" of her family and their desire and ability to manipulate her out of her money. The thought that he was alluding to her son didn't even cross my mind. When my brother mentioned my step-brother by name, my father raised his eyebrow in silent acknowledgment.

I defended my step-brother, due to the good relationship we had with him over the past 35 years. We'd always gotten along famously. My step-brother is incredibly charming, funny, and seemingly gets along with everyone. I truly believed that if there was any issue that came up regarding the trust and how the funds were spent, that they could be resolved through family discussion. How terribly wrong I was.

The four years following my father's death involved no shortage of "miscommunications" and issues with getting the trust formed and funded. However, the truth eventually came out. My step-mother and step-brother had been actively working to bypass the trust entirely, routing funds to a new bank account where he had the power of attorney—and complete control of the funds. When confronted, they claimed it was an accident, and that they didn't know they couldn't do that. Several weeks later, and we caught them trying to sell the house without us knowing, again, claiming that they didn't know better.

By then, my brother and I began to suspect that these people that we'd loved and trusted pretty much our whole lives had every intention of completely disregarding our father's wishes and were actively lying and manipulating us to do so. The worst part was that they were preying upon on our love and trust to do so. It's wild to look back, knowing what I know now, to realize that phone call or time spent with them for every birthday and holiday over those four years, was all part of their manipulation. They kept up the act that everything was normal, until enough concerning things happened that it was clear that everything, was indeed, very far from normal.

I immediately retained an attorney and threatened legal action, which somewhat impeded their scheme. Once they realized there was no way for them to get around setting up a trust, they finally ceased with their delay tactics, and we all met in the lobby of the bank. To say things were awkward would be an understatement. Seeing them face-to-face, it was clear that these people were complete strangers.

While their behavior up to that point was absolutely heinous, what followed was downright evil. As we sat in the lobby, out of nowhere, my step-brother casually mentioned that his new wife had recently formed a living trust. Then with chilling nonchalance he added, "Yeah, I told her she should just leave it all to me." The timing of this comment—while we were literally addressing his previous attempt to seize control of another trust—exposed his true nature. What's even worse, is that his new wife most likely formed a trust so that upon her passing her assets would go to her now five-year-old son, and not get "mistakenly" intercepted by our step-brother. The fact that he was helping to raise her child for the next few decades, while knowing that he was going to rob him blind and make his life a living hell, was just head-shakingly, jaw-droppingly evil.

However, it wasn't just what he said that I found abhorrent, it was the look he gave me when he said it. At that moment, his lifelong mask of "the nice guy" vanished. His eyes were like that of a shark: dark, cold, predatorial, and utterly devoid of emotion. His expression turned smug and contemptuous. His comment revealing his intention to repeat this pattern with his new wife and her son, and that he had no problem in doing so. At this point, I looked over at my step-mother, who refused to look at us, a gesture based in what I'd like to think is shame at being involved in his deception with us and the upcoming deception of his wife and step-son.

When our step-brother looked away, my brother and I shot each other a quick glance of incredulity. We both shook our heads and raised our eyebrows in stunned disbelief as to what was unfolding in front of us.

At that point it was clear that he didn't care about us, our father who cared for him like he was his son, or the relationship his children had with us. He didn't care that he had manipulated his mother and had destroyed her relationship with us—my brother being the one who frequently checked in on her, and who she'd call if she needed anything. He didn't care about his new wife or her son. He only cared about money. This realization was staggering: despite my professional background as a psychotherapist specializing in narcissistic abuse, I had been completely fooled by someone who viewed us merely as a means to an end.

When the Mask Slips

Narcissists are master social chameleons, constantly shifting their persona to manipulate those around them. They wear many masks, often portraying themselves as model citizens: the devoted parent, the pious church-goer, the selfless volunteer, the perfect spouse, or the life of the party. Yet those closest to them eventually discover a stark disconnect between these carefully crafted personas and their true actions.

This disparity creates immense frustration for those who know the narcissist intimately, especially as they watch others continue to praise and admire the false front. These "good deeds" and charming behaviors are nothing more than props in an elaborate performance; masks that can be donned or discarded at will.

The first glimpse behind the mask often comes as a shock—a sudden flash of anger, an unexpectedly cruel comment, or a calculatingly cold behavior that seems completely at odds with their public persona. These moments typically occur in private, with only the target witnessing the transformation. While others might occasionally catch glimpses of this darker side, they usually dismiss it as someone simply having an "off day."

These brief moments reveal the narcissist's true self: a personality built on deception, manipulation, and calculated cruelty. The contrast between their public and private faces can be stark and deeply unsettling.

The Chilling Reality

When narcissists fail to get their way or when their mask finally drops, the experience can be bone-chilling. Many describe encountering a dead-eyed stare as though this person had become possessed, or was demonic, or somehow inhuman. Experiencing this is terrifying and leaves a person in a state of confusion and fear, wondering what kind of monster they've been sharing their life with, and if they ever truly knew the person at all.

This loss of humanity isn't always visual. It might manifest in the cold tone of an email or the chilling cadence of a phone call. When this complete lack of empathy combines with an absence of remorse, the effect is terrifying. Targets often question whether they face serious danger—financially, emotionally, mentally, or physically. These fears are usually well-founded.

A person who completely disregards the feelings of others for their selfish gain will inevitably cause significant harm to those around them. What can be confusing is that as quickly as you saw their lack of humanity, you can see it return. Remember, their interactions with others is all a performance. This is why you see emotions come and go, seemingly at the flip of a switch.

If you ever have the feeling that you are in danger, that a person is "evil," or that they have dark intentions, do not try to minimize your concern. Especially if you have had moments where you've seen their mask slip before. It is not normal for a person to give off an "evil" or sinister vibe, let alone for those who feel that vibe to be mistaken.

Key Takeaways

1. **Narcissists are masterful social chameleons who can maintain a convincing "good person" facade for years or even decades.** Their public persona of being charming, funny, and likable can completely mask their true nature, fooling even trained professionals and close family members. Don't mistake likeability with good character.

2. **Trust your instincts when you catch glimpses of someone's darker side, even if they seem brief or an isolated incident.** Those small moments when the mask slips—a flash of cruelty, a calculating comment, or a cold stare—are actually important warnings. Don't dismiss these red flags as someone "having an off day," and don't let yourself be gaslit into doubting what you've witnessed. When you find yourself wondering if someone is evil, it's more than likely because they are.

Red Flag #13: You Wonder If You Might Be in Danger

Linda's Story

In 1996, Detective Linda Arndt responded to a 911 call from a woman reporting that her six-year-old daughter had been kidnapped. Within minutes, Detective Arndt arrived at the residence of John and Patsy Ramsey. When asked about the kidnapping of their daughter, JonBenét, Detective Arndt would later say that she witnessed no shortage of odd behavior from them—behavior that seemed strikingly incongruous with parents whose child was missing.

While his wife Patsy sobbed, John casually sorted through his mail and periodically paced around the house. Additionally, the couple never sought comfort from each other. Something else that Detective Arndt found strange was that the ransom note said that the kidnappers would call between 8am and 10am that morning to instruct them as to where to deliver the ransom money.

When 8am rolled around, neither John nor Patsy said anything. When 10am passed, they had no reaction—it was as if they had forgotten that the timeframe between 8am and 10am was significant. Again, Detective Arndt found this incredibly odd, as when someone is kidnapped and their loved ones receive a ransom note that specifies a time that the kidnappers will call, the loved ones are huddled around the phone anxiously watching the clock.

The most chilling moment came soon after she'd asked John, and his friend, Fleet White, to search the house again. Fleet's scream from the basement pierced the air, and John emerged carrying JonBenét's stiff and lifeless body. As he laid her on the living room floor, he gave Arndt a look that would haunt her for decades to come—an expression that she described as an "unspoken exchange." Immediately, she felt a level of primal fear within her, so much so that she instinctively felt for her gun, mentally counted her ammunition, and mapped escape routes in her mind. Her instincts were screaming at her that she was in danger. Despite her multiple requests for backup, she remained the lone police officer on the scene.

While Detective Arndt found John Ramsey's behavior strange leading up to his discovery of JonBenét's body, it was the way he looked at her that convinced her he was involved in his daughter's death. This encounter left Detective Arndt with profound fear for her own safety. In the months that followed, she actually had a will drawn up, fearing that the Ramseys, or even certain members of the Boulder Police Department, might hunt her down and kill her for knowing "the truth."

The Moment Everything Changes

For those of us who have experienced a narcissist's mask slipping or completely dropping, we know exactly what type of "unspoken exchange" she was referring to, as well as that level of primal fear she experienced. While having a feeling that someone is dangerous, or even a killer, might sound dramatic to someone who didn't experience this look or feeling this way, it's not something easily dismissed by those who have. Granted, these things aren't proof that someone is dangerous or even a killer, but that feeling is rarely wrong—and should be heeded. Watching Detective Arndt's interview where she recounts the events of that night, it's clear she is deeply traumatized.

In an interview with ABC News in 1999, Detective Arndt said, "I knew who killed JonBenét." However, she didn't specifically name John Ramsey, or anyone else, as the killer. We all know that a gut feeling isn't enough for a conviction, but it was strong enough for her to think that drafting a will and staying far away from him was a good decision.

Those of us who have encountered true predators understand the terror of that moment when the mask falls, and you see what lies beneath—that bottomless void where empathy should be. It's a moment that changes you forever, rewiring your understanding of what humans are capable of. Detective Arndt's reaction of counting her ammunition, planning tactical positions, and having a will drawn up might seem extreme to some. However, to those who have had the experience of feeling absolute certainty of danger, her response makes perfect sense.

Fear and Relationships

The Watts' Family Murders

In 2018, Chris Watts murdered his pregnant wife, Shanann, and their two young daughters, Bella and Celeste. It's theorized that Watts committed these murders so he could run off with his mistress and have a new life, free from the responsibilities that come with having a wife (or an ex-wife) and children.

However, a detail that isn't often discussed is that several days before the murders, an incident occurred that, in hindsight, carries disturbing significance: Watts texted Shanann a bizarre photo of a Barbie doll. The doll was positioned on their sofa, with a tissue covering her head and body, leaving only her feet exposed—eerily reminiscent of a corpse in a morgue. Shanann found the image strange enough to share it on social media with the caption "I don't know what to think about this" followed by a laughing emoji. Two days later he smothered her in their bed, wrapped her body in a sheet, and then dumped her in a shallow grave.

Disconcerting actions like the Barbie covered with sheets of tissue, as if dead, might be dismissed by some as dark humor, but they deserve to be taken more seriously. When someone "jokes" with you in a way that is darkly off-putting, there's a strong likely hood that their comments aren't misguided attempts at humor, but foreshadowing.

The Landscape of Fear

Fear starts to show up more often in your daily life. It's not the obvious kind of fear you see in movies, but a steady unease that affects how you go about your day. You begin second-guessing yourself more, wondering if you're remembering things correctly or if your concerns are valid.

Small things start adding up. Maybe they mention details about your day that you didn't share with them, or you notice they've been places you thought were just yours. You might find items in different spots at home or get messages that feel odd or uncomfortable. Each time something like this happens, you feel a little less secure.

Your thoughts pull in different directions. One part of you thinks you might be making too much of these things, that maybe you're just being overly suspicious. But another part of you, the part that's trying to keep you safe, senses that something isn't right. This feels different from regular relationship problems.

You begin looking back at what they've told you about their past relationships. Those stories about ex-partners that once seemed like unfortunate situations now feel like they might follow a pattern. The people you once felt sorry for, or who they said caused all the problems, might actually have been dealing with the same things you are now. Looking back, the pieces start forming a clearer picture.

The Breaking Point of Awareness

Oftentimes, the most terrifying revelations come in the most mundane of moments. A cold stare while chopping vegetables with a sharp knife. A casual comment about your potential disappearance. Threats veiled as jokes. Supposed dark humor about making you disappear or killing other people. Sometimes these are not random occurrences, but calculated displays of power designed to keep you off-balance and afraid. And at other times, moments like this happen by accident. You just happened to be there while they were thinking their sinister thoughts aloud.

Either way, there comes a moment of terrible clarity when everything snaps into focus. You realize the person beside you doesn't love you—they might not even like you—and they for sure don't care about you. People like this see others not as individuals but as a means to an end—tools to be used and discarded.

Some survivors describe it as an out-of-body experience. Watching this person you once loved reveal themselves as a heartless predator is absolutely terrifying. When the charming exterior falls away, what remains is cold, calculating, and potentially dangerous.

You begin to understand that your safety might be at risk. Not just emotionally but physically. The line between potential threat and immediate danger becomes frighteningly blurry.

Survival and Validation

Many who have survived dangerous relationships report the same phenomenon: a sense of danger long before any concrete evidence emerged. Your body knows things your conscious mind is still trying to rationalize. The most crucial step is trusting your instincts. Those feelings of unease are not paranoia—they're your body's sophisticated warning system. Generations of survival mechanisms have equipped you with an internal alarm, and when it is set off, it's vital we listen to its warning.

Key Takeaways

1. **Danger is not always visible.** The most dangerous individuals are often the most charming. Just because you can't point to concrete evidence doesn't mean the threat isn't real.

2. **If you feel unsafe, you are unsafe.** A healthy relationship is a safe relationship, and it feels safe on all levels: emotionally, physically, psychologically, spiritually, and financially. A healthy relationship doesn't make you question if you or others are in danger. If you feel unsafe, immediately get distance from the person with concerning behavior.

Character Red Flags

Sometimes the clearest picture of who someone really is, comes from everyday interactions with the people around them. These character red flags show up in regular conversations, casual comments, and how they treat people who can't do anything for them. You'll notice them when they're relaxed and aren't trying to make a particular impression on you.

The signs in this section reveal their actual values and beliefs about how people should be treated. When they're dismissive toward a server, when they talk poorly about an ex-partner, or when they show little concern for someone's problems, they're showing you what they really think about relationships and treating people fairly. These moments are glimpses into their real attitudes rather than isolated bad days.

Pay attention to these character traits. They often give you a preview of how you might be treated later on. When someone shows you that they think rules are for other people, that others exist mainly to help them, or that they only care about people who can benefit them, take note of what you're seeing. These character red flags are signs of who this person actually is when they aren't working to impress you.

Red Flag #14: Big Ego

Mia's Story

My first date with Jeremy was at a wine bar. Even though the sommelier was also the owner of the vineyard, and had worked there for decades, Jeremy spent a solid twenty minutes discussing wine with him—although it was more of a one-sided conversation where he was informing the sommelier about wine, wine storage, and the importance of different wine glasses. At the time, I was charmed by what I mistook for passion and expertise. I even defended him to my friends, saying he was just "confident" and "knowledgeable." What I didn't realize was that his need to be the expert in every room would eventually suffocate our relationship.

As we grew closer, his ego began seeping into every aspect of our lives together. He'd correct my pronunciation of common words, give me pointers on my field of expertise, and dismiss my friends as "intellectually unstimulating." When I achieved my promotion—something I'd worked towards for years—he managed to make it about himself, suggesting that his "mentorship" had played a crucial role, even though he worked in a completely different industry. The breaking point came during a dinner with my parents. Jeremy interrupted my father while he was sharing his story about immigrating to the US to share his theory about immigration reform. That night, I watched him talk over everyone, holding them hostage with lengthy stories about himself. I finally saw him clearly: a man who thought so highly of himself that there was no room for anyone else.

The Ego of a Narcissist

A narcissist's ego is like a magnificent castle built on sand: impressive and towering but fundamentally unstable. The prevailing theory on how a person becomes a narcissist is that it is a self-protective response to inconsistent nurturing or profound emotional wounds in childhood. Rather than develop a genuine, resilient sense of self-worth, they construct an idealized false self to protect against feelings of inadequacy, shame, or worthlessness. This false self is a fragile self-image, which explains why seemingly minor criticisms or slights can trigger such dramatic responses - each challenge threatens to expose the unstable foundation beneath their carefully maintained facade.

This fragility manifests in their constant need for external validation and control. Unlike someone with healthy self-esteem who can weather criticism and setbacks, a narcissist experiences these as existential threats. Consider how they might completely unravel over a casual comment about their appearance or fly into a rage when someone disregards their advice. What appears to others as an overreaction makes perfect sense when you understand that their grandiose self-image is like a balloon - one pinprick of reality can cause the whole thing to collapse. Some mental health professionals might say that a narcissist's elaborate systems of manipulation, gaslighting, and control are actually desperate attempts to maintain their inflated self-image and prevent anyone from exposing their deep sense of inadequacy.

However, psychological theories are just that: theories. Do Vladamir Putin, Kim Jong-un, or any other megalomaniac dictator have a deep sense of inadequacy? We can speculate, but we can't say for certain. And, additionally, does it matter? How and why personalities and personality disorders develop is only hypothesized, as these things are variable and can never be understood with certainty. And, at the end of the day, for those on the receiving end of abusive behavior, it truly doesn't matter. So don't let these psychological theories pull at your strings of empathy. If someone is hurting you, the correct response is to get out of harm's way, and not to try to figure out what deep-seated psychological trauma their behavior stems from or how you can somehow help them heal.

Harry's Story

For decades, my brother, William, had been the most successful of the three of us and he never let us forget it. He'd give us unsolicited financial advice during family gatherings and make subtle digs about our "simpler" lifestyle. This past Thanksgiving, our other brother, Luke, mentioned that he was promoted to a partner in his law firm, and although he didn't say it, we all knew that meant he'd be making more than William. The news hit William like a physical blow. We all knew he had a big ego, but we didn't realize how fragile it was until that moment.

William began questioning the legitimacy of Luke's new role, suggesting it was probably just an empty title. Luke fired back and said that, no, he'd have triple the pay, but he'd also have triple the work. When family members continued congratulating Luke, William's attacks became more direct. He brought up a twenty-year-old story about Luke cheating on a high school test, then began exposing random family secrets including Luke's wife's challenges with infertility, and how Luke's new position would probably add more stress to their already stressed marriage.

To say things were awkward by this point would be an understatement. Everyone at the table had their mouths hanging open in shock or gave each other wide-eyed side glances. Some older members got up and left the table under the guise of going for second servings. William was completely unraveling and was the only one who didn't see it.

William's wife was so embarrassed by his behavior that you could tell she just wanted to melt into the floor. She interrupted him and said they needed to go for some obviously made-up reason. What makes this experience extra ridiculous is that the next day, William sent a group text to Luke and me, informing us that we owed him an apology for ruining Thanksgiving. It's been three months, and William still refuses to acknowledge his behavior, instead telling relatives that his brother's "arrogance" had ruined Thanksgiving.

The Counterintuitive Truth

I am going to say something that's probably not going to make a lot of sense, so bear with me. All narcissists have huge egos, but not all of them act like it. In fact, many narcissists come across as the exact opposite of an egomaniac.

Take Sarah, for instance. She's constantly posting pictures on social media of herself with various homeless people, and writing how blessed she is to serve at a homeless shelter. Her posts get a lot of "likes," but it feels more like she's using her volunteer work to get validation and attention from others.

The "vulnerable" narcissist may come across as humble, gracious, complimentary, and dedicated to serving others. They're also the ones who seem to need constant reassurance and support, like a baby bird with a broken wing. However, everything a covert narcissist does serves their ego, even their apparent acts of selflessness and humility. Take the office narcissist who volunteers for every difficult project. On the surface, she appears helpful and dedicated. In reality, she's building a narrative of irreplaceability and collecting ammunition for future manipulation: Her good deeds become weapons. That time she covered your shift? She'll remind you about it for years. The money she lent you? It comes with invisible strings attached to your eternal gratitude.

For example, Connie is an aspiring writer and spends most of her days quietly convinced that her unfinished novel is a future masterpiece, though she rarely shares her work. When her writing group offers constructive feedback, she gets defensive, withdraws, and later tells her close friends that "they simply don't understand the depth of my artistic vision." She dismisses successful published authors, believing they are "commercial sellouts" and that her work is too layered for the masses to appreciate. When her friend got a book deal, Connie offered lukewarm congratulations, later sharing with her writing group that her friend's success was merely due to "pandering to popular taste."

Let's examine Connie's behavior through the lens of vulnerable narcissism:

1. **Covert sense of superiority.** She believes her work is more profound and meaningful than the work of others, yet expresses this through subtle dismissal ("commercial sellouts") rather than outright bragging about her accomplishments.

2. **Hypersensitivity to criticism.** When receiving feedback from her writing group, she withdraws rather than engages, protecting her fragile self-image by dismissing their input as a lack of understanding.

3. **Fantasy of unique specialness.** Connie believes she's exceptionally talented without evidence or achievements to support this.

4. **Self-sabotaging behavior.** She avoids finishing her work while claiming "the industry isn't ready," which protects her from potential rejection while maintaining her internal narrative of superiority.

5. **Envy and devaluation.** When her friend gets a book deal, Connie can't genuinely celebrate it and must devalue the achievement ("pandering to popular taste") to maintain her sense of superior talent.

6. **Passive expression of entitlement.** Rather than openly demanding recognition, Connie hints at her unrecognized genius while avoiding situations that might challenge this self-perception.

7. **Rationalization of failures.** Connie creates explanations for her lack of success that preserve her self-image as special and misunderstood, rather than confronting her role in her situation.

All these behaviors serve to protect her fragile self-esteem while maintaining her grandiose self-concept, which is characteristic of vulnerable narcissism.

The Narcissistic Injury Response

When a narcissist's ego is threatened, their response is often dramatically disproportionate to the situation. A gentle correction in a meeting might result in months of behind-the-scenes sabotage.

Key Takeaways

1. **A narcissist's ego can wear many masks, including false humility.** While some narcissists flaunt their superiority openly, others hide behind a facade of self-deprecation, excessive modesty, or victimhood. Don't be fooled by appearances; someone constantly talking about how humble they are usually has the biggest ego in the room.

2. **A narcissist's ego is simultaneously massive and fragile.** Despite their grandiose self-image, narcissists are extraordinarily sensitive to the slightest criticism or perceived slight. This combination of inflated self-importance and paper-thin ego makes them volatile and prone to extreme reactions over minor issues.

3. **The best way to handle a narcissist's ego is to maintain firm boundaries while avoiding direct confrontation.** Don't try to puncture their ego or prove them wrong; this typically leads to rage and retaliation. Instead, focus on protecting yourself through emotional or physical distance.

Red Flag #15: How They Listen (or Don't) to You

Jenna's Story

I once went on a first (and last) date with a guy named "Oliver." Oliver spent the whole two hours talking about himself without asking me a single question. When I finally got a word in and mentioned my recent promotion, he immediately spun the conversation back to himself, launching into a twenty-minute story about his career successes. He didn't even acknowledge what I'd said. The rudest moment came when I shared that I'd lost my mother last month: he cut me off mid-sentence to complain about his recent bout with Covid and how he felt like he was going to die. Then, not more than thirty minutes later, he asked if I had plans to visit my parents this weekend as if he hadn't heard or remembered what I'd just said about Mom.

Every time I tried to contribute to the conversation, I could tell he was waiting for his next opportunity to speak. By dessert, he'd asked me twice what I did for a living, each time seeming to hear this information for the first time. It was almost comical how nothing I said had registered in his mind.

The Problematic Listener

The way a narcissist listens can come in two different ways. The first type is the Oliver's of the world. These narcissists are obviously problematic, as they have no sincere interest in anyone else. When you talk, you can tell they aren't listening to a thing you say; they are only waiting (usually impatiently) for their turn to speak. Assuming they wait, they might just cut you off and redirect the conversation to themselves.

The impact of this behavior extends beyond rudeness. Those in regular contact with overt narcissists often experience a profound sense of invisibility and emotional neglect. Partners, close friends, and especially a narcissist's children may struggle with their own worth, questioning whether their thoughts and experiences matter, as the constant dismissal and invalidation by the narcissist creates a one-sided relationship dynamic that can deeply damage one's sense of self.

The other type of problematic listening that a narcissist can do is deceptively appealing. I call it "information gathering." This type of listening doesn't usually register as problematic in the relationship's early stages, making it difficult to recognize. They show an interest in what you are saying and then use that information against you in some way. Usually, they use it to create manufactured relatability or file it away to be used later as a weapon. The common thread between the two is that both types, overtly or covertly, have no genuinely compassionate interest in the other person.

Here's an example of the way a narcissist will listen and then use the information against you:

Kara opened up to Mason about her deepest wound, sharing how her ex-husband had died by suicide just before their divorce was finalized. As she confessed her lingering guilt over their last argument, Mason held her close, wiped her tears, and offered comfort and understanding. Then, three months later, when Kara confronted him about his controlling behavior and constant criticism, Mason deliberately twisted the knife in her most vulnerable spot. "No wonder your ex killed himself!" he spat, "He probably couldn't stand having to deal with all your whining!" Kara felt as though she had been punched in the stomach and rose to leave the room in tears. Mason watched with satisfaction, knowing he had "won" the fight.

The Covert Pattern: Strategic Information Gathering

By contrast, covert narcissists are very good listeners, especially at the beginning of relationships. As we saw with Kara, they may seem totally immersed and engaged, building a strong emotional rapport. This tactical listening has an agenda: whether it's intentional or not, they soak up information with the intention of weaponizing it later. For those that are intentional about gathering information about their partner only to strategically use it against them later, they tend to, first, create a type of pseudo-intimacy. They do this by revealing what appears to be vulnerable information about themselves. This creates a false feeling of trust and invites their victims to share intimate information.

They succeed in their approach because they are tapping into an inherent human need for connection and understanding. The covert narcissist is so skilled at mirroring actual empathy and interest that their victims will ignore their gut feeling about the artificially quickened pace of emotional closeness. Their pretend vulnerability is a sophisticated trap, an illusion of mutual trust that, when ultimately broken, is all the more devastating. The best example of this that I've found is the music video for the song "Liar" by Henry Rollins, which you can find on YouTube. I will warn you, however, that it can be really triggering.

The Long-Term Impact on Relationships

The aftermath of these relationships reveals their true nature. For targets of overt narcissists, the experience is like "screaming into the wind," as the overt narcissist repeatedly dismisses or redirects the target's thoughts, feelings, and concerns. Despite the obvious frustrations, however, something about the overt narcissist (for which there are numerous possible reasons including, perhaps, occasional glimmers of their charm) keeps the target attached.

With covert narcissists, the betrayal comes later, as vulnerabilities that have been shared in the past are converted into weapons within their arsenal of emotional manipulation. As one survivor commented, it can be especially insidious because it doesn't conform to the classic picture of abuse. Though no one gets hit or yelled at, there is constant chipping away at self-esteem through the strategic use of inside information.

The long-term consequences often extend far beyond the immediate relationship, affecting how survivors approach developing relationships with others. Understandably, many develop a deep-seated fear of vulnerability and sharing, having learned that their personal information could be weaponized against them. This trauma can create a pattern of emotional withdrawal that makes forming healthy relationships challenging, even years after the narcissistic relationship has ended.

Key Takeaways

1. **Just because someone asks you a question, doesn't mean you have to answer it.** You have a right to privacy. There is a deeply concerning trend I've seen in online dating where men are asking women what their "body count" (how many people they've slept with) is. This is a no-win question, as they already have a number in their mind in terms of how many is too many. And, even if you do have the "right" number, these types of men will feel insecure and, more than likely, still use that information against you at some point. Because at the core of this question is a deep-rooted misogyny, not just mere curiosity. It's okay to refuse to answer a question—especially one like this. If the other person has an issue with it, then they aren't for you.

2. **Healthy relationships develop naturally, with mutual respect for boundaries and no pressure for premature personal disclosures.** Anyone who pushes for deep, personal information too quickly or makes you feel guilty for maintaining privacy doesn't respect your boundaries. And if someone doesn't respect your boundaries, they don't respect you.

3. **You don't need to be an open book.** It's okay and healthy not to be an open book—especially right away. Getting to know you is a privilege, not a right, and it's a privilege that's best done in small bursts over time to ensure that the other person is responsibly handling what you are sharing with them.

Red Flag #16: Disrespectful

Drew's Story

Tony and I had been dating for four months, and everything had been going great. Then, one night in January, I was sick, so he brought me dinner. He came into my house with his wet and muddy boots, knowing that my house rule is that everyone takes their shoes off at the door. I was annoyed, but since he brought me dinner, I said nothing and figured he'd forgotten my house rule. I tried to hide my annoyance, but I didn't do a very good job.

His mood switched from happy to see me to irritated and rude. Out of the blue he told me that I should be grateful that he brought me dinner. There were some back-and-forth comments said by both of us after that. At one point, he told me that if I wanted to be a wife, I needed to start acting like one, whatever that meant. I didn't like his disrespectful tone and told him I thought it was time he left.

He didn't like that and continued to dig at me, telling me I should appreciate him more and that I needed to start "acting right." He continued to spiral no matter what I said to try and calm things down. At one point, he called me a loser for dating my abusive ex and said that I must like to be treated like crap, which is why I couldn't appreciate a good guy like him. He knew my ex was physically abusive and how hard that relationship was on me, and then here he was throwing it in my face. I was so hurt because that comment was such a low blow. What's wild is that he kept telling me I was disrespecting him during all this!

I was so upset and confused that the next day I called my best friend. I told her that his behavior reminded me of my ex's, but I couldn't pinpoint why. After our fight, Tony apologized, and my ex would have never done that. And Tony didn't threaten me or become physically violent, which my ex would have. My friend explained that the commonality was that both men didn't truly care about me, and they showed that by continually disrespecting me.

It sounds so obvious but hearing that what I had experienced was disrespectful behavior helped me identify a long-standing pattern in my life with what I've put up with from the men I've dated as well as with other people. Even though Tony apologized, his behavior crossed such a major line for me that I no longer felt emotionally safe with him—because who knows what cruel things he would have said to me in the future.

This experience reinforced that an abusive relationship can come in many forms. Just because there isn't physical violence, and even if there are apologies, a relationship can still be abusive. A healthy relationship is based in respect. I used to think this was too much to ask, but now I realize it's not. It's how mature adults interact with others.

When Disrespect Hides in Plain Sight

Disrespect often manifests in subtle yet devastating ways. Even if rules or policies are not explicitly violated, disrespectful behavior can be clearly hostile. In professional settings, this might look like someone deliberately excluding colleagues from important emails, taking credit for another person's work, or refusing to share crucial information. They might respond to detailed questions with curt one-word answers, deliberately misunderstand requests, or use unnecessarily technical language to confuse and assert dominance.

The patterns of disrespect often extend into physical behaviors and social dynamics. Someone might show contempt through exaggerated sighs, eye-rolling, or walking away mid-conversation. They might command, rather than request, with phrases like "Get me coffee," often accompanied by pointing or snapping their fingers. They might say "Figure it out," in a way that makes a person feel stupid, or like a nuisance, because they simply asked for help. In meetings or social gatherings, they might arrive late to deliberately interrupt, take phone calls while others are speaking, or create obvious cliques and exclusions.

These behaviors often escalate into more direct forms of verbal abuse, carefully disguised as help or constructive feedback. In professional relationships, this might manifest as "mentorship" with comments like "I'm the only one willing to tell you that your presentation style is really amateur." In personal relationships, they might say things like, "You're lucky I'm willing to point out your flaws, clearly no one else in your life cares enough to be honest with you." These tactics are particularly insidious because they're often masked with phrases like "I'm just being honest" or "This is coming from a place of love," making them difficult to challenge or address.

The accumulation of these behaviors creates an environment of perpetual inadequacy and self-doubt. The abuser might plant strategic doubts with comments like "Oh, you're attempting that project? That's... ambitious" or undermine through comparison: "Scarlett finished this type of project in half the time." They might express toxic concern with statements such as "I'll be there to fix things when this doesn't work out" or "I worry that you're not seeing your limitations clearly." Over time, these tactics erode the target's confidence and sense of reality, often leading to internalized criticism and increased isolation.

Key Takeaways

1. **Disrespectful behavior can take many forms.** Verbal disrespect involves dismissing feelings, making derogatory comments, hurtful teasing, being condescending, name-calling, and bringing up the past to cause harm (to name a few). Behavioral disrespect involves ignoring stated boundaries, invading space, and actively attempting to get a reaction out of someone. More subtle forms of disrespect can come disguised as "help" or "care" in the form of unsolicited advice that undermines judgment or doing favors that are leveraged for guilt-tripping.

2. **Disguised abuse is often more damaging than direct abuse**. The most insidious forms of disrespect are

those cloaked in concern, help, or care. These tactics are particularly harmful because they make the target question their reactions, creating confusion about whether abuse is occurring, or if they are being too sensitive.

3. **Response strategies for targets.** When encountering disrespectful behavior, consider implementing these protective strategies:

   • Hold clear boundaries by not explaining, defending, or justifying your decisions

   • Use "grey rock" answers – i.e., provide brief, factual, and unemotional answers that offer no emotional ammunition to the attacker

   • If they claim you are too sensitive, a good come back can be, "maybe you aren't sensitive enough"

   • Create a support network of people who can validate your experiences

   • Trust your instincts: if it feels disrespectful, then the person has crossed a line with you. It doesn't matter if they knowingly or unknowingly did so. What's important is that if you bring it up, that they don't do it again.

   • Keep in mind that you don't have to accept "help" that feels hurtful

   • Wherever you can, limit interaction with the problematic person

Red Flag #17: Emotionally Immature

Avery's Story

I once asked my husband, Mateo, to help with dinner. This led to him having what I've come to refer to as one of his adult temper tantrums—mind you this is a 45-year-old man I'm talking about. While this temper tantrum wasn't the first time he'd done this, it was the first time he'd ranted and raved over something so small. I seriously couldn't believe what I was seeing. He was stomping around the kitchen, slamming cabinets and loudly putting dishes away because I'd asked him to help with dinner. "You never appreciate anything I do!" he screamed, shoving a chair out of his way.

What made this situation beyond ridiculous was that, just that morning, I had overheard him bragging to a colleague about his emotional intelligence being the reason he was so successful in working with clients. Now, he was having a complete meltdown because I'd suggested he help with dinner. The disconnect between his professional facade and private behavior was striking. I'd grown used to living with two different Mateos: the polished executive who gave presentations about team building and workplace culture, and the man who would throw a tantrum if asked to help with dinner.

What an Adult Temper Tantrum Looks Like

When narcissists don't get their way, their tantrums can take seven main forms:

1. **Intimidation.** When a narcissist's rage turns physical, it's designed to intimidate (whether they consciously realize this or not). They'll slam doors and cabinets with explosive force, throw objects across rooms, and punch walls—all while claiming they're "not violent" because they haven't hit you directly. Their aggressive displays often include invading your physical space, blocking doorways to prevent you from leaving, or following you from room to room while yelling.

They might have issues with road rage—driving aggressively or erratically to punish you for "making them angry."

These displays of physical intimidation serve multiple purposes: they release their anger, satisfy their need for control, and create an environment of fear that makes you easier to manipulate. They're exceptionally skilled at ensuring their violence stops just short of direct physical assault, giving them plausible deniability while still achieving their goal of terrorizing you. Most disturbingly, they often seem to enjoy these displays of rage, using them as a form of theatrical performance designed to remind you of their potential for violence.

2. **Silent Warfare**. Sometimes, the loudest tantrums are silent. A narcissist might disappear for days without contact, give you the cold shoulder, or create unbearable tension when they are around. They'll ignore texts and calls while ensuring you know they're active on social media. At home, they'll sigh dramatically and roll their eyes, performing their silent treatment for maximum impact. They might deliberately disrupt your sleep or ignore you in front of others, all while claiming they're "just taking space."

3. **Emotional Manipulation**. Masters of emotional manipulation, narcissists can turn on tears at will, claiming betrayal and abandonment when faced with simple boundaries. Their temper tantrums can include threats of self-harm, playing the victim, and insisting no one loves them. They do their best to make you feel responsible for their emotional state while refusing to take responsibility for their behavior.

4. **Name Calling**. When narcissists attack with words, they often aim for your deepest vulnerabilities. The terms "crazy," "stupid," "worthless," "fat," or "ugly" aren't chosen in the heat of the moment. They're carefully selected from an arsenal of ammunition they've collected during

your moments of vulnerability and trust. Every insecurity you've shared, every past trauma you've confided, becomes a weapon in their verbal warfare. What makes their verbal assaults particularly devastating is how they can switch from a loving partner to a cruel opponent in an instant. One moment, they're calling you "the love of their life," and the next, they're unleashing the most hurtful insults imaginable.

5. **Social Attacks**. When private tantrums aren't getting the desired results, narcissists often take their performance public. They'll spread carefully crafted rumors, turn mutual friends against you, and launch social media smear campaigns. They excel at telling selective truths that paint them as victims while vilifying you. Some might even contact your workplace or recruit others (often called "flying monkeys") to harass you on their behalf.

6. **Professional Sabotage**. In professional settings, their tantrums become more calculated but equally destructive. They'll bad-mouth you to colleagues, undermine your work, and spread rumors throughout your industry. Some might contact your boss directly with false complaints, or sabotage important projects. They're experts at making you look incompetent while taking credit for your successes.

7. **Financial Warfare**

When other tactics fail, narcissists often resort to financial abuse. They'll threaten to cut off support, run up shared credit cards, or hide money. Some might make large purchases out of spite or refuse to pay shared bills. In more extreme cases, they'll drain joint accounts, withhold child support or alimony, or make false financial claims. They use money as both a weapon and punishment, often accusing you of being "materialistic" if you ask them to repay the money they owe you.

Psychological Mechanisms Behind the Tantrums

The root of these adult temper tantrums lies in four deep-seated psychological patterns:

1. **Fragile Self-Esteem:** Contrary to their outward appearance of confidence, narcissists have an extremely fragile self-image. Their sense of self is built on a thin veneer of grandiosity that can crack easily under criticism or perceived rejection. Tantrums are a protective response to prevent this fragile self-image from shattering.

2. **Entitlement:** Narcissists genuinely believe that they should get their way all the time. And if they can't get what they want, they attack the person who is telling them no.

3. **Emotional Dysregulation:** Narcissists struggle with managing their emotions effectively. When they cannot control a situation or receive the admiration they crave, they resort to explosive emotional outbursts as a primitive form of emotional regulation.

4. **Learned Manipulation:** Many narcissists have learned early in life that dramatic emotional displays can be an effective way to get what they want. These tantrums are often a learned behavior that has historically been used to manipulate others.

Key Takeaways

1. **Adult tantrums are about control, not emotion.** While a child's tantrum comes from genuine emotional overwhelm, an adult's tantrum is a calculated tool for manipulation. Notice how they can instantly switch it off when someone important (like their boss) walks in, proving they have more emotional control than they pretend.

2. **Big reactions to small requests are a way of training you not to make requests at all.** The size of the tantrum

often reveals the pettiness of their grievance. The more dramatically they react, the more likely their "grievance" is due to a reasonable boundary you've set.

3. **You can't prevent their tantrums, but you can protect yourself from being manipulated by them.** When a grown adult acts like a toddler, you don't need to treat them like a child. You don't need to negotiate. You don't need to try and reason with them. And you don't need to take responsibility for their emotions. Instead, set clear consequences for unacceptable behavior and follow through. Although, sometimes the safest and clearest consequence is moving out or leaving them when they aren't around.

Red Flag #18: Selfish

Jordan's Story

I didn't realize the depth of Eric's (my now ex-husband) selfishness until I had our son. The birth was difficult and long, and I was trying to heal from a second-degree tear, not to mention the stress from trying to figure out breastfeeding all while functioning on two hours of sleep.

During all this, Eric complained constantly about how the baby's crying was disrupting his sleep and how the house was becoming a disaster zone. Just five days after delivery, while I was still bleeding and in pain, Eric initiated sex, and when I explained I wasn't physically healed enough, he became irritated and accused me of "using the baby as an excuse" to neglect his "needs." He insisted that while the doctor had told us not to have sex for six weeks, that was only a guideline. We ended up having sex that night, even though I was in pain, and it wasn't enjoyable. Eric didn't care in the slightest and kept telling me that he'd make it quick.

A few days later, I was exhausted from trying to take care of the baby, the house, and Eric. I broke down crying, and he told me I was being insensitive as parenthood was hard on him too despite the fact he hadn't changed a single diaper or woken up for any night feedings. He even suggested I was being selfish for not considering his "physical needs" while I was literally wearing mesh underwear filled with ice packs to reduce postpartum swelling.

Narcissistic Selfishness

Narcissistic selfishness is not just about occasional self-centeredness. It is a profound relational dynamic where one individual's sense of self becomes, for others, a consuming black hole, drawing in and diminishing everything and everyone around them. Their selfishness goes far beyond simple self-interest, it impairs their ability to genuinely connect or empathize.

Here are ten examples of how narcissistic selfishness plays out in their behaviors and interactions:

1. **Constant Need for Attention, Admiration, and Validation.** Narcissists demand constant attention and admiration from others. They seek to be the center of attention in social situations, often monopolizing conversations or actions to ensure others are focused on them. For example, a narcissist at a party might dominate the conversation, telling exaggerated stories about their achievements while disregarding other contributions to the discussion. They may feel upset if they aren't the focus of attention or admiration.

2. **Exploiting Others for Personal Gain.** Narcissists often exploit people for their benefit, whether it's for status, money, or emotional validation. They may use others as tools to achieve their goals without regard for the other person's needs or feelings. For example, a narcissist might manipulate a colleague into doing all the work on a project, only to take the credit for the success. They might also use relationships for social status or financial gain without offering any genuine care or reciprocation.

3. **Lack of Empathy.** While not always obvious, narcissists lack sincere empathy for others, meaning they are often unable to understand or care about the emotions and needs of others. This lack of empathy enables them to be self-serving, without regard for how their actions impact those around them. For example, suppose a friend is going through a difficult time. Some narcissists might only show interest in the conversation if it somehow benefits them, perhaps using the opportunity to boast about how they overcame a similar experience or shift the focus back to their struggles.

4. **Entitlement and Expecting Special Treatment.** Narcissists believe they are entitled to special treatment and often expect others to cater to their needs, even if it

inconveniences or harms others. They have an inflated sense of their importance and frequently act as though the rules don't apply to them. For example, a narcissist might demand a special seating arrangement at a restaurant, expect to skip the line at an event, make unreasonable requests, and assume they will avoid the consequences of their actions, all because they believe they deserve better treatment than others.

5. **Manipulation and Gaslighting.** Narcissists often manipulate others to get what they want, using tactics such as gaslighting, guilt-tripping, or emotional blackmail. They aim to control situations and people to serve their desires without regard for others' autonomy or well-being. For example, a narcissistic partner might guilt-trip their significant other into spending more time with them, even though the partner has other commitments. They may twist the truth or lie to make the other person doubt their reality, ensuring they remain in control.

6. **Lack of Accountability.** Narcissists rarely take responsibility for their actions, especially when they have hurt someone. Instead, they deflect blame, deny their wrongdoing, or shift the blame onto others to avoid any consequences that might harm their self-image. For example, if a narcissist hurts someone's feelings with a thoughtless comment, they might respond by accusing the other person of being too sensitive or overreacting. They might never apologize or even acknowledge their behavior, instead focusing on how the other person is at fault.

7. **Dismissal of Other People's Needs.** From the narcissist's viewpoint, others are only tools to meet their needs rather than individuals with their own rights and emotions. This leaves narcissists to dismiss the needs or desires of others, prioritizing their own needs above everyone else's. For example, a narcissistic friend may cancel plans at the last minute to pursue something else they want to do without any concern for how it affects the other person. Even if the

other person is depending on them, the narcissist is focused on their own desires or convenience.

8. **Emotional Unavailability.** The narcissist expects others to provide emotional support but rarely offers the same in return. Having a relationship with a narcissist can be incredibly lonely, as they might expect you to affirm and support them constantly. Still, they might be unable or unwilling to reciprocate the emotional support when you are going through a tough time. They may return the conversation to their needs or avoid offering comfort altogether. And to add insult to injury, they may accuse you of being selfish because you needed emotional support from them.

9. **Lack of Reciprocity in Relationships.** In both personal and professional relationships, narcissists rarely offer equal give-and-take. They tend to take more than they give and may treat relationships as transactional, investing in others only to the extent that it serves their interests. For example, a narcissistic colleague might repeatedly ask for favors but never offer to help in return. They may expect others to support them in their career advancement but often offer little or no assistance to others in their work. If they do offer help, it's typically because it benefits them in some way.

10. **Breaking Boundaries.** Narcissists often disregard personal boundaries because they believe their wants and needs are more important than those of others. They may push others into situations they aren't comfortable with. A narcissist in a professional setting might demand to know personal details about someone's life or make inappropriate demands without considering the other person's privacy. They may pressure others into doing things they don't want to do, ranging from taking on tasks outside the person's scope of responsibility to pressuring them to give them another chance, give them access to their finances, get married, have sex, or have a child.

The selfishness of narcissists is deeply ingrained in their personality and is driven by their need to maintain a sense of superiority, control, and constant admiration. They tend to view others as tools or objects to satisfy their desires, with little regard for the needs or feelings of those around them. This extreme self-centeredness often leads to the narcissist exploiting and manipulating others while offering little in return.

Key Takeaways

1. **Selfishness is a sophisticated defense mechanism.** Narcissistic selfishness isn't simple self-centeredness but a complex psychological issue. We can't be sure of what, in somebody's personal history, causes narcissism. It might be shaped by childhood trauma, emotional neglect, deep-seated insecurities, or reasons we may never understand— but whatever it is, it never justifies the pain they inflict on others. Plenty of people experience all, or some, of the above and don't become narcissists. Your role is not to heal, cure, or transform their behavior. In fact, attempting to do so often further entangles you in their manipulative patterns and prolongs your suffering.

2. **Recognize the subtle manipulation tactics.** Narcissistic selfishness manifests through intricate manipulation techniques that can be hard to identify. The danger lies not in obvious aggression but in the gradual erosion of personal boundaries and self-worth through carefully crafted interactions that always center the narcissist's narrative.

3. **Reclaiming your power requires boundaries and self-compassion.** Healing from relationships with narcissistically selfish individuals is fundamentally about rediscovering your inherent value. This means establishing firm boundaries, refusing to internalize their narrative, and understanding that your worth is not determined by your ability to meet their ever-changing demands. Self-compassion becomes your strongest tool. Recognize that their behavior reflects their internal struggles, not your inadequacy.

Red Flag #19: Staggering Lack of Empathy

Quinn's Story

When my father passed away, Malik complained about going to the funeral since he had already organized a guys' weekend getaway. When I explained to him that I needed him to go to the reception since I required moral support, he said I was being manipulative. I was heartbroken, but he was upset and irritated by my show of emotion, so I attempted to hide my feelings.

In hindsight, I see all the warning signs I'd been ignoring. He would roll his eyes when I spoke about missing my dad. He'd change the subject whenever I tried to talk about my emotions concerning my dad's illness. He ended up cancelling his guys' weekend and coming to the funeral with me.

During the funeral, he was on the phone the whole time, noisily sighing and making a show of how absolutely put out he was. As my relatives got together to remember my father, and comfort one another, Malik hung back, every now and then asking when we could leave.

The worst, however, was not even his lack of compassion, which was just shocking that he could somehow make my dad's passing all about him. The worst part was that two weeks after the funeral, he complained that he wished I'd "get over" my dad's death already because my sex drive was almost non-existent. So, basically, my mourning was disrupting him getting laid.

At the time, I felt selfish—after all, my desire to have sex had dropped way off, and so I attempted to get in the mood so that we could have sex more often. However, I felt like a blow-up doll. He did not even try to check if I was in the mood. He just wanted to have an orgasm and thought that it was my role as his girlfriend to give him my body to do so, no matter how I felt.

That's when I finally realized it: this man I'd loved for two years was completely incapable of being interested in anyone other than himself. I realized that that Malik's behavior wasn't just thoughtless—it was lacking in empathy and compassion.

Understanding the Empathy Void

Empathy is the invisible thread that connects us, allowing us to understand and share in each other's emotional experiences. Empathy makes us wince when we see someone get hurt, tear up at others' joy, and reach out instinctively to comfort those in pain.

For narcissists, this fundamental human capacity is either missing or severely impaired. They move through the world, seeing others not as full human beings with their own complex emotional lives but as tools to be used for their purposes.

This lack of empathy isn't always evident at first. Some narcissists can perform empathy when it serves their interests, offering the right words and gestures. However, the mask inevitably slips, revealing a chilling emotional void beneath.

The Daily Reality of Living Without Empathy

In daily life, a narcissist's lack of empathy reveals itself in countless little but devastating ways. They dismiss others' emotions as overreactions, convert discussions of other people's tragedies into tales about themselves, and display utter indifference to the emotional hurt that they inflict.

In a crisis, their emotional emptiness is painfully obvious. When you are facing illness, loss, or personal crises, they may complain about how your crisis is inconvenient for them, switch the subject to their own problems, or just plain not care. Even when you're celebrating or in a good mood, their reaction isn't right. They may downplay your success, one-up your good news, or only be interested in how your success reflects on them.

While being invalidated and dismissed like this in a relationship is painful, growing up with a parent who lacks empathy leads to devastating effects. When a child has a narcissistic parent, they aren't allowed to have any thoughts, feelings, wants, or needs that conflict with their parent's. When they do, they are shamed, blamed, or punished. The result is that the child learns to keep quiet and show only the parts of themselves that their parent approves of.

Over time, the child learns to erase those parts of themselves altogether, because doing so becomes less painful than trying to suppress them. By the time that child reaches adulthood, they often struggle with knowing what their wants, needs, thoughts, and feelings even are. They can be so out-of-tune with themselves that they don't even recognize when they are in physical pain.

In short, empathy from others isn't just something that's nice to have. It's a requirement if we are to feel seen in a relationship. And, for a child, empathy is required so that they can understand that what they think, feel, want, and need is valid.

Key Takeaways

1. **Lack of empathy isn't the same as being occasionally insensitive or self-focused.** When someone consistently shows no genuine interest or concern for your emotional experiences, especially during significant life events, you're dealing with a deeper problem. This pattern of emotional disconnection doesn't improve with time or explanation.

2. **The absence of empathy creates a uniquely damaging form of emotional abuse.** A lack of empathy isn't just about having different emotional styles—it's about one person's fundamental inability to acknowledge and respect another's emotional experience. Trying to create a satisfying relationship with someone who lacks empathy is to set yourself up for loneliness and constant heartbreak.

3. **Recovery from an empathy-void relationship requires rebuilding trust in your emotional reality.** Recognize that

your feelings are valid and worthy of acknowledgment, even if your former partner couldn't or wouldn't recognize them. Healthy relationships include mutual emotional support and understanding, not constantly justifying your right to have feelings.

Red Flag #20: Jaw-Dropping Lack of Remorse

Lauren's Story

After my miscarriage, I was drowning in grief. My husband, Gabe, however, seemed untouched by our loss and my pain. When I shared how hurt I was by his indifference, he casually remarked that women have miscarriages every day and we could just "try again soon."

His words were so dismissive and felt like salt in an open wound. Devastated, I retreated from him, hoping he might recognize the depth of my sorrow. But when I finally tried talking to him about how deeply he had hurt me, his response was infuriatingly predictable.

"I'm sorry you're so sensitive," he said, his tone more exasperated than apologetic.

I called out the non-apology for what it was. "That's not an apology. That's blaming me for my pain."

Gabe's reaction was telling. He looked more annoyed than remorseful. "I don't understand why you're making such a big deal out of this," he said, frustration clear in his voice. "I said something insensitive. People do that. Move on."

There was no genuine acknowledgment of my suffering. No attempt to understand how his words had crushed me. To him, my grief was merely an inconvenience, my hurt feelings an overreaction.

When tears finally broke through my carefully maintained composure, he didn't try to comfort me. He didn't reach out. He simply sighed, "Here we go again," and walked away.

In that moment, I realized he wasn't just unempathetic. The harsh truth was that he felt absolutely no remorse for the emotional damage he'd caused. My pain meant nothing to him. Worse, he believed I was the problem for daring to be hurt by his callous words.

A Cold Indifference

A narcissist's profound absence of remorse manifests in ways that can devastate those around them. A mother might frantically call her narcissistic son about her cancer diagnosis, only to have him respond with annoyance about how her illness might affect his upcoming vacation plans. A husband might deliberately sabotage his wife's job interview because it threatened his sense of superiority, then blame her for being "too ambitious" when she confronts him. These aren't isolated incidents but rather manifestations of a deeper pattern of emotional disconnection and entitlement.

The Two Core Characteristics of Remorseless Behavior

1. Deep-Rooted Entitlement

Narcissists operate with an unshakeable belief in their supremacy, viewing the world as a stage where they are the perpetual star. A narcissistic CEO might lay off hundreds of employees right before the holidays, showing no concern for the families affected. A narcissistic mother might spend her children's college fund on cosmetic surgery, justifying it as her right to "maintain her image." They genuinely believe their desires supersede others' basic needs, often expressing shock or outrage when challenged about their selfish actions.

2. Emotional Disconnect

Their emotional void runs deeper than simple selfishness. A narcissistic partner might watch their spouse sob after discovering infidelity and feel nothing but annoyance at having to deal with the "dramatic" reaction. In professional settings, they might destroy a colleague's reputation with malicious gossip, and then express genuine confusion when others suggest they should feel guilty.

How these Two Characteristics Manifest in Relationships

Blame-Shifting Tactics

When confronted with their actions, narcissists deploy sophisticated blame-shifting strategies. A narcissistic husband might spend the family's savings on a sports car, then blame his wife for "not making enough money" when bills go unpaid. In professional contexts, they might miss crucial deadlines and craft elaborate explanations about how their team's "incompetence" forced their hand. These excuses function as calculated explanations that remove their responsibility and redirect blame to others.

Manipulation Through Apologies

Their apologies are masterclasses in manipulation. Consider a narcissistic friend who reveals your private struggles at a party to get attention or shift the conversation to themselves. When confronted, they might say, "I'm sorry you're so sensitive about your past," or "I apologize if you misunderstood my intentions." These non-apologies serve multiple purposes: they maintain the narcissist's image as reasonable while simultaneously invalidating your feelings and shifting blame to you for being "too sensitive."

Real-World Examples

In Personal Relationships:

The coldness in intimate relationships often emerges in shocking ways. Sylvia's experience typifies this pattern. After a five-year relationship, her narcissistic partner ended things via text right before she went into surgery to have an emergency hysterectomy, adding, "I don't want to make this into a big deal. I want someone who can have my children, and since you can no longer do that, I need to move on." When she confronted him about the timing, he replied, "Well, there's never a good time, and I didn't want your surgery to delay things."

In Professional Settings:

In workplaces, narcissistic remorselessness often takes calculated forms. A manager might take credit for a subordinate's project and gaslight them in front of executives: "I mentored you through this entire process. Are you really trying to claim my work as yours?" Another common scenario involves sabotage—like the department head who deliberately withheld crucial information from a promising employee, causing them to fail publicly, then expressed "concern" about their competence during performance reviews.

In Family Dynamics:

Family relationships reveal particularly cruel manifestations of remorselessness. A narcissistic father might skip his daughter's wedding because she refused to uninvite his ex-wife (her mother), then post photos of himself at a golf resort with the caption, "Best day ever!" A mother might tell her son's new wife at the wedding reception, "I give it six months. He always did have poor judgment," then act bewildered when her son becomes distant.

Key Takeaways

1. **It's all about them.** The narcissist's lack of remorse follows a distinct pattern that, once recognized, becomes impossible to unsee. They might rage at perceived slights to their ego while showing complete indifference to others' genuine pain. For example, a narcissistic mother might become hysterical over not being seated at the head table at her son's wedding but show no concern when her grandchild is hospitalized. Their remorselessness isn't random—it's systematic and predictable. They'll express more distress over a scratched car than a partner's grief, and more concern about their image than their child's emotional needs.

2. **When narcissists do show what appears to be remorse, it's typically performative, strategic, and usually something you have to drag out of them.** They might make a grand show of apologizing when witnesses are present, only to tell their victim privately that they "deserved" the mistreatment. A narcissistic spouse might buy expensive gifts after abusive behavior, not out of genuine regret but to maintain control and create confusion. Their "accountability" often includes phrases like "I'm sorry you feel that way" or "I apologize for whatever you think I did," carefully crafted to appear remorseful while actually accepting no responsibility.

3. **No amount of explaining, pleading, or providing evidence will create genuine remorse in someone incapable of feeling it.** The path forward involves accepting that you cannot appeal to emotions that don't exist. Instead, focus on your emotional safety and healing. Seek professional support if needed, and remember that their emotional void is their deficit, not yours. The most powerful response to someone incapable of remorse is often to remove yourself from their sphere of influence and reclaim your right to be treated with basic human dignity and respect.

Remember, their lack of remorse is a fundamental trait, as unchangeable as the color of their eyes. The sooner you accept this reality, the sooner you can begin making decisions that protect your emotional well-being rather than trying to evoke empathy from someone incapable of providing it.

Red Flag #21: Stubborn

Evangeline's Story

I never imagined our tax returns would become such a power struggle, but as April's deadline creeped closer, my husband, Trevor, became next to impossible to deal with. He kept telling me that he was going to handle getting our taxes done, but then nothing would happen. My mother who is a retired accountant had offered to help us last year, but Trevor refused. He didn't want her in "our business."

As a result, we racked up thousands of dollars in penalties and interest because we submitted our taxes so late. My mother called me often to make sure our taxes were getting done, because she knew how upset I was last year. I basically had to keep giving her vague reassurances that we were working on things, but the truth was I couldn't access what I needed, and Trevor refused to budge.

Trevor's stubbornness was absolutely infuriating. He would release information in infuriatingly incomplete batches, as if testing how little he could provide while still appearing cooperative. He'd hand over our W-2s but "forget" about the 1099 from his freelance work. He'd share bank statements but withhold the investment account documentation. Each time I'd point out what was missing, he'd act surprised, promise to find it, then conveniently become too busy to follow through.

His pattern of partial compliance was more infuriating than his earlier outright refusal. My poor mother was left trying to solve an incomplete puzzle. She'd start calculations she couldn't finish and was constantly having to revise her work. During our third video call, as I once again explained that we were still missing several critical statements, my mother's professional composure finally cracked.

"I can't help if I don't have everything," she said, her voice breaking as she began to cry. "I'm worried about you both. These gaps in your financial records, the disorganization... I'm afraid you're heading for serious trouble." Seeing my mother—always so capable and collected—reduced to tears of frustration made me so damn angry at Trevor.

When I confronted him about it, he accused my mother of creating drama and trying to make him look like the villain— completely glossing over that her tears came from genuine concern, not manipulation. I finally laid out the reality. I told him that his stubbornness wasn't just hurting us; it was taking its toll on my mom. I was so incredibly hurt and angry that he saw no problem with being such a stubborn jerk to the point where he'd made my mom cry.

The Unyielding Mind

The stubbornness of a narcissist isn't simple determination or strong-mindedness—it's an almost supernatural ability to deny reality itself in service of being "right."

For overt narcissists, this manifests as an unmistakable "my way or the highway" attitude. They plant their flag on a position and defend it as though their life depends on it, even as evidence to the contrary piles up around them.

Covert narcissists display their stubbornness more subtly, often appearing to bend while actually remaining rigid in their positions. They might seem to apologize or compromise, but these are usually tactical maneuvers rather than genuine concessions.

Eight Faces of Narcissistic Inflexibility

1. **Insisting They are Right:** Standing atop a mountain of evidence proving their mistake, they'll still insist they're right. Discussions become endless loops of defensiveness and deflection. They'll derail conversations, change subjects, or simply talk over others rather than acknowledge another perspective.

2. **Opinions Set in Stone:** Once they've declared a viewpoint, it becomes truth…at least in their mind. New facts, expert opinions, or changing circumstances bounce off their certainty like arrows off armor. To a narcissist, their perspective isn't just right; it's the only possible way to see things.

3. **Unwavering Standoffs:** Every discussion becomes a battlefield where surrender isn't an option. Even simple decisions like where to eat dinner can turn into hours-long standoffs because yielding to another's preference feels like defeat.

4. **Criticism as a Personal Attack:** Feedback triggers explosive defensiveness, whether it's a gentle suggestion or constructive criticism. Simple comments like "Maybe try it this way" can spark disproportionate reactions ranging from icy contempt to outright rage.

5. **The Inability to be Vulnerable:** Emotional openness represents a breach in their armor. They'd rather end relationships than admit to feeling hurt, maintaining their fortress of invulnerability at any cost.

6. **Rules for Thee but Not for Me:** Standard procedures and social norms slide off them like water off a duck. They'll park in handicapped spaces, cut lines, or ignore deadlines while insisting these rules simply don't apply to them. If others insist that they obey laws or social norms, they'll double down and insist that they know what they are doing, that what they are doing isn't a problem, or that they should not worry about it.

7. **"Sorry" Seems to Be the Hardest Word:** The word "sorry" seems physically painful for them to say. Instead of apologizing, they'll construct elaborate justifications or redirect blame, turning their obvious mistakes into everyone else's fault.

8. **Decisions Written in Stone:** Once they've chosen a course of action, they'll stick to it even if it leads straight off a cliff.

Changing plans would mean admitting their initial decision wasn't perfect.

The Impact of Unyielding Behavior

This relentless inflexibility creates a toxic environment where growth becomes impossible, and relationships wither under the strain. Team projects collapse as valuable input gets ignored, personal relationships crumble under the weight of unacknowledged wrongs, and simple interactions become exhausting battles of will.

For those dealing with narcissistic stubbornness, recognition becomes the first step toward protection. Their rigid stance stems from a need to maintain their fragile sense of superiority at any cost, regardless of facts or reality.

Key Takeaways:

1. **A narcissist's stubbornness goes far beyond normal determination or strong opinions.** They will go to extraordinary lengths to avoid admitting even minor mistakes, often constructing elaborate justifications and conspiracy theories rather than simply acknowledging their mistakes.

2. **Their inflexibility manifests in multiple ways, ranging from a refusal to apologize and being stubborn to rejecting all help and advice.** Their need to be right transcends logic, evidence, or relationships, turning even simple corrections into lengthy battles that can last for days or weeks.

3. **When dealing with someone showing these behaviors, recognize that their stubbornness isn't about facts or reality.** Don't exhaust yourself trying to prove your point with evidence or logic. Their resistance stems from a deep-seated need to maintain control, rather than from a genuine disagreement about facts. The healthiest response is often to disengage from these circular arguments and maintain your boundaries.

Red Flag #22: Arrogant

Ricardo's Story

I used to work with this absolutely insufferable woman named Misha, who always had to be seen as the smartest and most successful person in any room. And, of course, she couldn't stand not being the center of attention. I once gave a presentation, and at the end of it, she critiqued my methodology in front of everyone. The irony here is that the methodology that she said I should have used is the method I actually did use!

However, the only people who caught onto this were those who were familiar with statistical analysis—basically us data crunchers. Many of the higher ups were seemingly impressed with what she said, which was infuriating as she was talking nonsense, and they were gobbling it up.

Shortly after the meeting, my supervisor and I were refilling our coffee in the breakroom. While we were there, he congratulated me on my presentation. Misha had walked in right around this time, and not being able to handle anyone else getting a complement, she rushed over and tells me and my supervisor that I'd "gotten lucky" with my conclusions and offered to "mentor" me since I "clearly needed guidance" in proper research methods. My supervisor shot me a knowing glance and just gave her a polite smile before walking away.

What made it all so infuriating was how she'd frame her arrogance as helpfulness. During team meetings, she'd interrupt others mid-sentence with "Let me explain this in simpler terms for everyone," as if we were children struggling to grasp basic concepts.

In her office, she has a wall full of photos of herself with various executives. Most of the pictures were candid shots from company events where she'd positioned herself strategically in the background—so to everyone else it's clear that these photos don't show any type of closeness with these people—she just happens to be in the same place as them when the photo was taken. The kicker is that whenever anyone questions her decisions, she brings up her "close relationships with leadership" as a way to shut down any disagreement from others.

What really got me was that after I received my promotion, she sent an office-wide email "congratulating" me while making sure to remind everyone that she'd achieved the same position three years earlier than I had. It was exhausting how every conversation, every achievement, every moment had to somehow be about her and her superiority.

Understanding Narcissistic Arrogance

Have you ever met someone whose "confidence" feels more like a shield than a genuine trait, and their achievements more like weapons than accomplishments?

Have you ever shared good news with someone, only to watch them subtly twist the moment until you felt diminished rather than celebrated? Or perhaps you've encountered someone who treats knowledge like a competition, who must always be the expert in the room, even on topics they barely understand. Their "confidence" feels like a desperate need to prove their superiority rather than genuine self-assurance.

This kind of behavior isn't confidence or pride. Genuine confidence can coexist with the success of others. Whereas arrogance requires others to feel smaller for the narcissist to feel big. It's not enough for a narcissist to shine; they must dim everyone else's light in the process.

Arrogance lies at the core of narcissistic behavior, stemming from an inflated self-image and an unwavering sense of superiority. While this trait might not be immediately apparent, it invariably surfaces through their conviction that they're the smartest person in any room, and their belief that they can talk their way out of any consequence.

The best example I can think of for narcissistic arrogance, is Anthony Todt. Todt was sentenced to life in prison without the possibility of parole for killing his wife and three children. During his trial, his arrogance was off the chart, as he continued to maintain an attitude of superiority during his questioning.

At one point, he said that he walked in on his wife stabbing herself. When he asked her what she was doing she said, "I'm trying to stab myself in my vena cava." Of course, this statement doesn't make sense and far surpasses anything even close to being believable. No one who is stabbing themselves in the chest is going to be that articulate and use such precise medical language.

However, what is more believable is that Todt was using this moment to try to impress others with his knowledge of human anatomy. What was even more jaw-dropping, is that he seemed to believe his behavior and demeanor would somehow make him sympathetic to the jury. It did not.

Twelve Signs of Narcissistic Arrogance

1. **Believing they Are Always Right.** Narcissists frequently interrupt conversations to assert their opinions as absolute truth. They dismiss opposing viewpoints and may belittle those who disagree, even those who are experts in whatever topic is being discussed. Their certainty in their correctness remains unshakeable, regardless of evidence to the contrary.

   For example, Sam is an accountant with no medical training, yet he'll argue confidently (and at great length) with his sister Chloe, a practicing physician, about complex medical issues. When presented with peer-reviewed research that contradicts his views, he dismisses it with, "Those studies are flawed. You need to do your own research." When asked for his sources, he cites questionable websites. When others try to contribute to the conversation, he talks over them or waves away their points with, "Let me explain why you're wrong about this." Even when proven wrong with concrete evidence, he'll shift the argument or claim he "meant something else," never admitting his mistake.

2. **Exaggerating Achievements.** Watch for constant exaggeration of accomplishments and appropriation of others' successes. They might claim to have been the "key to success" for their children with whom they have had little to no relationship. They might also embellish their credentials with prestigious, but unverifiable, or questionable achievements.

For example, Tom is a mid-level marketing manager who transforms every minor task into an epic achievement. During a recent project presentation, he claimed he "single-handedly saved the company millions" by catching a minor error in an email that was to go out to a big client. At office parties, he regularly interrupts colleagues' stories about their successes to redirect attention to his "more impressive" accomplishments. At a co-worker's retirement party, Tom announced that he'd been headhunted by three Fortune 500 companies (which no one could verify). He keeps a carefully curated LinkedIn profile filled with inflated titles and responsibilities, claiming he "led global initiatives" when, in reality, he participated in online team meetings where some of the other participants were based overseas. He even embellished his college, one-semester, study abroad program by stating he had "extensive international business experience."

3. **Expecting Special Treatment.** Their perceived superiority leads to demands for special treatment. A narcissist might bypass standard procedures or expect others to accommodate their schedule, believing their time and needs hold greater importance than anyone else's.

For example, Lisa is a Realtor who believes standard rules are beneath her. At restaurants, she regularly demands to be seated immediately, regardless of the waitlist, often announcing, "Do you know who I am? I bring all my high-end clients here." When her son's school enforced a strict pickup time policy, she filed multiple complaints, insisting her schedule was "too important" to accommodate standard procedures. During a recent flight, she berated flight attendants for not upgrading her to first class because there was an empty seat, although she didn't want to pay for it. At her gym, she refuses to wipe down equipment after use, telling others, "That's what the cleaning staff is for."

4. **Disregarding Others' Opinions or Needs.** They routinely ignore or invalidate others' perspectives, seeing their own view as paramount. In relationships, this might mean unilaterally making decisions about shared concerns like finances or travel, assuming their preferences naturally take precedence.

   For example, Phillip, the department head at a tech company, epitomizes this trait. During a crucial project meeting, when his junior developer suggested a more efficient coding solution, Phillip didn't just disagree – he laughed and said, "Let's stick to ideas from people who actually understand programming" and then later implemented the coding suggestion, passing it off as his own. Even when customer feedback contradicts his vision for a product, he dismisses it as "users not understanding what they really need." At home, he consistently overrules his wife's parenting decisions without discussion, saying, "Women are too emotional about these things." When his teenage daughter expressed interest in business school, he went back on his promise to help her pay for tuition and, instead, encouraged her to enroll in nursing school at a junior college, declaring, "I know what's best for your future."

5. **Talking Down to Others.** Their speech often carries a patronizing tone, treating others as intellectually inferior. They might use phrases like "I'll explain this slowly so you

can understand," or adopt a deliberately simplified speaking style to emphasize perceived superiority.

6. **Refusing to Apologize.** Admitting mistakes threatens their self-image of perfection. Rather than apologize, they'll often blame others for being "too sensitive" or deflect responsibility entirely. Even clear wrongdoing, like a last-minute cancellation, gets reframed as others' overreactions. Take for example, Rachel, a department store manager whose refusal to acknowledge mistakes has created a toxic workplace. When she ordered the wrong seasonal inventory, costing the store thousands, she blamed her staff for "not properly explaining the ordering system" she'd used for five years. After missing her daughter's piano recital because she was scrolling through social media, she told her crying child, "You should have reminded me more clearly. This is a learning experience for you." During a dinner party, she spilled wine on her friend's white carpet, but instead of apologizing, she criticized her host for "having impractical furnishings."

7. **Name Dropping and Boasting.** They frequently name-drop and highlight connections to prestigious individuals or institutions. Social gatherings become opportunities to showcase their proximity to power or fame, expecting admiration in return.

   For example, Miles, an investment banker, has turned name-dropping into an art form. At his cousin's posh wedding, he loudly complained about how it didn't measure up to the "exclusive charity gala" he allegedly attended with celebrities (though no photos exist). During parent-teacher conferences, he steers every conversation toward his "close friendship" with the school board president, whom he met once at a fundraiser. His social media is carefully curated with strategic photos taken outside of luxury hotels. And he regularly posts about "private meetings" with executives who don't know his name. Even his children's play dates become opportunities to brag about his "insider connections" to high-end preschools, often making other parents uncomfortable.

8. **Power Through Intimidation.** They maintain superiority by making others feel small. In leadership positions, this manifests as using authority to suppress challenges or wielding knowledge as a weapon to control conversations. Ruby, a non-profit director, uses intimidation like a finely tuned instrument. In meetings, she regularly reminds her staff about their "replaceable" status, saying things like "There are hundreds of people who would be grateful for your position." When a talented employee received praise from the board, Ruby began assigning them menial tasks and excluding them from important meetings, later explaining, "I need to remind people of the hierarchy here." She keeps detailed notes of minor mistakes to use as leverage during evaluations, often bringing up incidents from months ago to justify denying promotions. Even in volunteer committees at her church, she creates unnecessary power structures and threatens to withhold her participation unless given leadership roles.

9. **Refusing to Acknowledge Others' Success.** Others' achievements trigger their insecurity, leading them to ignore or diminish these accomplishments. A narcissistic sibling might consistently downplay their family members' successes while demanding a celebration of their own.

Consider Amanda, the regional sales director who can't stand anyone else's success stealing her spotlight. When her colleague won "Employee of the Year," she spent the entire celebration dinner telling stories about her past awards, then sent an office-wide email "clarifying" that her sales numbers were still higher.

At her sister's college graduation, she interrupted the family photos to announce her minor promotion. During team meetings, she visibly withdraws or checks her phone when others share successes, yet she expects full attention during her updates.

When her best friend got engaged, Amanda immediately posted about her relationship milestones, then criticized her friend's ring as "hopelessly practical" and laughed, saying that she must really love him if she agreed to marry him based on how small the diamond was.

10. **Obsession with Their Image.** The narcissist's preoccupation with image goes beyond healthy self-care, extending into an all-consuming focus on maintaining a perfect appearance both in person and online.

Take Elijah, who spends more time positioning himself for photos than being authentically engaged in life. His social media presence is meticulously curated; he'll take dozens of photos to get the perfect "candid" shot, delete posts that don't get enough engagement within an hour, and regularly pays for professional editing of casual family photos before sharing them.

During work meetings, he's visibly distracted by his reflection in the conference room windows, adjusting his tie or hair mid-conversation. His Instagram grid follows a careful color scheme, and he'll plan outings or even skip events based on whether they'll provide "social media worthy" content.

What makes this behavior particularly revealing isn't just the attention to appearance but how maintaining this perfect image takes precedence over genuine connections and experiences; he's more concerned with documenting and presenting the moment than living it.

11. **Boundary Violations.** A narcissist's sense of entitlement leads them to disregard personal boundaries. They might show up uninvited, make unreasonable demands, or ignore

requests for privacy, believing their desires supersede others' rights. For example, when Jannette's son and his wife bought a new home, she insisted on having a key. During her divorce, she continued using her ex-husband's credit cards, arguing that their separation didn't change her lifestyle requirements. At work, she regularly walks into private meetings unannounced, telling others that closed-door policies didn't apply to upper-level management like her.

12. **Perceived Envy.** They assume others envy their success, appearance, or lifestyle, often without basis. This belief reinforces their sense of superiority and leads them to interpret any lack of admiration as jealousy.

For example, Peter turns every situation into evidence that others envy him and his girlfriend, Sarah. When his friends' relationships hit rough patches, instead of showing empathy, he smugly tells Sarah, "No one has the connection we do." At social gatherings, if another couple receives attention, Peter immediately starts whispering to Sarah about how "they're just trying to compete with us" or "they're copying what we did first." If Sarah's friends achieve career success, Peter insists they only worked harder because "they're trying to prove something" to him and Sarah. When they lose touch with couples they used to be close with, Peter spins stories about how "they couldn't handle seeing a truly happy couple" or "they stopped hanging out because they're jealous of our relationship." Any criticism or distance from others gets reframed as jealousy, never as a response to his behavior. This pattern prevents genuine friendships, as every achievement by others becomes a threat, and every normal social interaction gets twisted into a competition that, in Peter's mind, others are desperate to win. What makes this particularly toxic is how it gradually isolates them from genuine connections, as Peter's constant projection of envy onto others reveals more about his insecurities than any actual feelings from their social circle.

The Impact

Narcissists create toxic environments in all types of relationships. Their entitlement and self-centeredness lead to strained personal connections, hostile workplaces, broken social bonds, and emotional harm to others. Since they can't see people as equals and constantly need to feel superior, healthy relationships become virtually impossible.

Recognizing these twelve narcissistic behaviors helps us spot toxic patterns early, before they damage our sense of reality and self-worth. What makes these behaviors so harmful isn't just their impact on single interactions, but how they gradually change relationship dynamics until the narcissist's warped perspective becomes dominant.

To protect yourself, don't waste time arguing with their arrogance; instead, hold firmly to reality. When someone needs you to feel inferior for them to feel superior, when they constantly demand validation, or when their "confidence" undermines your self-worth, these aren't signs of strength but of a fragile ego trying to maintain its false image.

Key Takeaways:

1. **Healthy confidence lifts others up, while narcissistic arrogance requires pushing others down.** Real success doesn't demand constant acknowledgment, true strength doesn't need to diminish others, and genuine self-worth never requires someone else to feel worthless.

2. **Narcissistic arrogance manifests in specific, recognizable patterns, from refusing to acknowledge others' successes to demanding special treatment and violating boundaries.** Don't bother trying to explain to a narcissist why their arrogance is a problem, as they will more than likely think you are jealous of them. Instead, try not to let their arrogance bother you.

Red Flag #23: A Giant Hypocrite

River's Story

My relationship with Casey ended after I realized what a sexist hypocrite he really was. I'd mentioned I had lunch with a male coworker—the same kind of lunch Casey regularly had with his female coworkers and other female "friends." But while Casey's lunches were "just networking" or hanging out with friends, mine was apparently "emotional cheating."

As I watched him storm around our apartment and demand to see my phone, I remembered how, just last month, he'd refused to show me his messages after weeks of being overly secretive with his phone. "That was different," he said. He claimed I didn't need to see his phone and that I just needed to trust him, whereas now he didn't trust me and saw no problem with going through my phone.

Of course, he found nothing on my phone but still demanded that I never go out to lunch with male coworkers again. At that point, his hypocrisy was crystal clear. When I tried to point this out, Casey would twist the conversation so skillfully that I'd end up apologizing for even bringing it up. He'd tell me that I was paranoid and that "my jealousy was really unattractive."

In Casey's mind, any woman that spent time with men outside of their partner was a form of cheating. We argued about his views on women and his hypocrisy in general for several weeks before I finally ended things with him. I realized that not only was his hypocrisy infuriating, but his sexism would probably only get worse with time, not better.

Different Rules for Them

In the world of a narcissist, fairness is a foreign concept. They operate like corrupt judges, creating and enforcing rules that somehow always favor themselves. A narcissist might:

- Demand you share your location 24/7 while refusing to tell you where they're going

- Expect you to introduce them to all your friends while keeping parts of their social life mysteriously private

- Interrogate you about every coworker while having regular "work dinners" with their colleagues

- Require you to account for every dollar you spend while spending freely, or hiding their financial activities

- Explode if you like someone's social media post, but regularly message and flirt with others online

- Insist you cancel plans with friends when they need you, but disappear when you're having a crisis

- Demand immediate responses to their texts while taking hours or days to reply to yours

- Expect you to be understanding about their ex being in their life while accusing you of cheating if you mention your ex

- Monitor your clothing choices and criticize anything "too revealing" while openly flirting with others in front of you

- Require your undivided attention when they're speaking but regularly interrupt or ignore you

These double standards form the foundation of how narcissists view relationships. In their minds, they are special, unique, and therefore deserving of privileges and exceptions that shouldn't apply to others. These double standards extend beyond privacy to every aspect of the relationship. They expect instant forgiveness for their mistakes while holding lifelong grudges over your smallest infractions. Their sense of entitlement runs so deep that when confronted about these inconsistencies, they'll often respond with genuine confusion or anger, as if it's absurd to suggest they should be bound by the same rules they impose on others.

The Art of Never Being Wrong

When confronted with their hypocrisy, narcissists demonstrate an almost Olympic-level ability to dodge accountability. Their arsenal of defense mechanisms includes gaslighting ("I never said that"), projection ("You're the one who always does this"), and selective memory ("That's not how it happened"). No matter how clear the evidence or how many witnesses, they will never fully admit to holding double standards.

Their explanations involve complex mental gymnastics that would almost be impressive if they weren't so damaging. They might admit to a behavior but insist their version was somehow nobler or more justified: "Yes, I had lunch with Sarah from work, but that's different because it was about business. Your lunch with Tom was clearly personal." Or they'll create elaborate scenarios that cast them as the victim even when they're clearly the aggressor: "I only called you a bunch of names because I thought you were going to break up with me."

The phrase "that's different" becomes their shield, wielded with absolute conviction yet never accompanied by a logical explanation of what makes their situation unique. They'll rewrite entire histories, claiming they never said things you clearly remember, or insisting their actions were justified by circumstances that never existed. When backed into a corner with undeniable evidence, they'll shift tactics: "Why are you so obsessed with being right?" or "You always have to make everything about you."

Most disturbingly, they deliver these illogical explanations with such unwavering confidence that targets often find themselves questioning their memory and judgment. Their need to be right is so fundamental to their personality that they'll create entire alternative realities rather than acknowledge their contradictions. Even in group settings where others witness their hypocrisy, they'll maintain their position with such conviction that people often give up challenging them simply to avoid the exhausting circular arguments that follow.

The result is a relationship where the facts become unclear, with the narcissist controlling the narrative. They'll deny video evidence, challenge written proof, and dismiss multiple witnesses, all while staying completely certain they're right. This goes beyond being stubborn to show a basic inability to accept any version of events that challenges their sense of superiority and entitlement.

The Forgiveness Trap

The narcissist's manipulation of forgiveness reveals perhaps their most damaging double standard. They demand immediate and complete absolution for their transgressions, often before they've even finished apologizing. Your hesitation to forgive instantly is viewed as a character flaw on your part, proof that you're "unforgiving," "hold grudges," or are "making too big a deal" out of their behavior.

Their apologies come with built-in escape clauses: "I'm sorry you feel that way" or "I wouldn't have done it if you hadn't made me." These non-apologies are quickly followed by demands that you "move on" and "stop bringing up the past." Meanwhile, they keep a mental ledger of your every mistake, ready to reference them months or years later as justification for their current bad behavior.

The dynamic becomes especially toxic when they use your past forgiveness against you: "You forgave me for the affair I had ten years ago, so why can't you "forgive" (get past) the one you just caught me having?" This creates a pattern where each act of forgiveness becomes ammunition for future transgressions. They'll pressure you to "get over" their betrayals or wrong doings while bringing up your minor infractions from years ago as if they happened yesterday.

This one-sided system of forgiveness serves to keep you perpetually off-balance and seeking their approval. You find yourself apologizing for things that don't warrant an apology while they refuse to acknowledge clear wrongdoing. The more you forgive, the more entitled they become to your forgiveness, creating an endless cycle where your capacity for understanding becomes a weapon used against you.

Key Takeaways

1. **When someone shows you they operate by different rules than they expect you to follow, this is a problem.** Double standards aren't mistakes or misunderstandings—they're deliberate tactics of control. Pay attention when someone consistently excuses in themselves what they condemn in you.

2. **The moment you notice a double standard, call it out calmly and directly.** Don't waste time trying to understand or justify their hypocrisy. Instead, simply state what you observe: "You expect me to forgive your behavior immediately, but you're still angry about my lunch with a coworker from three months ago. This double standard isn't acceptable to me." Your power lies not in making them understand or change, but in clearly acknowledging the hypocrisy and deciding what boundaries you need to set for yourself. *Keep in mind that continuing to call someone out for their behavior and expecting them to change isn't a boundary.* <u>A true boundary has a deal breaker, meaning, it has an action attached to where you distance yourself in some way, shape, or form from damaging behavior.</u>

3. **In balanced relationships, rules and expectations are mutual.** If you find yourself constantly explaining or apologizing for things your partner does freely, you're in a one-sided relationship.

Red Flag #24: Low to No Regard for Laws or Social Contracts

Andy's Story

My ex, Andy, used to drive while texting. If I said anything about it, he'd laugh and say I was overreacting. And, at times, if I showed that his driving made me nervous, he'd drive even more recklessly. I thought about all the other signs I'd overlooked: how he used handicapped parking spots because they were "convenient," bragged about avoiding taxes, and stiffed contractors right before jobs were finished because he decided they didn't deserve full payment. Each incident came with an explanation that made me question whether I was being too strict about rules. Sitting in that car as we came close to hitting other vehicles, I could see that his disregard for rules came from a sense of entitlement that affected everyone around him.

One night, after we made it home, I lay awake thinking about years of similar incidents: how he cheated on his ex-wife multiple times during their marriage, which he said was her fault; the small businesses he refused to pay because they "should have known better than to trust a handshake deal;" the neighbor's fence he tore down without permission because it "blocked his view." Each time, he'd made me feel like I was being uptight for questioning his actions, like following basic rules and showing common decency made me weak.

His contempt for rules went beyond traffic laws. He seemed to believe he was above the basic agreements that help society function. He broke rules and took pride in treating every law, boundary, or social expectation as something that didn't apply to him. He genuinely believed he was always right, which meant he'd never change.

The Rules Don't Apply to Me

Narcissists operate with a fundamental belief that laws and social contracts are optional guidelines that apply to others but not to them. This worldview manifests in both small and large ways, from parking in fire lanes because they're "just running in for a minute," to committing tax fraud because they "already pay too much." What makes this behavior particularly insidious is how they present it not as rule-breaking but as intelligent opportunism. "Only smart people know how to work the system," they'll say, or "You have to make your own rules to get ahead."

Their justifications often come wrapped in a veneer of superiority. They'll frame rule-following as a weakness, using phrases like "Don't be a sheep" or "The system is rigged anyway, so why play by their rules?" This reframing serves two purposes: it elevates their rule-breaking to seem like clever rebellion rather than selfish entitlement, and it makes others feel naive for following rules. A narcissist might mock their partner for waiting at a red light at 2 am or ridicule an employee who refuses to fudge numbers on a report.

The most dangerous aspect of this mindset is how contagious it can become. People around the narcissist often find themselves gradually accepting increasingly unethical behavior as normal. What starts as justifying small infractions ("Maybe he's right, that handicap spot was empty anyway") can evolve into excusing serious violations of ethics and law. They create an environment where questioning their behavior marks you as rigid, unsophisticated, or unable to see the "bigger picture." This normalization of rule-breaking often leaves their partners, employees, or children with a distorted sense of right and wrong that can take years to unravel.

When confronted about their behavior, they'll often employ sophisticated manipulation tactics. They might point to successful people who've broken rules ("Every successful person bends the law sometimes"), appeal to flexibility ("You need to learn to think outside the box"), or attack the legitimacy of the rules themselves

("Those laws are just there to control people"). These arguments can sound compelling, especially when delivered with the narcissist's characteristic confidence, making it difficult for others to maintain their ethical bearings.

Their contempt for rules extends beyond just breaking them; they often feel compelled to demonstrate their superiority over those who follow the rules. They might deliberately create situations where others are forced to either break rules or face negative consequences, taking pleasure in corrupting others' ethical standards. For example, a narcissistic boss might pressure employees to lie on reports and then mock those who refuse as not being "team players." Or a narcissistic partner might push their spouse to participate in tax fraud and then use this complicity to ensure silence about other unethical behaviors.

The Dangerous Belief in Their Invincibility

They operate with an almost magical thinking about their specialness. "I won't get caught" becomes their mantra, not because they're particularly careful or clever, but because they truly believe they're immune to the consequences that affect "ordinary" people. A narcissist might drive drunk while insisting they "drive better after a few drinks" or refuse to wear a seatbelt because they're "too good a driver to crash."

This sense of invulnerability makes them particularly dangerous because they'll take risks not just with their safety, but the safety of others as well. They'll text while driving with their children in the car, invest others' retirement funds in obvious scams, or ignore crucial safety protocols at work. When disasters inevitably occur, they're genuinely shocked; not just acting surprised, but truly unable to comprehend how their special status didn't protect them. One narcissist might say, "I can't believe this happened to ME," while another insists, "They can't send someone like ME to jail."

The depth of this delusion becomes apparent in their response to near-misses or warning signs. Instead of seeing close calls as wake-up calls, they interpret their escapes as further proof of their invincibility. A narcissist might nearly cause a major accident while speeding, then take their survival as confirmation that they're "just that good at driving." They'll use these experiences to double down on their risky behavior rather than learn from them, creating an increasingly dangerous spiral of risk-taking.

Their belief in their invulnerability often extends to legal and financial consequences as well. They might ignore court orders, violate restraining orders, or continue illegal business practices even after being fined or warned. In their minds, they're simply too smart, too special, or too well-connected for serious consequences to stick. They'll often point to previous escapes from consequences as proof: "See? Nothing bad happened last time. They can't touch me."

Perhaps most chilling is how this sense of invincibility affects their response to others' tragedies. When they hear about someone else facing consequences for similar behavior—a drunk driver going to jail, a fraudster being caught, a reckless driver causing a fatal accident—they remain unmoved. Instead of seeing these as cautionary tales, they'll often explain away why that person's fate doesn't apply to them: "Well, they weren't as careful as I am" or "They just weren't smart enough." This inability to learn from others' experiences makes them particularly resistant to change and especially dangerous to those around them.

Key Takeaways

1. **A person's attitude toward small rules often reveals how they'll handle bigger ones.** When someone regularly disregards traffic laws, parking rules, or other daily social contracts, they're showing you their fundamental belief that rules don't apply to them. These aren't isolated incidents but glimpses of a dangerous pattern of entitlement.

2. **Don't expect loyalty from someone who can't even give you honesty.** Someone who isn't honest with you won't

be loyal to you either. Honesty is a fundamental aspect of healthy relationships. If a person fails at this basic level of trustworthiness, they're unlikely to demonstrate more complex commitments like loyalty.

3. **Contempt for rule-followers is a serious red flag.** When someone mocks others for following rules, or brags about breaking them, they're revealing not just their unethical behavior but their disdain for basic social contracts that keep society functioning. It is only a matter of time before their behavior and worldview negatively impacts you.

4. **Trust actions over explanations**. No matter how convincing their justifications might sound in the moment, patterns of disregarding rules and laws reveal someone's true character. If someone regularly puts their wants above others' safety and well-being, believe what their actions are telling you about their values.

Abuse and Control Tactics (The Devalue Phase)

The shift from idealization to devaluation rarely happens overnight, although it can. Usually, the devaluation phase of the cycle of narcissistic abuse is a gradual erosion of the respect and care you once received. The idealization phase is now replaced by criticism, manipulation, and control. This is where the mask begins to slip, and you start to see glimpses of who they really are beneath the charm. What once felt like passionate love now feels suffocating and unpredictable.

The tactics in this section represent deliberate attempts to undermine your confidence, isolate you from support systems, and establish dominance in the relationship. These behaviors often start small and escalate over time, making them difficult to recognize at first. You might find yourself making excuses for their actions or believing that you've somehow caused their change in behavior. The confusion is intentional; it keeps you off balance and easier to control.

Pay attention to these patterns of abuse and control. They reveal the true purpose behind the earlier love-bombing and idealization. When someone begins to monitor your activities, criticize your appearance, or turn your loved ones against you, they're systematically breaking down your independence and self-worth. These aren't signs of a relationship going through a rough patch. They're calculated strategies designed to make you dependent on their approval and afraid to leave. Recognizing these tactics is essential to understanding that the problem lies with them, and that you deserve to be treated with consistent respect and kindness.

Red Flag #25: Gaslighting

Emily's Story

The crazymaking started when I found another text from a woman on Jim's phone. This text, like the one before it, was supposedly from this woman that he had been seeing before we started dating. When I asked Jim about the now second text, he'd swore he'd stopped talking to her, and said he didn't know what I was talking about. When I confronted him about it, he pulled up a completely different series of text messages and denied ever having received a second text from her.

I'm embarrassed to say it, but he was so convincing that I believed him and even apologized for doubting him! That night, I couldn't sleep. I kept thinking about the text that I was fairly positive I saw. Finally, around 2am, I got out of bed, snuck his phone into the bathroom with me and went through it. I felt guilty for doing this, but for the sake of my sanity, I knew I had to.

While I couldn't find the conversation that I first saw, I did find lots of nude pics she'd sent him. Most of them were in folders that he'd named "work." I also discovered that he had her number saved in his phone under the name "Kenneth-Work." So, clearly, he was hiding her and his communication with her. I took pictures of all this information on my phone and then emailed it to myself, so I had proof before he could delete it and tell me those didn't exist, either.

Then, last month, I found a hotel receipt in his car, and when I asked him about it, he had this whole elaborate story about a business lunch. He was so logical, so certain about every detail, that I ended up believing him. Then, last week, I asked him about the receipt and if he kept it for tax purposes, and this is what really got me: he told me there never was a receipt at all. He said I must have dreamed it up.

He kept telling me my anxiety was making me paranoid. And you want to know the scariest part? Sometimes, I catch myself wondering if he's right. Maybe I am just imagining everything. When my therapist told me about the term "gaslighting" so much made sense. I didn't realize there was a word to describe what I was experiencing.

We've been broken up for about six months now, but I still find myself questioning parts of the relationship and wondering what was real and if I really did imagine certain things.

The Origins of Gaslighting

The term "gaslighting" originates from Patrick Hamilton's 1938 play *Gas Light* and its renowned 1944 film adaptation *Gaslight* starring Ingrid Bergman. In the story, a husband systematically manipulates his wife by secretly dimming and brightening their home's gas-powered lights while persistently denying any changes are occurring. As she notices the flickering lights, he dismisses her observations, claiming she's imagining things. This systematic denial of her reality, combined with other psychological manipulations, eventually causes her to question her sanity.

How Gaslighting Works

Much like in the film, modern narcissists employ similar tactics of reality distortion. They twist the truth, omit crucial facts, or convince their targets they are wrong, crazy, overreacting, or paranoid. Through this persistent manipulation, targets gradually lose faith in their judgment often becoming dependent on the narcissist to define their reality.

Narcissists typically gaslight for four primary reasons:

1. To evade consequences for their actions.

2. To maintain power and control over their target.

3. For their amusement.

4. To boost their ego and sense of superiority.

Rather than accepting responsibility, they deny or deflect, eventually leading their targets to accept the narcissist's distorted version of events as truth.

This manipulation creates two devastating effects:

1. Targets lose trust in their perceptions and become increasingly dependent on the narcissist for validation.

2. Problematic behavior becomes normalized in the relationship. This is a process known as "managing down of expectations" which causing targets to remain in unhealthy situations far longer than they otherwise might.

Gaslighting Across Different Relationships

Romantic Relationships

Common phrases include:

1. "I never said that; you must be remembering wrong" (when you remembered correctly)

2. "You're too sensitive, I was obviously joking" (after saying something hurtful)

3. "You're paranoid; she's just a friend" (while actively cheating)

4. "You must be crazy to think I would do something like that" (when caught lying)

Workplace

Typical scenarios involve:

• Claiming that previous approvals or authorization never happened

- Shifting blame with statements like "You must have misunderstood the deadline" (when you didn't)

- Undermining confidence with phrases like "Everyone else understands what I want, why can't you?" (when everyone else is confused, or no one else has acknowledged their understanding)

- Taking credit for others' work while claiming, "You never mentioned this was your idea" (when you had originally presented the idea as your own)

Family Relationships

Common tactics include:

- Denying past events: "That never happened; you're misremembering things" (when the events in question did happen)

- Manipulative care: "I only want what's best for you" (while undermining choices)

- Rewriting history: "That's not how it happened." (when that's exactly how it happened)

- Creating isolation: "No one else in the family has a problem with this" (when the people who understand what's going on do have a problem with it)

The Long-Term Impact

The most insidious aspect of gaslighting is its cumulative effect. When it occurs over extended periods, or comes from authority figures and trusted individuals, it can create profound long-lasting damage. Targets often develop pervasive paranoia, mistrust, and insecurity. This erosion of self-trust can extend beyond the immediate relationship, affecting their ability to trust anyone, including their closest confidants and even themselves.

Key Takeaways

1. **Gaslighting isn't just about lying—it's about making the target doubt their reality and sanity.** While all manipulators lie, gaslighters take it further by systematically undermining your trust in your perceptions and memories. When you find yourself obsessively documenting events or questioning your clear memories, you're likely experiencing gaslighting rather than simple dishonesty.

2. **The most dangerous gaslighting often comes wrapped in expressions of care and concern.** Watch for phrases like "I'm worried about your mental health." These seemingly supportive statements are designed to make you doubt yourself while positioning them as the caring, concerned party.

3. **The goal of gaslighting is to create a world where the target becomes dependent on the gaslighter to define reality.** Through persistent reality distortion, gaslighters aim to make their targets so unsure of their judgment that they rely on the gaslighter to tell them what's real and what isn't. This dependence makes it incredibly difficult for victims to trust their own instincts enough to leave the relationship, even when they have clear evidence of wrongdoing.

4. **Your instincts and memories are valid, and you can reclaim your reality by documenting your experiences and seeking outside perspectives.** Start keeping a detailed journal of events as they happen, including dates, times, and exact quotes—gaslighters rely on their targets' confusion and self-doubt. While they will still argue with facts and proof, the documentation you gather can help you to stay grounded in the truth. Share your experiences with trusted friends, family members, or a therapist who can provide reality checks and help you maintain your grip on the truth. Keep in mind that someone who genuinely cares about you will be empathetic when you're hurting, not tell you that your feelings are wrong or that you're imagining things.

Red Flag #26: They Keep Things Vague

Taylor's Story

I met Jason at a gallery opening in October. What started as a whirlwind romance quickly became a nightmare. Those first few weeks were intoxicating—late-night conversations stretching until dawn and lengthy texts where we made lots of future plans. I felt like I'd finally found someone who truly saw me.

But then things began to shift. The long messages and conversations became fewer and fewer. Daily messages became sporadic, replaced by shortened responses and "busy with work" explanations. When I tried to talk about where our relationship was heading, Jason would redirect the conversation. I'd get comments like, "Why do we need to label what we have?" Or "Isn't this perfect just as it is?"

The confusion deepened when he invited me to his sister's wedding as his date. There I was, meeting his entire family, helping his mother pin her corsage, and even being included in family photos. Yet when I changed my Facebook status to "In a Relationship," he texted immediately, asking me to remove it. "I'm just private about my personal life," he explained. "Besides, social media ruins real connections." This came from someone who posted daily about his workout routines and pictures of what he had for lunch.

Looking back, I see how Jason kept me suspended in uncertainty. He'd give me just enough hope to stay invested—a key to his apartment here, a mention of future travel plans there—but never enough security to feel stable. One weekend, he would plan an elaborate surprise birthday celebration for me and make dinner reservations at my dream restaurant. The next week, he'd be unreachable, only to resurface with vague excuses about phone issues or work emergencies.

When I expressed hurt over being excluded from his company Christmas party, he dismissed my feelings: "We never said we were exclusive. You're creating expectations that were never there." When mutual friends asked about our relationship, I found myself echoing his vague responses: "We're just enjoying each other's company," or "We're seeing where things go."

The truth was, I didn't know where things were going. I only knew that I was constantly walking on eggshells, trying to be perfect enough to earn the consistency and commitment he'd hinted at but never fully offered. It took me months to realize this was his way of simultaneously being in a relationship with me but keeping the door open.

Power Through Vagueness

Keeping things vague is a classic manipulation tactic employed by narcissists that serves multiple self-serving purposes. The vagueness often manifests in contradictory behaviors and statements that leave their partner confused and constantly seeking clarity. For example, a narcissist might introduce their partner to family members and plan future trips together but then become evasive when asked about relationship status or refuse to acknowledge the relationship on social media.

By keeping things vague, they create a power dynamic where they hold all the control. Meanwhile, their partner remains in a state of uncertainty and emotional dependence, holding onto hope that given enough time they'll become serious with them. This allows the narcissist to continue exploring other options and maintaining multiple relationships in a guilt-free way, while keeping their primary partner invested through intermittent reinforcement and the promise of something more concrete in the future.

This push-pull dynamic keeps their partner constantly off-balance and working harder to earn the narcissist's intermittent displays of affection. Narcissists also use vagueness as protection against accountability. Without clearly defined relationships and boundaries, they can more easily gaslight their partners when conflicts arise.

If confronted about their behavior with other potential romantic interests, they can claim there was never an agreement of exclusivity. If their partner expresses hurt about being excluded from important events or decisions, they can dismiss these feelings by saying the partner was expecting too much from an undefined relationship. This pattern of avoiding responsibility while maintaining control is central to narcissistic abuse.

Key Takeaways

1. **Inconsistency is a red Flag.** When someone's actions and words don't align, trust the pattern of their actions, not the sporadic displays of love and romance.

2. **Privacy can be a smokescreen for control.** There's a crucial difference between someone who values privacy across all aspects of their life and someone who selectively uses privacy as an excuse. Genuine privacy preferences are consistent; selective privacy in relationships, while being public in other areas, often masks ulterior motives.

3. **Clear communication should never feel like a threat.** In a healthy relationship, discussing expectations and defining the relationship shouldn't feel like walking through a minefield. Even if they aren't ready for exclusivity in a relationship, a partner who values you will make that clear, as that want you to feel secure, not confused.

Red Flag #27: Things Must Be Done Their Way

Naomi's Story

It took me a while to see John's behavior as controlling. I think it's because I grew up without a father, and so, initially, I saw John's "over-involvement" in my life as a form of care and concern. It wasn't until I found myself having a lot of anxiety over texting my sister, Karen, about our weekend plans that I realized something wasn't right.

John didn't like my sister. I think he thought she was a bad influence because she wasn't particularly fond of him. I knew that if I'd told him I was having a sisters' weekend, he'd get upset, and I'd spend hours defending myself, my sister, and my relationship with him. I knew this conversation was inevitable and that it'd be exhausting. Just the thought of it was sucking my energy.

I found myself continually rehashing all kinds of conversations with John as to my sisters' weekend. I knew that as soon as I told John, the next week would be full of subtle comments about my "divided loyalties." If I told him Karen and I had planned this trip, but then canceled on her to keep the peace with John, he'd act extra loving and attentive. Of course, whenever I chose him over my sister, he'd act this way, but it felt gross. It was like he was praising me for doing the right thing.

I'd become so used to everything having to be his way, that even making the smallest decision was anxiety inducing. The month before, when I'd gone to my niece's birthday party without him, he spent the entire next day giving me the silent treatment, then casually mentioned how his ex "never prioritized other people over their relationship." The fact that he'd been the one to decline the invitation didn't matter. In his mind, I should have skipped it too, proving my loyalty by isolating myself alongside him.

I was so tired of being put in this position where every decision I wanted to make for me needed to meet his approval. The more I thought about how much time and energy situations like this soaked up, the angrier I got. Relationships shouldn't have to be this difficult. I just wanted to go to my niece's birthday party. I just wanted to spend a weekend with my sister. These things weren't a big deal, and yet, I felt like I was continually having to navigate a minefield.

Understanding the Control Playbook

Narcissists like John don't just want influence in a relationship—they demand complete control. This control isn't always obvious; it often starts subtly, masked as care or concern, before gradually tightening like a noose around their partner's autonomy. Every rule, restriction, and manipulation serve a purpose in their quest for dominance. Whether through charm, isolation, or emotional manipulation, their ultimate goal is to create a world where their partner's every decision requires their approval.

The Six Pillars of Control

There are six primary tactics narcissist's use to maintain control. I remember it by using the acronym "I CHIVE."

1. Isolation from support systems.

2. Charm to lower defenses.

3. Hope through false promises about the future.

4. Intimidation when gentler methods fail.

5. Violence (emotional or physical).

6. Emotional manipulation using fear, obligation, guilt, love, or pity.

These tactics aren't used randomly—they're deployed strategically with different tools for different situations. When charm doesn't work, they switch to intimidation. When guilt fails, they try isolation.

The most insidious aspect is how they blend these tactics, making it hard for targets to recognize the manipulation. A single conversation might contain elements of charm, guilt, and subtle threats, all woven together so skillfully that you leave feeling like you're the unreasonable one.

Over time, this constant control erodes their partner's sense of self. Simple decisions become sources of anxiety. Independent thoughts feel dangerous. Even basic choices, such as what to wear, who to talk to, and how to spend free time become filtered through the lens of "What would they think?"

The control extends beyond actions to emotions themselves. Targets learn to doubt their feelings, constantly questioning if they're "overreacting" or "being too sensitive." Their emotional reality becomes secondary to keeping their controller happy.

The isolation compounds the damage. As friends and family are slowly pushed away, victims lose their external reality checks, making it harder to recognize just how problematic their relationship is.

Here are 9 examples of how a narcissist can be controlling:

1. **Dictating How You Spend Your Time.** Whenever Naomi made plans with friends or family, John would interfere. If she had something scheduled that didn't involve him, he'd try and make her feel guilty, saying things like, "I thought you'd want to spend time with me," or "You never have time for me anymore." He'd make her feel like she was abandoning him, even though she had every right to have a life outside their relationship.

2. **Making All the Decisions.** John insisted on making all the decisions, even the smallest ones, such as where they should

eat, what movie to watch, or how they should decorate the house. If Naomi suggested something different, he'd shoot it down immediately or complain that she never took his wants and needs into consideration.

3. **Controlling What You Wear.** John dictated what Naomi could wear, especially when they went out. If she wore something he disapproved of, he'd criticize her, saying it was too sexy, or, at other times, that it wasn't sexy enough. He'd often suggest more 'appropriate' clothing, making her feel self-conscious and as though she was constantly making the wrong decision.

4. **Monitoring Your Actions.** John constantly asked where Naomi was, who she was with, and what she was doing, even if she was just running errands. He'd text or call multiple times a day to check in, making her feel like she was under surveillance. If she didn't respond right away, he'd accuse her of ignoring him or being secretive.

5. **Manipulating Your Emotions.** If Naomi ever disagreed with John or expressed any dissatisfaction, he'd turn it around on her, making her feel unreasonable or ungrateful. He'd use emotional manipulation to make her feel like she was the problem, saying things like, "You're overreacting," or "I can't do anything right for you." She found herself constantly trying to appease him to avoid conflict.

6. **Limiting Your Social Interactions.** John would subtly discourage Naomi from spending time with friends or family, saying things like, "They don't want us to be together," or "You always choose them over me." Over time, she became isolated because he made her feel like she couldn't have relationships with anyone outside of him, because if she did, she was being selfish and inconsiderate to John. In his mind, they were a couple, and they needed to act like a "unified front" when it came to making decisions. While Naomi agreed on being in alignment with major decisions,

she only felt this way to a point. She felt she was entitled to have her own life outside of John, and rightly so.

7. **Minimizing, Gaslighting, and Denying Your Reality.** Whenever Naomi brought up an issue, John would minimize or deny things that had happened, making her feel like she was imagining things. If he had done something hurtful, he'd say, "That never happened," "You're remembering it wrong," or "You're playing the victim and trying to make me look like the bad guy." After a while, Naomi completely doubted herself. She wasn't sure if the autonomy she wanted was reasonable or if she was selfish and struggled to work as a team like John so often told her.

8. **Using Rewards and Punishments.** John would reward Naomi with affection, praise, or attention when she behaved the way he wanted, but if she didn't comply with his wishes, he'd withdraw affection or give her the silent treatment. She felt like she was walking on eggshells, always trying to get back into his good graces.

9. **Isolation from Others.** Whenever Naomi made new friends or started getting closer to someone, John would subtly make negative comments about them, trying to make her doubt their intentions or their worth. He'd say things like, "I don't trust them," or "they're using you." Slowly, she started distancing herself from others because he made her feel like they were the problem, and that Naomi had terrible judgment when it came to befriending others.

Key Takeaways:

1. **Manipulation creates dependency through control:** Narcissists use criticism, emotional manipulation, and approval-seeking dynamics to make you feel like your actions, feelings, and thoughts need their permission, gradually eroding your personal boundaries and self-confidence.

2. **Healthy relationships feel calm and supportive**: In good relationships, you feel nourished, maintain your autonomy, and have space for your own life, wants, needs, and feelings without constantly seeking approval.

3. **Chronic anxiety about approval signals toxicity**: If you're continually anxious, afraid to be yourself, or worried about whether your partner approves of your decisions, this is a red flag that the relationship dynamic is unhealthy and potentially abusive.

Red Flag #28: Jealous and Possessive

Layla's Story

In the early months of our relationship, Theo's attentiveness had seemed like devotion. He wanted to communicate with me on a regular basis, which was so refreshing—especially considering my last relationship was with a man who went for long stretches of time without responding. Theo wanted to know every aspect of my day and wanted to be included in all of my plans.

He framed his behavior as deep love and an investment in our connection. I felt as though he truly cared. But gradually, these gestures of "care" began to feel suffocating. His texts shifted from "I miss you" to "Who are you with?"

There was no good answer to this question. If I was with female friends or colleagues, he'd think that they were being a bad influence on me. If I was with male friends or colleagues, he'd be so "concerned," I could hear it in his voice. I knew when I'd get home I would have to answer all kinds of questions about who this person was, how I knew them, if they were married or single, and on and on.

He'd explain that his "insecurity" came from loving me so deeply that he was terrified of losing me. At the time, I didn't see his behavior as jealousy or possessiveness. I saw it as him being insecure and chalked it up to his ex cheating on him as well as him having an anxious style of attachment due to his upbringing. I felt bad for him, after all, it must be exhausting to be so hypervigilant about your partner all the time. And for those reasons, I tried my best to constantly reassure him.

The possessiveness crept in so gradually that I didn't notice how much of myself I was sacrificing to maintain Theo's fragile sense of security. I stopped mentioning casual interactions with friends or coworkers to avoid his hours of questioning. I began declining invitations to after-work gatherings where I knew men would be present, not wanting to deal with Theo's cold silence and pointed comments afterward about what I wore, who else was there, if we'd ever gone out before, and on and on.

When my best friend gently pointed out that I had been a lot less social over the past few months, I defended Theo's behavior, explaining that he'd been hurt before and just needed extra reassurance. I didn't mind not seeing my male colleagues alone after work. I could see how that was walking the line of being inappropriate. I also agreed with not spending time with my male friends alone; that we'd need to be in a group.

I didn't argue with Theo when he wanted me to stop spending time with my single friends because they wanted to go out to the club. When we stopped going to the club, and started meeting up for brunch, Theo still had a problem with this, as he was afraid they were encouraging me to leave him. Overtime, I quit hanging out with them. Then it was certain members of my family that he felt were a bad influence, and I stopped seeing them too.

When my mother pointed out that he was isolating me, I was defensive and thought she misunderstood our relationship. He wasn't isolating me, I was distancing myself willingly from others. At the time, I thought me doing so was my choice. And it was, but I was distancing myself from them because of Theo's reasons.

What was so hard for me to see was that even though his reasons were unfounded, I could understand his thought process behind them. The reality was that I was cutting ties because, even though I knew my intentions were good, I wanted him to feel secure. I also didn't want the draining conversations that would follow when I'd get home from spending time with people he had concerns about.

But late at night, lying awake beside him, I kept thinking about what my mom said, and she was right. I was becoming isolated. It didn't matter that Theo wasn't isolating me directly, I was isolating myself to keep the peace, and that was still a problem. I couldn't ignore the growing hollowness in my chest, that in trying to prove my loyalty, I was slowly erasing myself and my life.

Jealousy and Possessiveness as an Early Red Flag

Narcissists often exhibit signs of jealousy or possessiveness early on in a relationship, especially if you give attention to others. They might react negatively if you spend time with friends, talk to someone of the opposite sex, or even mention others in a positive light.

Abusive people tend to isolate their partners in direct and indirect ways. Isolation can happen in many ways; jealousy and possessiveness being two of the most common. Sometimes, an abusive person will insist that their target quit their job, move in with them, or stop seeing their friends and family.

However, it's just as common that the target isolates themselves in an attempt to keep the peace in their relationship, which is what's going on in Layla's case. The challenge when a target isolates themselves is that they think they are doing it willingly, so it can be difficult for them to see the problem for what it is.

As time passes, what at first seems like benign jealousy and possessiveness, can become malignant and spread. They may start to monitor your interactions with others, reading your journal, tracking your location, checking your phone, reading your emails, stalking your social media and the social media of friends to see if you are with them, making accusations or demanding that you prioritize them over all other relationships.

If unchecked, jealousy and possessiveness lead to contempt and controlling behaviors. While controlling behaviors can feel stifling and anxiety-inducing, contempt in a relationship is what leads to dangerous and deadly behavior. Contempt is at the core of an abuser's mindset, which is "You deserve my abuse."

Of course, when they have consequences for their abusive actions, they may take some ownership as to what they did being a problem, but they'll blame it on the target, saying something along the lines of, "Look at what you made me do."

Key Takeaways:

1. **Jealousy and possessiveness aren't signs of caring; they are signs of control. No amount of changing your behavior will fix someone else's jealousy. Their insecurity is theirs, not yours.**

2. **Control in a relationship rarely starts with obvious restrictions.** It begins with subtle manipulations disguised as love or concern. Watch for how they react when you make independent decisions or spend time with others without them. If you find yourself constantly justifying normal activities or feeling guilty about having a life outside the relationship, you're likely experiencing controlling behavior.

3. **Controlling patterns tend to get worse with time, not better.** What often starts as subtle methods of control, often seen as "micromanagement" can evolve into systematic attempts to isolate you, undermine your self-confidence, and create conflict over seemingly harmless interactions.

4. **Jealousy can quickly become dangerous.** When a possessive partner claims that you are being "provocative" or "attention-seeking," they may feel justified in using aggression to "put you in your place." This warped reasoning reveals a particularly toxic mindset that can lead to escalating abuse.

5. **Healthy relationships enhance your freedom; they don't restrict it.** A partner who truly loves you will support your independence and respect your right to make your own decisions. Any relationship that requires you to make yourself smaller or give up your autonomy to keep the peace isn't love. It's control.

Red Flag #29: The Silent Treatment

Rachel's Story

I'd been dating Leo for about three months when we went to a dinner party at my friend's house. There were six of us altogether, and we were deciding what game to play. I had mentioned that I'd rather play Scrabble instead of the card game Leo wanted. The look he gave me was ice cold, like I'd just deeply insulted him in front of everyone. I was really taken aback by the look he gave me, as I couldn't believe he was so upset over something so small.

The next day, I felt really bad about the whole thing, so I texted him to apologize. But he completely ignored me. For two days I tried texting and calling but he wouldn't answer. Later, when we were finally together, he acted like I wasn't even there. He barely looked at me, and would only give me one-word answers. This kind of behavior was so out of the ordinary for him, as he wasn't normally cold and distant. I had never been around someone who gave me the silent treatment before, but that's exactly what he was doing. And his silence was meant to punish me. He wanted me to feel terrible for disagreeing with him and expected me to keep apologizing until he decided I'd groveled enough. It was like he wouldn't be satisfied until I was begging for his forgiveness all over my choice in a board game.

Understanding the Silent Treatment

Most targets have experienced the silent treatment at some point in a relationship, and many may have even felt that they have even given it in response to being frustrated or exhausted with a narcissist.

However, there is a difference between giving the silent treatment, staying quiet to keep the peace, and needing space and time to think before you respond. The difference between these is:

- The silent treatment is designed to punish someone. The goal of the silent treatment is to create an icy and hostile environment where the person on the receiving end of it feels like they are holding their breath until the other person tells them it's okay to breathe.

- Staying quiet to keep the peace is a survival strategy designed to protect your wellbeing as well as to keep the relationship going. A person who stays quiet to keep the peace isn't trying to punish the other person; in fact, it's the opposite: they are trying to stay out of "trouble."

- Needing space to think before responding is exactly that: it's needing some breathing room so you can collect your thoughts before you respond. If a person needs space, they are able to verbalize this, and during this time, they don't create a tense environment.

So why do narcissists give the silent treatment?

Narcissists will use the silent treatment to punish their target whenever the target has brought up any concerns they may have about the narcissist's behavior or their relationship. This teaches the target to never bring up any issues, no matter how problematic.

There are four main reasons why narcissists use the silent treatment:

1. **To assert their power and control over their target.** The silent treatment is a great way for narcissists to make sure that the relationship is being played on their terms. After all, with their silence they are now in control of the communication and the target's anxiety that tends to go along with it. During this time, the target is often left to scramble to apologize, or to try and somehow make things better—anything to just get their partner to reopen communication again.

2. **It gives them time to line up additional supply.** Narcissists tend to have a harem of other people that they

use, abuse, exploit, or cheat with. It's common for them to have multiple people in their pipeline. These people are known as "narcissistic supply" and are often lined up as a plan a, b, c, d, and so on. Narcissists might pick a fight with the target. They might accuse the target of some bad behavior, and announce that they need a break from the relationship to re-evaluate things. Then, during this "break" the narcissist goes off and cheats, during which time the narcissist refuses to communicate with the target. The narcissist might also twist things by saying something like "I'm so offended that you would confront me about texting another woman that, I figured, if I was going to be blamed for it, I might as well do it!"

In the narcissist's mind, they always feel entitled and justified to cheat, or do anything else for that matter. There are no laws or social contracts that keep their behavior in check. They want what they want and have no problem lying, cheating, or stealing to get it. What's worse is that they tend to enjoy deceiving others because it's yet another way for them to feel smug and superior because, in their mind, they are winning. Of course, they are winning at a game that only they are playing and that no one else knows about, so it's hard to comprehend that they would take so much satisfaction in hurting other people. But that's a narcissist for you.

3. **It allows the narcissist to show their new target how unhinged the former one is.** This is especially true if the former target is being reactive to having all communication abruptly turned off. The narcissist is able to take these phone calls and texts and show the new target what a mess the former target really is, which backs up the narcissist's narrative that the former target is the problem.

There might come a point where the narcissist eventually gets tired of "playing" with the new target. Or perhaps the narcissist decides they want to "play" with both targets simultaneously. When the narcissist returns to the prior target, something predictable happens. The prior target feels immense relief and showers the narcissist with all kinds of ingratiating behavior. They do this in a desperate attempt to keep the narcissist around, as their relief at being "chosen" again overrides their better judgment.

More often than not, if a narcissist isn't spending time with you, they are spending that time working on someone else. And since love bombing takes a lot of time and energy, it's easier for them to do when their partner isn't expecting them to engage with them in any way. During the silent treatment, the narcissists can be gone for days at a time, telling the target that they just need time to think or that they are so hurt by the target's words. They may even say that, yes, they are seeing someone else, and how can the target blame them? After all, if the target wasn't so stupid, fat, ugly, depressed, anxious, etc., or if the other person hadn't thrown themselves at the narcissist, then they would have never cheated. These kinds of actions cut deep, and if the target is still trying to hold onto crumbs of what they think is a relationship, then they will continue to try and twist themselves into an emotional pretzel to make things work. Take, for example, Johanna's situation:

"It took me several years to fully understand what was happening. At first, I thought it was just a coincidence, but, almost like clockwork, Jerry would pick a fight around Valentine's Day or Christmas. It was always over something trivial, something that didn't warrant him ignoring me for days. One day, I happened to find his laptop open and saw pictures of him with another woman and two kids. It turned out he had another family! That's when it hit me—every time he started a fight, it was because he was trying to juggle two families. The only excuse he could come up with to leave the house for days on end was to provoke an argument, then claim the relationship wasn't working and he needed space. And on her end, well, I ended up speaking to her, and he had told her that he had to take frequent business trips for his job!"

4. **To manage down expectations.** The silent treatment is crazy-making and torturous, and targets of it will often do anything to make it stop. The narcissist knows this and is then able to give the bare minimum (crumbs of attention/affection) to the target, and the target is now relieved that things are back to "normal." However, it's important to realize that now their relationship "normal" has hit a new low. The target is all too happy to pick up those crumbs, thinking that maybe this time, things will be different. And the target would be right: things will be different, although not in a good way. Things will be worse. The narcissist is letting their true selfish selves shine through, and in doing so, they slowly train the target to expect less and less of them while they get away with more and more. Take for example Merideth's experience:

> *"I got into therapy because I had recently gotten out of an abusive relationship. I was shocked to realize that there were many patterns of the same kinds of behavior that my mother used to do, but I never saw it that way before. For example, when I was in college, I told my mother that I was planning on going into art and design. She became upset and gave me the silent treatment for months. When she began talking to me again, she'd tried to push me into becoming a teacher—like her. At the time, I didn't see her behavior as controlling or even problematic; I thought I really was being selfish and stupid for wanting to get a degree in art and design, and that I should have been more sensitive to how she felt! I now see things differently and also realize that I've been controlled much of my life by her and by other men who have treated me in the same way."*

It's important to always remember that a relationship with a narcissist is a one-sided relationship, where the narcissist will insist that the target make them their top priority while the target remains their last priority.

Key Takeaways

1. **The silent treatment is not a healthy request for space. It's a form of emotional abuse designed to punish and control.** When someone needs genuine space to process their emotions, they can communicate this clearly without creating a hostile environment. The difference lies in the intent: while taking space is about self-care and eventual resolution, the silent treatment is about punishment and power.

2. **When a narcissist goes silent, they're often using this time to engage with other sources of attention and supply.** Their disappearing act isn't just about punishing you; it's frequently a cover for pursuing other relationships. The silence serves multiple purposes: it lets them focus their energy elsewhere while simultaneously training their current target to accept less and less attention.

3. **The silent treatment is designed to make you lower your standards and accept crumbs of attention as if they were a feast.** Through this pattern of withdrawal and return, narcissists gradually condition their targets to feel grateful for even minimal engagement or basic decency. Remember that while crumbs might seem better than nothing, they only serve to keep you emotionally starving in the relationship.

Red Flag #30: Triangulation

Elena's Story

For months, I thought I was losing my mind. Every time I confronted Miguel about his late-night texts to his co-worker/ friend Nora, he would tell me that she was going through a rough divorce and needed support. And he'd show me what I now know were carefully selected messages between them that painted him as a supportive friend.

But of course, at the time, he claimed that his texts were appropriate, and he was simply supporting a friend who happened to be "needy" and "clingy" (his words). I had met Nora before at the company Christmas party, and she seemed nice enough, but I still wasn't a fan of him texting her—not to mention the around-the-clock texts seemed a bit much, especially to a man who was in a relationship.

Miguel promised to encourage her to lean on some of her other friends for support, and I thought she had done just that as the texts decreased to almost nothing. I kind of felt bad, as I knew what it's like to go through a divorce and to need that support. I questioned myself if I was being jealous, possessive, and even controlling by not wanting him to talk to her as much as he was.

But then I ran into Nora at a coffee shop, and we got to talking. And as our chat unfolded, we discovered we'd both been told very different stories about what was going on. She believed Miguel was on the verge of leaving me, his abusive girlfriend who was so "unstable" that she'd continually threaten to commit suicide in an attempt to get him to stay. And, as his story went, that Nora needed to be patient and understanding while he worked up the courage and strength to leave this abusive relationship he was in. My jaw was hanging open, and I can only imagine the look on my face.

Both of us slowly realized we weren't fighting over a man; we were being played by one who had carefully orchestrated our mutual distrust, feeding each of us a different version of reality while positioning himself as the innocent victim caught between us. The sick feeling in my stomach grew as Nora and I compared stories, uncovering lie after carefully constructed lie.

It was like watching a house of cards collapse—each revelation exposing another deception, another way he'd pitted us against each other while maintaining his image of innocence—the "good guy" caught in the middle. The relief of finally understanding why things never quite added up was, well, a relief, but at the same time I was so angry I could hardly think straight.

As I scrolled through her phone, I saw months of texts and how he'd strategically shared just enough truth with me to make his lies believable. And, of course, he deleted all the texts from her that alluded to their relationship. What enraged me was how he gaslit me about the whole thing and how he had the nerve to lie next to me in bed, after we'd made love, to text her! The lack of respect for me was just so over the top it was ridiculous.

Understanding Triangulation

Triangulation is a dysfunctional communication technique where three people are involved in a two-person conflict. Triangulation can happen in any relationship and isn't always used to manipulate or harm others. However, problematic people, tend to use triangulation to stir the proverbial pot. In this dynamic, the narcissist pits two people against each other, with the goal of planting seeds of doubt or insecurity within each, making one believe the other is the problem. For example, a narcissistic parent might turn two of their children against each other, or a narcissist could create conflict between their spouse and the person they are cheating with.

Triangulation is a powerful manipulation tactic for several reasons. It deflects blame away from the narcissist and feeds their ego by creating chaos and drama. The narcissist thrives on conflict and tension, feeling empowered by the control they have over others and the ability to cause stress and division. They enjoy being the center of attention and the cause of the turmoil because it reinforces their sense of power.

Sarah's Story

Sarah noticed something was off when her sister Kate suddenly became distant. Whenever Sarah tried to make plans, Kate had an excuse. Finally, during a family dinner, Kate made a cold comment about how Sarah had called her a "self-centered drama queen." Sarah was stunned; she'd never said anything like that. It turned out their mother had been telling Kate that Sarah was constantly criticizing her behind her back, while telling Sarah that Kate was jealous of her success. Their mother had spent months feeding each sister a different story, creating tension and distrust between them while positioning herself as each sister's loyal confidante. It wasn't until the sisters finally talked directly that they discovered their mother had been deliberately driving them apart, likely because she felt threatened by their close relationship.

What's particularly manipulative about this situation is that both sisters had been fuming at each other rather than questioning their mother, who was the actual source of the conflict. That's the essence of triangulation: the manipulator stays clean while the other two parties direct their anger at each other.

Triangulation serves four main purposes for the narcissist:

- It entertains them.

- It boosts their ego.

- It shifts responsibility away from them.

- It gives them power and control over both the situation and the people involved.

When narcissists implement triangulation in romantic relationships, they may make each target feel like a potential threat to the other. If you have "lost" the narcissist to the other target, don't focus on "winning" them back. When you feel like you need to win back your partner, you are not in a relationship—you're caught in a game that you will lose as long as they are in your life.

Here are common examples of how narcissists use triangulation to manipulate relationships:

Family Triangulation:

1. Tells each sibling different stories about what the other said about them.

2. Plays favorite parent/child games, constantly shifting who's the "good one."

3. Says, "Your sibling thinks you're being unreasonable" (when your sibling never said this).

4. Creates competition between children for their love/approval.

Romantic Relationships:

1. Constantly mentions their ex: "My ex would never complain about this."

2. Talks about how others find them attractive: "My coworker said she'd date me in a second."

3. Creates jealousy by keeping backups: "You know, Sarah really understands me."

4. Compares current partner unfavorably to real, or imaginary, others.

Workplace:

1. Tells each coworker different versions of conversations.

2. Uses phrases like "Everyone thinks your work isn't up to standard" (but won't say who).

3. Plays favorites, creating competition for their approval.

4. Spreads different rumors to different departments to create conflict.

Friend Groups:

1. Tells Friend A: "Friend B said they're worried about you."

2. Creates artificial competition between friends for their time/attention.

3. Uses phrases like "Everyone agrees with me about this." (When no one was consulted.)

4. Shares private information selectively to create mistrust. For example, a problematic manager might tell one team member privately: "I shouldn't tell you this, but Sarah complained about your presentation to the executives. I defended you, of course. Just keep this between us—I wouldn't want to create tension in the team."

Extended Family:

1. Tells their own family false stories about their in-laws, and vice versa.

2. Creates competition between grandparents for access to grandchildren.

3. Shares different versions of events to different family members.

4. Uses holiday invitations and gifts to create rivalry and tension.

Social Media:

- Posts cryptic messages designed to plant seeds of doubt and insecurity with the goal of making multiple people think this concerning message is about them.

- Tags specific people to make others feel excluded.

- Shares private conversations publicly to create drama.

- Uses public praise of some to make others feel insecure.

The goal is always to:

1. Keep people off-balance and insecure.

2. Prevent direct communication between parties.

3. Position themselves as the information gatekeeper.

4. Create dependency on their approval.

5. Generate conflict they can control.

6. Isolate people from each other.

Here are five more examples of how a narcissist uses triangulation:

1. **Jealousy Manipulation:**

   "Whenever I started to feel close to someone else, like a friend or family member, he would subtly bring up how much attention he was getting from other women, or how his ex always used to do something for him. It was like he wanted me to feel threatened by these other people. He'd say things like, 'She always thought I was perfect, unlike you,' or 'You should be more like her.' It made me feel like I was in competition, and insecure about myself and our relationship."

2. **Playing Victim to Family/Friends:**

   "Anytime we had an argument, he would immediately go to his family and tell them a completely one-sided version of the story, leaving out

key details that would radically change the story; instead, he portrayed himself as the innocent victim and me as the selfish, unhinged bad guy. Then, when I'd confront him about it, he'd say, 'Well, my sister says you're too emotional about everything,' or 'My mom said you are making a big deal out of nothing.' It felt like he was getting his family to take sides and see me as the problem."

3. Creating Rivalries:

"She would often say things like, 'Why can't you be more like my friend? He's always so supportive and understanding' or 'My coworker is really good at this; I wish you could learn from her.' It made me feel inadequate and like I was constantly being compared to others. Sometimes, she'd even talk about how 'one of her exes' did things better than me. It felt like everyone else she'd ever dated was so much better than me."

4. Pitting People Against Each Other:

"When my friend and I had a falling out, he'd bring up how much my friend 'complained' about me and how she wasn't a good friend to me. But then, when I talked to my friend about it, she'd say he was saying similar things about me to her! He would always create a divide, making me feel like everyone was against me, or that I had to choose sides, but really, he was just stirring the pot to keep me isolated and dependent on him."

5. Using a Child as a Pawn:

"When we disagreed, he would talk to our child about it, trying to make them pick sides. He'd say things like, 'Mom's upset with me again, but I guess that's just how she is,' or 'I really wish your mom would understand me.' It was like he was using our child to manipulate me, making me feel guilty for being upset, and creating confusion for our child, too."

These examples show how narcissists use triangulation to manipulate relationships, create jealousy, foster dependency, and turn others against the person they're controlling. It makes the targeted person question their reality, feel insecure, and like they're at fault.

Key Takeaways

1. **Look for indicators of triangulation.** If someone constantly shares stories about what others supposedly said about you, or frequently compares you unfavorably to others, they're likely using triangulation to maintain control.

2. **The most powerful defense against triangulation is to establish direct communication channels with the people involved, where you can.** When someone tells you "Everyone thinks" or "She said" something about you, make it a practice to verify this information firsthand rather than accepting it as truth. Reach out directly to the person you're supposedly in conflict with, and you'll often discover that the "conflict" was manufactured by the manipulator. Anyone who tries to discourage direct communication, or becomes angry when you talk to others directly, is likely using triangulation to maintain control.

Red Flag #31: Accuses You of Doing Things You Aren't Doing

Julia's Story

When my husband first accused me of having an affair, I was really taken aback. Here I was, juggling a full-time job and our children's packed sports schedules when my husband began insisting I was having an affair. The accusation was so absurd I thought he was joking.

I remember laughing and telling him I didn't have the time or the energy for an affair. He didn't think my response was funny, and instead, he thought I was mocking him. Again, I thought he was still kidding around with me, but when he made it clear he wasn't, I felt bad.

I assumed something I'd done or said gave him this impression. His ex-wife had cheated on him, and I didn't want to contribute to any lingering insecurities he might have had from that. I gave him access to my phone, told him he could turn on a location tracker on my phone, and let him go through all of my emails and social media accounts.

This didn't give him the peace of mind I was hoping it would. This only make him more jealous, paranoid, and insecure.

The truth finally emerged one evening when he left his laptop open, revealing his ongoing affair with a coworker. I was shocked, devastated, and enraged. I couldn't believe the nerve he had to accuse me of cheating.

I went to such great lengths to reassure him when here he was, cheating on me with seemingly no guilt and no remorse. The big lesson I learned in all this is that sometimes the loudest accusations are actually confessions in disguise.

Understanding the Smoke and Mirrors

Projection serves as a psychological defense mechanism where individuals attribute their uncomfortable thoughts, feelings, or actions to others. For narcissists, this projection goes beyond a simple defense mechanism; it becomes a sophisticated tool for manipulation and control.

When narcissists engage in projection, they create an elaborate smokescreen that serves two purposes: it deflects attention from their behavior while simultaneously undermining their target's sense of reality. This double blow often leaves victims defending themselves against false accusations while the narcissist walks free.

The most insidious aspect of narcissistic projection is their persistence. It's a sustained campaign of accusations that slowly erodes their target's confidence.

The Eight Faces of Narcissistic Projection

1. **The Cheating Partner**. Perhaps the most common form of narcissistic projection involves infidelity. The cheating partner becomes increasingly paranoid about their spouse's loyalty, often imposing strict rules and demands for "transparency" while hiding their indiscretions. Their knowledge of their wrongdoing manifests as an obsession with their partner's potential betrayal.

2. **The Liar Who Accuses Others of Lying**. Narcissists who regularly deceive others often become preoccupied with catching others in lies. They scrutinize every word, looking for inconsistencies, while their web of deception grows ever larger. Their heightened suspicion of others serves as a mirror reflecting their own dishonesty.

3. **The Finger-Pointer**. A narcissist secretly draining joint accounts or making reckless purchases might suddenly become hypercritical of their partner's spending habits.

They'll demand detailed explanations for minor expenses while concealing their financial misdeeds.

4. **The Responsibility Dodger.** Watch for the narcissist who constantly criticizes others' work ethic or responsibility, while neglecting their duties. Their vocal complaints about others' perceived laziness often mask their avoidance of responsibilities.

5. **The Emotional Manipulator.** These narcissists excel at projecting their emotional instability onto others. After their angry outburst, they'll accuse their target of being "too emotional" or "unstable." This projection allows them to avoid accountability while controlling others.

6. **The Controller.** While imposing rigid restrictions on their partner's behavior, these narcissists often accuse others of being controlling or possessive. Their accusations reveal their deep-seated fears of losing control.

7. **The Envious Eye.** The success of others often triggers a narcissist's feelings of inadequacy. Rather than acknowledging their envy, they'll accuse others of being jealous of them, completely inverting the dynamic to protect their fragile ego.

8. **The Blame Shifter.** Masters of avoiding responsibility, these narcissists immediately shift blame for any conflict onto others. After creating chaos, they'll accuse others of "starting drama" or "always causing problems."

Key Takeaways

1. **Projection reveals more about the accuser than the accused.** Their accusations are often unconscious confessions of their behavior and insecurities. When they make seemingly random yet oddly specific accusations, they're usually describing their actions. Understanding this helps you recognize that their accusations are reflections of their reality, not yours.

2. **The most telling projections are those that seem to come out of nowhere and persist despite evidence to the contrary.** Pay attention to accusations that appear suddenly without provocation or focus on behaviors you've never exhibited. These accusations often intensify when you question the narcissist's activities, serving as a smokescreen for their misconduct.

The key to protecting yourself from projection is recognizing it as a defense mechanism rather than a legitimate attack. Narcissists aren't typically plotting to accuse you of their misdeeds; their minds automatically deflect uncomfortable truths about their behavior by projecting these traits onto you. Once you understand this, you can stop exhausting yourself by defending against false accusations and instead see them as indicators of the narcissist's behavior.

Red Flag #32: Lying

My Story

About 15 years ago, I dated a man who told me he was a member of some top-secret sniper unit in the military. I believed him because we lived close to a military base where high-level security clearances weren't unusual. But things didn't add up.

At one point he got very sick and needed to go to the doctor, but refused because he didn't have health insurance. When I asked him why he didn't have military health insurance, he said it was because he was part of the German military. Again, I didn't question this because the base close to us had a large German military presence, and I didn't know anything about their health insurance.

I mentioned that I thought it was odd that the German military wouldn't give their members health insurance, and he said that his unit was so top secret that they didn't have a record of him. I should have known then that he was full of it, but again, I didn't know much about the German military, and I had no way of verifying anything, so I let it slide.

Shortly after this, I asked him about a scar he had, and he said it was from a gunshot. Another time, he was sobbing, and I asked him what was going on. He said that he'd done awful things as a soldier…awful things to children. I was really concerned about this and assumed he was referring to children being casualties, somehow caught in the crossfire.

At one point, I mentioned his military service to his mother, and she was confused. She told me he'd never been in the military. We broke up shortly after when I also discovered that he was on multiple dating sites and had committed tax fraud.

What disturbed me the most was how compelling his story was about the horrors of war. For all of that to be false is just wild. And, honestly, I wonder if his crying about what he did to children was some sort of confession.

Understanding the Narcissist's Relationship with Truth

Lying comes in many forms: half-truths, spinning the truth, lying by omission, and flat-out lies, to name a few.

Most narcissists are liars, and compulsive ones at that. If you've been around them for any length of time, then you know what I mean. They'll lie about their age. They'll lie about what they had for lunch. They'll lie about why they came home two hours late. They'll say something to your face, and then they'll deny that they ever said it. They'll lie about the smallest, most unimportant things that normal people would never even think to lie about. They'll even lie when the truth would serve them better.

So, how do you know when a narcissist is telling the truth? The answer is you won't ever know. Narcissists rarely, if ever, tell the full truth. This is because they are driven by power and control. Keeping the truth to themselves allows them to keep control. Perhaps the most common example of this is with murderers who are behind bars. These people have nothing to lose as they are already locked up for life, and yet they won't tell where their victim's remains are. The reason behind this is power and control. This level of withholding the truth is common with narcissists, no matter how extreme their behavior. The best you are likely to get is what's known as "trickle truthing," where they slowly drip the truth out, usually based on what they think you know.

More than likely, you will never get the whole truth from a narcissist. Instead, you'll only be given variations of the truth, and they will only ever admit to the bare minimum required. If you don't accept one version of the story, they'll offer you another, and then another, until either you give in to one of their versions or become so worn down by the hoops you have to jump through to get to the truth that you eventually give up.

Narcissists don't lie for the same reasons "normal" people lie. Normal people lie to get out of trouble, to avoid confrontation, or to make themselves look better. While narcissists also lie for these reasons, they might also lie because it's fun to see what they can get others to believe.

Their lies are a series of small wins that serve to boost their insatiable ego. It's a little way for them to feel smug and superior that they were able to trick you. Of course, where there are small lies, there are also much bigger ones that you haven't seen yet.

A confrontation with a narcissist is a dizzying game of trying to nail jello to the wall. They will tell you the truth is story A. And then when confronted with more facts, the truth moves to story B, then to story C. If you then believe story C, then they'll claim that is the truth (even though it's not). But if you push, you'll get stories D, E, F, and G.

To be in a relationship with a narcissist means to never ever really know what's going on. It's a one-sided relationship where everyone loses except them. How this looks in action:

A narcissist gets caught texting some woman on their phone. He admits to having contact with the woman but denies it's anything more than just texts.

Then you find out they've been swapping nude pictures. Once confronted, he might admit to texts and nude pictures, but it was just that one time.

Then you find out that he met her at a motel. Once confronted, he admits to meeting her at a motel, but nothing happened–he felt guilty and just couldn't bring himself to cheat.

Then you find out she's pregnant. Once confronted, he admits to having sex with her, but just one time, and, besides, she threw herself at him. He was drunk, and he only cheated because you never had time for him.

Then you find out that he's taken her on trips around the world and racked up over $15,000 in credit card debt on a joint card you didn't even know you had. Once confronted, he admits that he's been seeing her for a bit, but she was just a friend back then…and why are you doing all this digging? Obviously, you have trust issues.

And besides, he started using drugs again, so his behavior isn't his fault; it's the drugs. He needs to get into rehab so this never happens again. And on and on it goes.

The Seven Categories of a Narcissist's Lies

What I've noticed over the years is that the lies narcissists tell tend to fall into seven categories:

1. **Military Service and Heroic Acts of Duty**. Narcissists often fabricate or exaggerate government positions or military service, claiming involvement with the CIA, FBI, or in classified missions or special units. These stories typically include elaborate details and emotional performances to make their tales more convincing. If they did actually join the military or work for the government, then odds are they've milked it for all it's worth, talking about their position or service or inflating what they did.

   "My ex told everyone about his time in Vietnam, sharing detailed war stories that brought people to tears. Years later, I discovered he'd stolen these stories from his best friend, who actually served. It was my first clue that I was dealing with a pathological liar."

2. **Religious and Spiritual Deception**. Narcissists often claim deep religious or spiritual convictions, taking leadership positions in religious communities while privately violating the very principles they preach.

   "My grandfather was a Baptist minister who quoted scripture, and preached hellfire and brimstone. People loved his charismatic personality, but they didn't see the serial cheater who moved our family different churches in different towns to escape scandals. While we lived in poverty, he always dressed impeccably and bought expensive cars. We

knew it was only a matter of time before he lost whatever house or car we had to the bank.

3. **Lies About Academic and Professional Achievements.** The need to appear successful drives many narcissists to lie about their education and business achievements, creating elaborate stories of professional success.

> *"My ex told everyone he had two PhDs. He actually had one, but apparently, that wasn't impressive enough for him. His constant need to embellish his achievements revealed his deep insecurity."*

> *"My ex-wife tells people she turned down Harvard Medical School to attend our local university's nursing program because she wanted to be closer to her family. Everyone who knows her knows it's completely false, but she maintains the story with absolute conviction."*

4. **Stories Stolen from Others.** Narcissists frequently appropriate others' experiences, achievements, and ideas, presenting them as their own, even in front of people who know the truth.

> *"When we first started dating, my ex told me about his childhood battle with cancer. Five years later, I learned his sister was the one who had cancer—not him. He'd simply stolen her experience and made it his own."*

5. **Outlandish Tales.** Some narcissists tell stories so incredible that they strain credibility, yet they maintain these tales with absolute conviction.

> *"Our nursing program director would tell the most unbelievable stories. Once, she claimed a wolf approached her at a campfire and communicated with her telepathically. Another time, she described racing on a snowmobile to deliver a baby in the wilderness, carrying the baby and the placenta in her jacket pocket! Yet she told these tales with such conviction that some students believed her."*

6. **Financial Fantasies**. Many narcissists create elaborate illusions of wealth while hiding financial instability.

> *"My ex drove a BMW convertible and wore expensive watches, looking every bit the successful businessman. After moving in together, I discovered he couldn't write checks anywhere in town because he'd bounced so many. His BMW had a 21% interest rate, and he was basically living on credit cards. He cared more about maintaining appearances than paying basic bills."*

7. **Major Illnesses**. Narcissists sometimes fabricate serious medical conditions to gain sympathy, control, or attention from others. This manipulation can continue for years, fooling even medical professionals and close family members.

> *"My mother convinced everyone she had MS for nearly a decade. She used it to get constant care from me and my siblings, made us feel guilty when we couldn't help, and collected donations from church members. When her lies unraveled, she simply moved to another state and started claiming she had lupus instead."*

Key Takeaways

1. **Narcissistic lying isn't just about deception—it's about power and control.** While normal people lie to avoid consequences or conflict, narcissists lie as a way of life, even about things that don't matter. Their lies are designed to maintain control over their narrative and keep others off-balance.

2. **The most revealing lies are often the smallest ones.** When someone lies about inconsequential things—what they had for lunch, where they went shopping, or basic facts that could easily be verified—it's a warning sign of pathological lying. These small lies are practice runs for bigger deceptions and are indicators that truth itself holds no value for them.

3. **Reclaim your power by shifting your focus from uncovering their lies to trusting your reality.** Instead of exhausting yourself trying to prove their deceptions, or getting them to admit the truth, document what you know to be true and trust your observations. If you aren't ready to leave, keep a dated journal of events, save screenshots or emails, and confide in trusted friends who can help validate your experiences.

Red Flag #33: Financial Control or Exploitation

Lee's Story

In the six months since Mark had moved in, my savings had dwindled from $40,000 to barely $3,000. Each withdrawal had seemed reasonable at the time—helping with his car payment and insurance after he lost his job, covering his portion of the rent while he "got back on his feet," and lending him money for his daughter's medical bills.

Whenever I asked him if he'd be able to repay me soon, he'd spin things around and accuse me of being pushy, rude, or greedy. Because I sincerely felt bad for him, and thought all this was temporary, and that we were building a life together, I kept trying to smooth things out between us.

In the end, he broke up with me, saying that he wasn't ready for a relationship. At first, I was devastated and did all I could to be understanding and give him his space.

Then I heard from a mutual friend that he had a new girlfriend and was already living with her! When I heard this, an ice-cold wave washed over me. I realized that his string of financial emergencies hadn't been bad luck; it was a calculated pattern of exploitation, and I was never going to see the money I'd loaned him.

The Art of Financial Manipulation

Narcissists approach finances like they approach everything else: as a tool for control and exploitation. Their patterns often begin subtly, testing boundaries with small requests that seem reasonable in isolation.

Unlike regular financial struggles, a narcissist's money problems are perpetual, yet somehow never their fault. There's always someone else to blame such as an ex who ruined their credit, a business partner who betrayed them, or a bank that made a mistake.

The most telling sign is their reaction when questioned about finances. A person who is genuinely struggling financially might feel shame or demonstrate a willingness to change. Narcissists, on the other hand, respond with indignation, gaslighting, or by turning the tables to make you feel guilty for asking.

Many narcissists create elaborate narratives about their past financial success. They'll tell stories about their former businesses, high-powered careers, or investment wins. Yet their current reality never quite matches these tales.

Their explanations for the disconnect between their claimed success and the current situation often involve complex conspiracies or betrayals. They might claim a sister sold their business "out from under them" or that a jealous partner ruined their career.

The truth usually reveals itself through their basic financial incompetence such as bouncing checks, maxing out credit cards, or showing fundamental ignorance about business practices that someone with their claimed experience would know.

The Two Faces of Financial Abuse

Financial abuse typically manifests in two ways: mooching or controlling. The moochers consistently live beyond their means, relying on others to bail them out while maintaining an image of success.

The financial controllers, on the other hand, might have money but use it as a weapon. They monitor every penny their partner spends while freely spending on themselves, or they ensure their partner remains financially dependent on them.

Sandra's Story

About two years into our marriage Marcus and I sat down to discuss our finances. I had always worked full-time, but now with a baby on the way, we needed to figure out what to do as my paycheck would only be slightly more than childcare costs. Since he made about twice as much as me, we both agreed I'd stay home with our child. However, shortly after I quit my job, he then began using my financial dependence against me. During fights, he would threaten to cut off my access to money completely, saying things like "Maybe you'll learn to appreciate what I do for you" or "Don't forget who pays for everything around here."

When things between us were good, he would "allow" me to go out to lunch with my friends or buy something new for myself. But when things were bad, he'd throw those purchases in my face, saying that I was ungrateful. I was afraid to spend money on anything for myself because it always led to conversations that involved me justifying every dime I spent and him lecturing me about being extravagant, selfish, or unappreciative since he "paid for everything around here." I felt trapped, guilty, and like a bad wife. I hated being completely dependent on someone who treated buying even basic necessities like a favor he was doing for me.

Marcus controlled every dollar that came into our household, and he made sure I knew it. I had to ask permission for everything, including groceries, gas money, and even buying shampoo. He gave me a small weekly allowance that barely covered the basics, then questioned every purchase like he was conducting an audit. When I wanted to take a photography class or buy new clothes, Marcus would shut me down, lecturing me about being "irresponsible with money" and telling me to "be grateful for what I had." But he had no problem spending money on himself. He'd buy expensive tools, have nights out with coworkers, and whatever gadgets caught his eye. He checked our bank statements constantly and would grill me about every purchase, making me feel like I was stealing when I bought anything he hadn't pre-approved.

For years, I bought into his narrative that his issues with my spending was about the budget. It wasn't until I saw a movie online that was about an abusive relationship and the husband was controlling his wife in a similar way. Then I realized what was going on was financial abuse and was really about power, and not our budget.

Red Flags in Early Dating

The signs often appear on first dates, though they're easy to dismiss. Watch for disconnects between their claims and reality, like driving an expensive car but being unable to fill the gas tank, or wearing flashy accessories but needing help to pay rent.

Pay attention to how they talk about money. Narcissists often name-drop expensive brands, talk about large sums of money they've handled, or share dramatic stories about financial betrayals early in dating.

Their interest in your financial situation might seem excessive, masked as concern or planning for the future. They might push to know your salary, savings, or property values.

When "Loans" Become Losses

The transition from dating to financial exploitation often begins with "emergency" loans. These start small and seem legitimate such as car repairs, medical bills, or temporary help with rent.

Once you agree to one loan, the emergencies multiply. Each one comes with a compelling story and promises of repayment, but somehow, there's always another crisis before they can pay you back.

The manipulation intensifies if you hesitate to help or ask about repayment. They might accuse you of not caring about them, compare you to others who would help, or remind you of times they've helped you.

Key Takeaways

1. **Financial abuse often starts with seemingly reasonable requests for temporary help.** Watch for patterns of emergencies that never end, and loans that are never repaid. A narcissist will always have compelling stories about why they need money now, and why they can't pay it back yet.

2. **Be wary of someone whose financial reality doesn't match their claims of success.** When someone talks about their financial success or past wealth, while bouncing checks and living off others, they're showing you who they really are. Remember, actions speak louder than words.

3. **You can protect yourself by maintaining firm financial boundaries from the start.** Keep your accounts separate, document any loans with written agreements, and set clear limits on how much you're willing to help. Remember that you're not responsible for another adult's financial well-being. Additionally, someone who makes you feel guilty for having boundaries with your money is waving some red flags. Trust your instincts when something feels off about someone's financial situation or requests, as your gut is usually right.

Red Flag #34: When Words, Actions, and Feelings Don't Align

My Story

After my father passed away from pancreatic cancer, my step-brother got a large tattoo of our father's last name—our last name—on his arm in tribute. At the time, this seemed like a profound gesture of love and respect; permanently marking his body to honor our father's memory.

However, over the next four years, my brother and I uncovered a disturbing reality. During the very period when my step-brother was getting this memorial tattoo, he and my step-mother were not only actively working against my father's final wishes, but they were also exploiting the trust and love we had for them.

They had deliberately circumvented the will, attempting to steal both money and the family home from the estate. This betrayal was especially shocking given that we had maintained a close, seemingly loving relationship for 35 years.

So, they weren't just disrespecting our father; they were fine with causing us major emotional and financial harm as well. Not to mention committing numerous potential felonies along the way. And, in addition to the tattoo, they were posting on social media about how much they loved and missed our father. The disconnect and the hypocrisy were enraging.

This wasn't the only time he'd hypocritically tattooed himself. He had two other tattoos showing the world his seemingly strong moral compass. He had his wedding ring tattooed on his finger before later having an ongoing affair. And he has a large cross on his back despite ongoing behavior that contradicts basic Christian values.

At the time, I kept asking myself, "Who does that?" Why on Earth would he get a tattoo of our last name on his arm if he truly didn't care about our dad or us? Knowing what I now know, it seemed more like a sick trophy reminding himself of the hurt he caused us.

Clearly, the tattoo wasn't about honoring our father at all. While it may actually be a sick trophy of sorts, I think it's also a form of self-deception; a permanent sign meant to convince both himself and others that he was the loving, devoted son he wanted to appear to be, even as his actions behind the scenes proved otherwise.

This tattoo served as visible "proof" that he could point to while actively undermining everything our father had worked for and wished for his family.

My big takeaway from this experience was how some people use visible symbols and grand gestures not as genuine expressions of love or grief but as props in their performance. These outward displays mask and attempt to compensate for their true actions and character.

Reaction Formation

Reaction formation is a psychological defense mechanism where a person unconsciously adopts behaviors, thoughts, or emotions that are the opposite of their true feelings. This defense mechanism allows for the original feeling to remain unconscious. This is done to reduce anxiety or internal conflict by masking undesirable feelings with exaggerated, outwardly opposite behaviors. In other words, when someone feels a certain way that is too uncomfortable to acknowledge, such as guilt, shame, or anger, they may instead act in ways that express the opposite emotion or behavior, often to the point of excess. In the case of most narcissists, they are concerned about their public image, but they are also concerned about how they see themselves.

Some examples of this would be:

- Someone posting on social media about how happily married they are while the reality is they are unhappy, and divorce is on the horizon.

- A pastor who preaches about morality, but who is cheating on his wife.

- Someone who feels deep anger towards a coworker, but acts overly kind or affectionate towards them instead.

- A person who has repressed same-sex attraction might express extreme homophobic views.

Narcissists and Reaction Formation

For narcissists, reaction formation is frequently used to cope with vulnerabilities, insecurities, and feelings of inadequacy. Since narcissists rely heavily on maintaining a grandiose self-image and seeking admiration, they often feel compelled to hide any emotions or behaviors that might contradict their perceived perfection or superiority. Here's how reaction formation may manifest in narcissistic individuals:

1. **Exaggerated Confidence to Mask Insecurity.** Narcissists may appear outwardly arrogant or overly confident, but this can be a defense against deep-seated insecurities. The more vulnerable they feel, the more they may exaggerate their confidence and self-assuredness to protect their fragile self-esteem. For example, a narcissist who feels unsure about their skills might overly boast about their accomplishments, emphasizing how much better they are than others to cover up their underlying self-doubt.

2. **Pretend Altruism to Hide Selfishness.** Narcissists might engage in acts of apparent kindness or generosity, but these actions are often motivated by a desire to receive admiration, praise, or control rather than genuine care for others. The narcissist might act overly humble or self-sacrificing, pretending to be altruistic to avoid being seen as selfish or egotistical. For example, a narcissist may donate to charity or volunteer for a cause, not out of a true desire to help others, but because they want to be admired or seen as a benevolent figure.

3. **Excessive Empathy to Mask Emotional Detachment.** Narcissists may present themselves as excessively empathetic, or emotionally attuned to others' feelings, to mask their lack of genuine empathy. They might go to great lengths to appear compassionate, but this is often a facade designed to manage how they are viewed by others. For example, a narcissist may pretend to deeply care about a friend's struggles, offering over-the-top sympathy, just to maintain the image of being understanding and kind-hearted.

4. **Hostility Toward Others to Conceal Feelings of Inferiority.** Narcissists who feel insecure or inferior to others may react with hostility, contempt, or criticism to conceal these feelings. They may project a sense of superiority by belittling others, even if these feelings stem from their internal struggles with self-worth. For example, a narcissist might belittle someone for their appearance or intelligence, even though the narcissist internally feels inadequate and is attempting to defend against those feelings by putting others down.

5. **Hyper-Competitiveness to Conceal Fear of Failure.** Narcissists often have a deep fear of failure or being perceived as unsuccessful. To counteract this, they may become excessively competitive and driven to prove they are the best at everything. This intense drive often masks their fear of inadequacy and their underlying sense of vulnerability. For example, a narcissist might go to great lengths to outdo everyone else in a professional setting, not because they genuinely care about being the best, but because they fear being seen as incompetent or incapable.

6. **Grandiosity to Conceal Self-Loathing.** It's thought that at the core of many narcissists, lies a profound self-loathing or emptiness, which they are often unwilling to acknowledge. To protect themselves from these feelings, they project grandiosity and an inflated sense of self-worth. The more they feel internally inadequate, the more they may present

themselves as being invincible, perfect, or superior to others. For example, a narcissist might frequently talk about how they are destined for greatness, or how others could never measure up to them, despite deep feelings of worthlessness.

Key Takeaways

1. **Reaction formation in narcissists involves creating elaborate displays that directly contradict their true actions and feelings.** They may make grand public gestures of love, loyalty, or devotion while simultaneously betraying those same values in private. The narcissist may use these displays as both a shield against the possible judgement of others, and/or a form of self-deception.

2. **The more extreme or theatrical the display, the more it may be masking opposite behaviors or intentions.** An example of this is a little boy who harasses a girl in his class, when he actually likes her. For adults, it might be telling you how they want to marry you, and then you never hear from them again, or they speak at great lengths about their morality when they actually have none, these over-the-top demonstrations often serve to cover up contradictory actions happening behind the scenes.

3. **When someone's public displays and private actions don't align, trust the actions rather than the performance.** While grand gestures and public declarations can be convincing, they're not proof of genuine feelings or intentions. Pay attention to the concrete actions and behaviors that occur when they think no one is watching, as this is the truth as to who they really are.

Red Flag #35: Concern with Public Image

April's Story

Here's your text split into several shorter paragraphs:

For decades, I thought my mother's behavior was normal. She'd spend forever getting ready just to go to the store, making sure she looked perfect in case she ran into anyone she knew. She'd volunteer for everything at school and talk loudly about all the good things she did, while texting me complaints about how I was standing or what I was wearing.

At home she'd yell at me for the smallest things, but the second we were around other people, she'd put on this fake sweet voice and act like we were the closest family in the world. She'd hug everyone and ask about their kids, then spend the whole car ride home talking about how stupid they were.

Every time we went anywhere, it turned into this performance where I had to smile and act happy while she told everyone what a great mom she was. She'd go on and on about our "special bond" to whoever would listen.

But at home, she basically ignored me and my brother, and when she did give us any attention it was because we did something wrong. The worst part was that she actually seemed to believe her own lies that she was this amazing parent and person.

If I ever did anything that made her look bad, or if I seemed unhappy when people were watching, she'd lose it when I was alone with her. What I felt or needed didn't matter at all; I was just there to make her look good.

I suppose deep down I thought that if I was good enough at playing my part in her play that she'd love me, but that never happened. Instead, all she saw were my flaws, and she hated me for them.

It wasn't until I was well into adulthood that I realized how much of a people pleaser I was and how much damage that trait had caused in my life.

The Narcissist's Public Image: A Study in Deception

The Perfect Persona

A narcissist often meticulously crafts their public image. They present themselves as the ideal friend, partner, or professional. To others, they might seem so perfect that they're too good to be true. In social settings, they are charming and are happy to lend a helping hand. They're the first to volunteer at their child's school, the colleague who brings coffee for everyone, or the neighbor who organizes community events. They are the kind of girl/guy you'd want to introduce to your best friend, someone you can't wait to introduce to your parents, father or mother of the year, or the kind of person you'd call if you needed anything. This carefully curated image serves as their armor, protecting their fragile ego while also enabling their manipulative behavior.

In today's digital age, narcissists expertly utilize social media to reinforce their carefully constructed image. They post carefully selected photos of family moments while privately terrorizing those closest to them. They share inspirational quotes about kindness while bullying subordinates; or they broadcast their charitable acts while privately exploiting others. Each post serves to strengthen their public persona while gaslighting their targets.

However, behind closed doors, a stark contrast emerges between their public facade and private behavior. While society sees a charismatic leader or devoted parent, their targets experience a completely different person. At home, they might berate their spouse or emotionally abuse and manipulate their children. At work, they might undermine colleagues while maintaining a reputation as the office mentor. This Jekyll and Hyde existence allows them to maintain control while keeping their targets off-balance and questioning their reality.

The Smear Campaign

When their mask slips or a target threatens to expose them, narcissists launch sophisticated smear campaigns to maintain their reputation. They might paint their ex-spouse as unstable during a divorce, label a former employee as incompetent after they quit, or portray their adult children as ungrateful when they establish boundaries. Their years of image cultivation pay off as society often believes their version of events, leaving their targets isolated and discredited.

The narcissist's image management extends to recruiting others to their cause. They cultivate a network of enablers, who are often referred to as "flying monkeys" who unwittingly support their false narrative. These might include family members who excuse their behavior, colleagues who defend their actions, or new partners who believe they've found their soulmate. These allies become powerful tools in discrediting the target's experiences and maintaining the narcissist's facade.

Protection Through Preemption

To safeguard their image, narcissists often preemptively discredit potential threats. They might casually mention their spouse's "emotional instability" long before any marital issues become public or subtly undermine a colleague's credibility before any overt workplace conflicts arise. This strategic groundwork ensures that if their target ever speaks out, others are already primed to doubt their story.

When one target is discarded or leaves, the narcissist quickly moves on, presenting their new relationship as "different" and "special." They convince everyone, including their new target, that previous relationship failures were entirely the fault of this "crazy" other person. The cycle continues as they repeat the same patterns:

love-bombing, devaluation, and discard, all while maintaining their sterling public reputation.

Key Takeaways

1. **The public-private split is deliberate and strategic.** Narcissists don't accidentally maintain two different personas: it's a calculated strategy. Their charming public image isn't just a mask; it's a weapon they actively use to discredit their targets and maintain control. Understanding this duality helps targets recognize that their private experiences with the narcissist, no matter how different from the public perception, are valid.

2. **Image management serves multiple purposes.** The narcissist's dedication to their public image goes beyond simple vanity. It serves as both a shield and a sword: protecting them from exposure while enabling them to continue their abusive behavior. Their carefully curated reputation acts as insurance against future accusations, preemptively discrediting potential whistleblowers, and ensuring they maintain access to new targets. This understanding helps explain why narcissists invest so much energy in maintaining their public facade, even when it seems exhausting.

3. **Build a support network of people who know your truth, ideally before any potential smear campaign begins.** For targets of narcissistic abuse, knowledge of these image management tactics is crucial for self-protection. Document everything, as your reality will likely be challenged by the narcissist's well-crafted public persona. There will be people who believe and support you, and there will be those who, no matter how much proof you have, will continue to support the narcissist. I know it's hard, but try to let go of the idea of trying to convince everyone that the narcissist is bad. Take that energy and redirect it into your healing.

Red Flag #36: Insults and Put Downs

Evie's Story

Here's your text split into shorter paragraphs:

I never saw the trap I was walking into with Jason. It started subtly; the way he'd make me question every text message I sent, turning simple communication into an anxiety-inducing ordeal. I'd stare at my phone for ages, debating whether adding a single emoji would make me seem "too needy" or if asking about weekend plans would make me "demanding."

When I finally confessed how stressed I felt about communicating with him, his response was crushing: "You're a mix between too much and too sensitive, but I love you anyway." Looking back now, I realize this was just the beginning of how he would systematically tear me down.

As our relationship progressed, Jason's "constructive criticism" became increasingly cruel and seemingly calculated. When I landed a major promotion at work, one I'd spent years working toward, his response cut deep: "The only reason you got the position was because your boss wants to sleep with you. Did you really think it was because of your 'business strategy'? God, you're delusional."

Even dress shopping for my sister's wedding became an exercise in humiliation. As I stepped out of the dressing room in what I thought was a beautiful dress, he looked me up and down with cold eyes and said, "That dress would've looked good on you about 20 pounds ago."

The worst part? I was so conditioned to accept these verbal assaults as "helpful feedback" that I actually thanked him for being "honest" with me.

When my anxiety finally drove me to seek therapy, his contempt was immediate: "Really? Are you that sensitive that you can't handle honest feedback without having a therapist walk you through it? Is that really who you want to be?"

Sometimes I catch glimpses of who I used to be before I met Jason: confident, self-assured, unafraid to be myself. The journey back to the "old me" has been long, but at least now I can see his "honest critiques" for the calculated attacks designed to break me down into someone smaller, someone easier to control.

The Narcissist's Playbook: Understanding Their 5-Part Insult Strategy

Looking at the pattern of narcissistic insults is like examining a carefully crafted weapon—each barb is designed not just to hurt but to achieve specific psychological goals. These aren't random outbursts of cruelty; they're calculated tools used to tear you down.

1. **Feeding Their Ego.** When they criticize you, they're simultaneously reinforcing their own perceived superiority. When they diminish your achievements, they're artificially inflating their accomplishments. Think of it like they're climbing a ladder using your shoulders as steps—each time they push you down, they rise higher…well, at least in their own mind.

2. **Controlling and Manipulating.** Insults function as a form of control. They learn which words make you flinch, which topics make you doubt yourself, and which criticisms send you into a spiral of self-questioning.

3. **Projecting Their Insecurities.** Pay attention to what they criticize most often; it usually reveals their deepest insecurities. When they repeatedly mock your intelligence, they're likely insecure about their own. When they constantly critique your social skills, they're probably deeply insecure about their social standing. Their insults are often a projection screen displaying their own worst fears about themselves.

4. **Distorting Reality.** Through constant criticism, they slowly rewrite your understanding of yourself. Today's "you're not very good at public speaking" becomes next month's reluctance for you to speak up in meetings, which transforms into next year's complete avoidance of any public role. Criticism like this doesn't only hurt in the moment; it's a systematic destruction of your self-image.

5. **Maintaining Superiority.** In their world, relationships are never partnerships; they're hierarchies. Their insults serve to continually reinforce their position at the top of this imagined pyramid. Every criticism, put-down, and dismissive comment is another brick in the wall they build between what they believe is, their superiority and your enforced inferiority.

Understanding these strategies doesn't just help you recognize them—it helps disarm them. When you understand that their insults reveal more about their insecurities and desperate need for control than your flaws, they lose their power to shape your reality.

Categories of Cruelty

Here are 10 examples of how a narcissist might use insults and put-downs:

1. Undermining Your Achievements:

"Whenever I would share something I was proud of, like a work achievement or personal milestone, he'd downplay it. He'd say things like, 'Anyone could have done that,' or 'It's not a big deal. I've done way more impressive things.' It made me feel like my accomplishments were meaningless, and that nothing I did would ever be good enough."

2. Criticizing Appearance:

"My mother would constantly criticize my looks, even if I made the effort to dress well or look nice. She'd make snide comments like, 'You've

really let yourself go.' Even when I tried my best, she would always find something to pick on to make me feel unattractive or insecure. It got to the point that I'd wear baggier and baggier clothes in an attempt to hide my body from her criticism."

3. **Belittling Your Opinions or Thoughts:**

"If I ever shared my thoughts or opinions, especially on things I cared about, he'd make me feel stupid for even speaking up. He'd say, 'That's just a dumb idea,' or 'You don't really know what you're talking about, do you?' It made me feel like my voice didn't matter, and that I was inferior to him."

4. **Making You Feel Inadequate:**

"If I made a mistake, no matter how small, my boss would exaggerate it and make it feel like I had ruined everything. He'd say, 'How could you be so dumb?' or 'That's such a simple thing, I don't know why you can't get it right.' He would never let me forget the mistakes I made, and I continually felt as though I wasn't competent or capable.»

5. **Disparaging Family and Friends:**

"If I spent time with family or friends, she'd make rude comments about them, saying things like, 'Your family is so weird,' or 'Why do you always hang out with those losers?' She would try to make me feel embarrassed or guilty for my relationships, subtly putting me down for enjoying time with people who cared about me."

6. **Using Sarcasm to Discredit You:**

"He would often use sarcasm to insult me without directly saying anything. For example, if I asked for help with something, he'd say, 'Oh, sure, let me drop everything just to help you. What would you do without me?' I truly believe it was his way of making me feel dependent and incompetent."

7. **Mocking Your Emotions:**

"Whenever I expressed my feelings, especially if I was upset or hurt, he would mock me. He'd imitate my voice or say, 'Oh, I'm so sorry. Did I hurt your delicate little feelings?' or 'Are you seriously crying over that?' It made me feel like I wasn't allowed to have emotions or that I was overreacting to everything."

8. Comparing You to Others:

"He would frequently compare me to other people, especially exes or acquaintances, in a way that made me feel inferior. He'd say things like, 'Well, [insert ex's name] would never act like that,' or 'You know, [insert friend's name] has her life together, unlike you.' It made me feel like I was always falling short, and no matter what I did, someone else was always better."

9. Diminishing Your Needs:

"If I asked for something, whether it was attention, affection, or help, he would make me feel selfish for wanting anything. He'd say things like, 'You always want something; it's never enough for you,' or 'Why can't you just be grateful for what I give you?' It made me feel guilty for even voicing my needs, as if I was being unreasonable or demanding."

10. Using Humor to Hide Insults:

«He'd often disguise his insults as jokes, saying things like, 'I'm just kidding. But you know, you are a little crazy,' or 'You're so dramatic. I'm glad I'm not as sensitive as you.' At first, it seemed harmless, but over time, I started realizing how much it hurt to constantly be the butt of his 'jokes.'»

The Impact on You

Being the target of constant put-downs and insults is soul-crushing. Here is the impact this kind of behavior can have if left unchecked:

1. Erodes your self-esteem

2. Makes you doubt your perceptions and abilities

3. Keeps you walking on eggshells

4. Creates anxiety and depression

5. Makes you dependent on the narcissist for validation

Recognizing the Reality

These patterns of put-downs share a common thread: they're designed to create doubt. Doubt in your perceptions, doubt in your worth, doubt in your right to feel hurt. *The narcissist's goal isn't just to hurt you, it's to make you question whether you're hurt at all—and then if you determine that you are, in fact, hurt, they'll blame you for it.*

Understanding these patterns is the first step toward breaking free. When you can name the tactics, they lose some of their power. You start to see how "I'm just trying to help" can be a weapon; how "just joking" can be a shield for cruelty; and how "loving concern" can be a mask for control.

Remember: Your feelings aren't "too sensitive." Your reactions aren't "dramatic." That knot in your stomach when they speak isn't just anxiety; it's your intuition screaming that something is wrong. Trust it. The first step to reclaiming your reality is recognizing when someone else is trying to rewrite it.

Breaking Free from the Insult Cycle

So, what's a person to do when they're caught in this web of insults and put downs? Here's your battle plan:

1. **Recognize the Pattern.** The first step is seeing the insults for what they are—a manipulation tactic, not truth.

2. **Don't Take the Bait.** Your reaction is what they're after. Don't give it to them. A blank stare can be your new superpower.

3. **Rebuild Your Self-Esteem.** Start challenging those negative messages. Do your best not to internalize hurtful comments. Don't let their words become your inner voice.

4. **Set Boundaries.** If you feel safe to do so, make it clear that insults are not acceptable. If they try to wriggle out of being accountable for their actions, and they will, make it known that you don't care if they were "joking," or having a bad day, or didn't mean to hurt you—that you want the hurtful comments to stop. If they don't stop, which they probably won't, be ready to enforce your boundaries—meaning, limiting or cutting contact.

5. **Seek Support.** Get yourself into therapy and/or join a support group. You need a reality check from supportive people who aren't trying to manipulate you or further put you down.

6. **Plan Your Exit.** If this is a relationship you can leave, start planning your escape. You deserve better than to be someone's verbal, emotional, or even physical punching bag.

Remember, their insults are a reflection of their unresolved issues, not your worth. You're not the problem here; they are. While they might think their opinions are universal truths, the real truth is that their reality is filtered through their insecurities and entitlement. But here's the kicker: the moment you see this dysfunction for what it is, their power starts to crumble.

In actuality, you are the one with all the power. You can decide that you're not playing this twisted game anymore. You have the right to be treated with respect and kindness. And you have the strength to walk away from anyone who thinks it's okay to tear you down to build themselves up.

Key Takeaways

1. **Pay attention to how you feel after interacting with them.** That knot in your stomach when they speak, the anxiety before sending a text, the constant self-editing— these aren't signs that you're too sensitive; they're your inner wisdom trying to protect you. If you consistently feel smaller, less confident, or find yourself second-guessing everything, you're likely experiencing this form of emotional erosion.

2. **Other people don't get to decide if you are too sensitive.** When someone tells you you're being "too sensitive" or "can't take a joke," they're attempting to get you to accept that their hurtful behavior is okay—and it truly might be how they joke or interact with others. However, this doesn't mean that their way of behaving has to be okay with you. After all, while they say you are too sensitive, the reality is they might not be sensitive enough. Trust your feelings and remember that in healthy relationships, you don't have to constantly defend your right to feel hurt.

Red Flag #37: They Seem to Enjoy Hurting You

Amber's Story

I met Ryan on a dating app, and his first message was about how glad he was to have found me. He claimed he'd been searching his whole life for a woman like me. Of course, I recognized the pickup line for what it was, but it felt fun to flirt.

We spoke about the challenges of online dating, and I told him I never imagined that I'd be looking to date again. I told him how my husband had died several years earlier and how he was an amazing man and that moving forward in life without him had been incredibly difficult. He sympathized with me and told me about how his wife had left him out of the blue about three years ago and he was still trying to recover from that.

This seemingly authentic connection kicked off communication between us that became a rollercoaster of epic highs and confusing lows. It started as playful banter about our "future marriage"—we'd joke about wedding plans and what we'd argue about as a couple. He'd laugh and say he'd do anything to make his wife happy—even going to farmer's markets and antique shops if that's what I wanted.

I guess I had my guard down, because I didn't take what we were saying seriously. It was all a big, fun, flirty joke...at least at first. Joking about having a life together and being his future wife went on for weeks.

However, at one point we spoke about previous relationships. He casually mentioned his recent hookups, always with a dismissive tone. He'd laugh about how awkward things would get when these women became "obsessed" with him after just a few dates, calling him nonstop when he'd already lost interest. "They just couldn't handle that it was never going to be serious," he'd say, almost with amusement in his voice.

But then he'd switch gears completely when talking about us. He began calling me his "wife" and "favorite person" with what seemed like genuine emotion during our video calls. When I mentioned I told my friends that we were "kinda dating" he seemed a little offended. "We aren't dating, I'm your future husband."

He'd make elaborate plans for romantic getaways and weekend trips, only to cancel at the last minute with dramatic excuses. I even purchased airline tickets for two of these planned trips, losing money when the cancellations came too late for refunds. He'd apologize profusely and promise to reimburse me, but the money never came.

Despite the constant disappointments, when we did talk, he'd paint vivid pictures of our future—describing our life in detail, planning our children's names, and sending me photos of engagement rings, asking which style I preferred "for when the time comes." We both worked from home, and he'd tell me that he worried he wouldn't be able to focus on work as he was so attracted to me.

During our marathon phone calls, he'd map out our entire life together—where we'd live, how we'd merge our finances, and what our wedding vows would say. He'd send me links to dream houses saying things like "this will be ours soon" and "I can't wait to wake up next to you every morning."

What had started as lighthearted jokes about marriage turned into detailed conversations about our shared future, complete with specific timelines and heartfelt promises. He'd call me late at night just to whisper about how he'd never felt this connected to anyone and how I was "the one" he'd been waiting for his whole life.

The intensity was intoxicating. Here was someone who saw our future so clearly and seemed to want it desperately. I'm embarrassed to say it, but all this talk was over the phone or video calls. We hadn't even met yet.

Once we did meet, the chemistry was off the charts. We had the best sex of my life, and the next day everything changed. He stopped calling or texting. Days passed without a word, and I began to panic, genuinely worried something terrible had happened to him.

Had he been in an accident? Was he seriously ill? I called and texted, my anxiety growing with each hour of silence. When he finally responded after nearly a week, it was a brief, emotionless text: "Hey, been busy with work. Talk soon."

No explanation for his disappearance, no acknowledgment of my frantic concern, no mention of our intimate time together or any of our elaborate future plans. It became crystal clear that he was blowing me off, and suddenly his earlier casual jokes about women becoming "obsessed" after sex took on a chilling new meaning.

I found myself becoming one of those many women who were obsessed with him. I sent text after text begging him for clarity and doing whatever I could to regain his attention. Thoughts of him consumed my day. I hated that I was so fixated on him.

I found myself trying to deny the reality that he was blowing me off. I told myself that maybe he really was busy, and found myself checking my phone every few hours throughout the night. After about five days of this, it became clear that he never had any intentions of a future with me, and that this had been his game plan all along.

What devastated me most was realizing how intentionally he'd orchestrated everything—taking me from sympathizing about the loss of my husband to playful jokes to serious emotional investment, only to yank it all away once he'd gotten what he wanted. It was like he'd wanted to take me to the highest emotional high possible and then pull the rug out from underneath me just to watch how hard I'd fall.

He'd carefully studied my responses during our conversations, learning exactly how to make me feel chosen and special, only to turn around and make me feel worthless and foolish for believing in the future he'd so convincingly created.

Looking back, I think the cruelty was always the point. What he really seemed to get off on was the psychological game itself—building someone up just to tear them down, creating deep trust just to betray it, offering love just to snatch it away at the moment of greatest vulnerability.

It was like he was conducting a calculated experiment to see just how gullible and emotionally invested he could make me. The way he'd seemed to savor every detail of our future planning, the intensity with which he'd painted our life together, all of it was designed to maximize the eventual devastation.

My emotional destruction wasn't an unfortunate side effect of his pursuit of sex—it was the entire goal. He was getting genuine pleasure from engineering my suffering, and that realization was almost more devastating than the abandonment itself.

The Pleasure in Others' Pain

There's a particular breed of narcissist who doesn't just manipulate for control or validation; they actively derive pleasure from causing their target pain. These sadistic narcissists are calculated in their cruelty. They study their targets, learning every insecurity and vulnerability, then craft their attacks for maximum damage.

The goal isn't just to diminish their target; it's to break them completely. They frequently push boundaries, each time going slightly further to see how much damage they can inflict. What starts as "playful" teasing or "helpful" feedback evolves into vicious character assassination, then escalates to deliberate psychological torture.

For example, they might share private information publicly to humiliate their target, or create situations designed to trigger panic attacks, all while maintaining their innocence that they didn't mean to cause harm.

Another tactic is bringing the target to the highest of highs by promising an ideal future such as a vacation or marriage, and once the target has fully bought into the fantasy and/or paid for it, the narcissist cancels. Pulling the plans away causes the target to suffer financially, emotionally, and sometimes psychologically.

For the narcissist, the goal is to get the target to have an intense emotional reaction: anger, sadness, fear, or debilitating levels of concern. Their goal is to get the target to have the biggest, most explosive reaction as possible, because the more upset the target is, the more superior the narcissist feels.

Some narcissists take this sadistic behavior to extreme levels, deliberately pushing their targets toward self-destruction. They might encourage self-harming behaviors or attempt to push their target to suicide.

The most chilling aspect is how these sadistic narcissists can maintain a sparkling public image. They're skilled at appearing charming and concerned, while systematically destroying their target behind closed doors. They may even position themselves as the worried partner, telling friends and family they're "so concerned" about their target's deteriorating mental health, conveniently leaving out their role in causing that deterioration.

These abusers often select their targets carefully, looking for individuals with specific vulnerabilities they can exploit. They're drawn to people with histories of trauma, knowing these individuals might be more susceptible to manipulation and less likely to trust their perceptions.

They tend to seek out highly empathetic people who will continually try to understand and forgive their behavior, even in the face of escalating cruelty. Although, this is not always the case.

Sometimes, a sadistic narcissist will pursue a target that has healthy self-esteem, is confident, and has a strong inner circle. For these types of narcissists, the fun involves breaking a tough target.

Jane's Story

My divorce from Marcus brought out a particular kind of sadism in him. Towards the tail end of our relationship, things were at their worst. He knew how insecure I felt about my body after having our baby, so he'd deliberately focus on that. "Look at yourself," he'd tell me, "your body is all stretched out and used up. No one's ever going to want you now." The more I'd break down, the more energized he seemed to get, following me from room to room as I tried to escape, detailing all my perceived flaws. When he found me crying in the bathroom one night, he leaned against the door frame and casually suggested that I was "pathetic and should just end it all."

When I confronted him about his affair, he asked how I could blame him. He told me she was the exact opposite of me: she was fun, young, and "smokin' hot." He would tell me that I wasn't only a terrible wife but a terrible mother too, and that our child would be better off without me. The truth is that I had severe postpartum depression and had days where doing the bare minimum was exhausting, and because of that I began to believe him; that maybe our child was better off without me. But he didn't believe postpartum depression was a real condition. He thought that it was just something I was using as an excuse. And that there was something fundamentally wrong with me for not being able to pull myself together.

What makes me sad is that, at the time, I didn't see his cruel and sadistic comments for what they were. I saw them as the truth, because each awful comment did have a kernel of truth to it. It took many years of therapy for me to rebuild my self-worth. Frankly, I don't know how I made it out of that relationship alive because he really had me believing that I was this disgusting person, and terrible mother, and that there was no hope in sight for me.

The Lasting Trauma

Many targets of sadistic narcissists end up with severe PTSD, depression, anxiety, and suicidal thoughts long after the relationship ends. The calculated nature of the abuse, combined with the evident pleasure their abuser took in causing them pain, creates particularly deep trauma. Recovery often requires understanding that this level of cruelty says everything about the abuser and nothing about the target's worth.

What makes these relationships especially devastating is how the sadistic narcissist can convince their target that they deserve the abuse. They manipulate their victims into believing that the cruelty is justified, that it's somehow an expression of love, necessary feedback, or the natural result of the target's behavior. This twisted dynamic can make it incredibly difficult for targets to recognize the abuse for what it is, let alone escape it.

Key Takeaways

1. **The most dangerous type of narcissist is the one who actively enjoys causing pain.** These sadistic narcissists deliberately time their attacks for maximum emotional damage and take visible pleasure in watching their target's suffering, often showing excitement when landing particularly devastating blows. They will target your vulnerabilities, weaponizing them against you.

2. **If you encounter a sadistic narcissist, remember that their cruelty reflects their pathology, not your worth.** Don't try to understand or fix them. And try your best not to absorb the hurtful things they've said or done. Their calculated attacks, and evident pleasure in causing pain, are about their disturbed psychology, not your value as a person. The most important step you can take is to drastically limit or completely cut contact with them, as these individuals rarely change and often escalate their abuse over time.

3. **Don't try to get them to understand their actions are hurting you, as doing so will only make things worse.** Oftentimes, the default advice given when someone is hurting us is to make our boundaries known. This is the last thing you want to do with a sadistic person. They know they are hurting you, so letting them know their tactics are working will make things worse, not better. Focus instead on protecting yourself and seeking support from trusted friends, family members, or mental health professionals who can help you navigate the aftermath of this particularly toxic form of abuse.

Red Flag #38: Crazy-Making Conversations

Sasha's Story

My relationship with Mitchell was the most confusing, exhausting, and infuriating relationship I've ever been in. I remember repeatedly telling my best friend, my therapist, and even Mitchell himself that I'd never had a dynamic like this one before.

I'm normally a laid-back and go-with-the-flow kind of person, and yet, conversations with Mitchell seemed to frequently go off the rails to where we'd get into these conversations from hell. I've never been so angry before.

I remember one time yelling at him, in sheer frustration, that I didn't know why things were so difficult between us and why my best efforts weren't making things better.

For example, the last fight we got in was over me asking him to text me if he was going to be home late. I woke up around 1 am and realized he wasn't home, so I texted him saying I was worried and for him to text me. He ended up coming home at 3 am.

When I told him I was upset that he didn't text me to let me know he was going to be out late with his friends, he twisted the conversation into an exhausting spiral that lasted for hours. First came the deflection about my lunch with my sister last week, then accusations that I was "controlling" and "suffocating" him.

When I tried to redirect the conversation back to his broken promise, he switched to cruel sarcasm: "Well, we can't all be perfect like you, can we?" What started as a simple request for communication had spiraled into a maze of accusations, deflections, and guilt, leaving me second-guessing myself and wondering if I truly was the unreasonable, controlling partner he described.

I found myself rereading those texts several times, trying to pinpoint where things went off track. When I told my therapist what happened and how Mitchell was now giving me the silent treatment, she explained that Mitchell was manipulative and broke down all the forms of manipulation she saw in his texts.

Having a name for the different ways our conversations got confusing helped tremendously. I was no longer in the dark about what was going on or why.

Understanding Crazy-Making Conversations

Crazy-making conversations are those maddening exchanges where the discussion veers off track, nothing gets resolved, and the person who initially raised the issue is left feeling unheard and frustrated to tears.

These conversations commonly include disrespectful behaviors ranging from angry outbursts and sarcasm to dismissive attitudes, blame-shifting, and the minimization of concerns, to name a few.

It's the kind of communication where the other person belittles or invalidates you with a tone of "What's wrong with you? You're overreacting," "That didn't happen," or "If it did happen, it's all your fault." In these moments, the target of the conversation feels alone in their reality, without anyone to confirm that their feelings and perspectives are valid.

As the conversation unfolds, blame-shifting often takes over, with the original issue being sidelined in favor of accusing the target of something entirely different. The person who brought up the concern often finds themselves having to defend their words and actions, feeling that if they can just explain themselves or make their partner see and stay on the issue at hand, that the relationship will improve.

However, because the partner lacks the desire to work things out in good faith and isn't willing to engage with an open mind and work towards a solution, these conversations never lead to a resolution. Instead, the cycle continues, leaving one person constantly trying to work towards a solution while the other remains inflexible.

The result leaves the person on the receiving end feeling isolated in their reality, questioning their perceptions and emotional responses. They often end these conversations feeling frustrated to tears, with a knot in their stomach, an overwhelming desire to escape, or fearful to bring anything up in the future.

They dread how their concern gets shifted around to where they are in the hot seat and are now stuck in hours-long conversations where they feel they must defend themselves. The most unsettling part is how reasonable or workable it can feel in the moment, as though if you could only be clearer about what you said or need from them, that a solution is possible.

These aren't random communication failures. They're calculated tactics designed to maintain control and to ensure that they get their way. The result is that you feel perpetually off balance, confused, in a scramble to get things back on track, and desperate for the "conversation" to end.

Like a magic trick, these techniques only work when you don't know what to look for. So, let's get rid of the smoke and mirrors so you can see reality clearly.

10 Tactics of Crazy-Making Conversations

1. Withholding.

> Think of trying to complete a puzzle while someone deliberately hides pieces. That's withholding. When confronted about suspicious behavior, they respond with "There's nothing to talk about" or "I don't know what you mean," even when evidence suggests otherwise. The truth comes out in tiny drops - a phenomenon called "trickle truthing" where each small admission is followed by new denials, only to be revealed later as lies.

You might catch them in a lie about their whereabouts, only to receive a small piece of truth ("Okay, yes, I was at the bar") followed by more lies about who they were with. This pattern continues until you're exhausted from trying to piece together what really happened. The psychological toll of constantly hunting for truth leaves you feeling paranoid and questioning your judgment.

2. **Countering.**

Imagine playing a game with someone who changes the rules midway through. This is countering. What this looks like in motion is that *even when you agree with them, they'll find something to dispute.* If you say "you're right," they'll argue that you're agreeing for the wrong reasons, or they'll shift to a different topic. For them, the goal isn't to reach an understanding; it's to maintain control or to start a fight. You might find yourself in an argument about dishes, which somehow becomes about your tone of voice, which then morphs into a debate about something that happened three years ago. These conversations leave you feeling like you're trapped in an endless maze where the walls keep shifting. By the end, you can't even remember what the original discussion was about.

3. **Discounting.**

This is like having someone tell you you're not hungry when your stomach is growling. They systematically dismiss your feelings with phrases like "You're too sensitive" or "It's not that big a deal." Each dismissal chips away at your trust in your emotional and physical responses. Over time, you start to preface your feelings with "Maybe I'm overreacting, but..." or "I know this sounds silly..." Their dismissal becomes your inner voice, creating a constant state of second-guessing your own emotions. You might find yourself apologizing for having feelings at all, as if your emotional responses are a character flaw rather than a normal human experience.

4. **Verbal Abuse as Jokes.**

Picture someone throwing rocks at you while claiming they're just having fun, and that you're the one who is ruining a good time. That's what it feels like when verbal abuse is disguised as a joke or no big deal. Everything hurtful comes wrapped in "just kidding" or "can't you take a joke?" When they mock your intelligence or appearance in front of others, you're painted as overly sensitive for not laughing along. This creates a double bind where defending yourself makes you seem like the problem. They might say something cutting about your career choices, then roll their eyes when you react, saying, "Learn to take a joke. Everyone else is laughing." The 'humor' serves as both a weapon and a shield, making you feel simultaneously hurt and guilty for feeling hurt.

5. **Blocking and Diverting.**

Like a train being switched to a different track, they derail meaningful conversations before they can reach their destination. "We've already discussed this" or "You always bring this up" become barriers to addressing real issues. When confronted about their behavior, they might suddenly remember an urgent task or develop a headache. They excel at changing topics just as you're about to make a point, leaving you feeling like you're chasing a conversation that's always just out of reach. The pattern becomes so predictable that you start doubting whether to bring up issues at all.

6. **Accusing and Blaming.**

Watch how skillfully they turn every situation around until, somehow, you're the one apologizing. You approach them about their hurtful behavior, and suddenly, you're defending yourself against accusations of being "controlling" or "never satisfied." They might arrive home late without calling, but end up making you apologize for being worried.

The mental gymnastics leave you so disoriented that you find yourself apologizing for things that clearly weren't your fault. By the end of many conversations, you're somehow comforting them about how your reasonable request made them feel attacked.

7. **Judging and Criticizing.**

Their criticism comes wrapped as a concern. "I'm just trying to help you improve" becomes the preface to a barrage of judgments about everything from your parenting to your career choices. Watch how they offer "constructive feedback" about things you can't change, like your laugh or your personality traits. These comments often come with a side of comparison. They might say things such as, "I just want you to be as successful as my father" or "Your sister always manages to look so put together." The result is a constant state of trying to improve yourself to meet impossible standards.

8. **Trivializing.**

They can turn any victory you may have into a defeat. Land a promotion? "Well, they were desperate to fill the position." Complete a marathon? "It's not like you won it." Their responses to your achievements follow a predictable pattern: acknowledge briefly, then immediately diminish. The impact is like watching a balloon slowly deflate: your initial excitement fades into self-doubt. You gradually stop sharing good news altogether, knowing it will only be used to make you feel smaller. Even major life milestones become moments you dread sharing, anticipating how they'll be reduced to nothing.

9. **Threatening.**

Their threats come wrapped in plausible deniability. They might claim that they are "just being honest" or "telling you what could happen." They might casually mention how easy it would be to find someone else, or how their ex is still interested. Watch how they use your deepest fears as leverage: "Maybe I should give you something to really be jealous about" or "If you keep acting this way, don't be surprised if I leave." These aren't just words; they're emotional landmines designed to keep you walking on eggshells.

10. **Name Calling.**

This goes beyond obvious insults to include subtle digs that corrode your self-image. They might use pet names that actually mask criticism. For example, they might "jokingly" call you names such as, "Drama Queen" or "Princess." The tone matters as much as the words; they can make even your name sound like an insult. You might find yourself answering to these belittling names, normalizing the disrespect until it becomes part of your identity.

Understanding Reactive Abuse

In the face of constant manipulation and crazy-making behavior, even the most level-headed person may eventually snap. This phenomenon, known as reactive abuse, occurs when targets respond to prolonged crazy-making conversations with behavior that might appear aggressive or unstable to outsiders.

The manipulator often deliberately provokes these reactions, pushing the target to a breaking point through sustained crazy-making behavior. Once the target reacts, the abuser can then point to this response as proof that the victim is "crazy" or "abusive," effectively deflecting from their manipulative behavior.

This dynamic creates a particularly vicious cycle, as victims then struggle with guilt over their reactions, questioning whether they're actually the abusive ones in the relationship. This confusion further entrenches them in the toxic dynamic, making it harder to recognize and escape the manipulation.

Key Takeaways

1. **You cannot reason with someone who is deliberately trying to confuse you, avoid accountability, refuses to understand what you are saying, or avoids working towards a solution.** No amount of careful explanation or perfect wording will make a manipulative person suddenly develop empathy or take responsibility for their actions. These individuals aren't engaging in these behaviors out of ignorance; they're making conscious choices to avoid accountability and maintain control. The tears, frustration, and confusion they cause aren't accidental side effects; they're intentional and designed to break you down and do things their way.

2. **The only way to win this game is to refuse to play.** This might mean setting firm boundaries, seeking professional support, or ultimately removing yourself from the relationship entirely. Remember, you can disengage from any conversation at any time. If the conversation feels circular and the issue isn't getting resolved, you don't have to keep at it until you explode in either anger or tears. You can tell the other person that you need to continue this conversation later (if at all). ....And if you do continue it, it can help to do so in a clear, concise, bullet point, written format. This way it's harder for them to spin the topic off course.

3. **Any dynamic that leaves you constantly questioning your sanity is not a dynamic worth preserving.** Your emotional stability and mental health deserve protection. If you find yourself repeatedly trying to explain why someone's behavior is harmful, or why your issues with them never seem to get resolved while they show no interest in understanding or changing, it's time to recognize that the problem isn't your communication skills; it's their choice to remain destructive.

Red Flag #39: Intense Anger/Intimidation

Lauren's Story

Cole and I had been on and off for seven years. I felt like I could never leave for good because we had a three-year-old daughter together. He'd always had a bad temper, and when we moved to California and I began making new friends and going out with them, he didn't like this at all.

Over time, my friends grew to intensely dislike him. He was controlling and put me down a lot, sometimes in front of them.

Once, he told me how during our last breakup, he had sex with a stripper and how she was better than me in every way. I was beyond devastated, and him telling me that hit all of my emotional insecurities. And he told me this in front of our daughter.

The whole situation was awful. I realized then that I had to leave; that I couldn't have her grow up around this.

Things with Cole were quiet for about a week, and it seemed like we were going to break up for good. He even told me to move on with my life and to date other people because he was "done with me."

And, so, about three months later, I started dating James, a mutual friend of ours. Neither of us wanted to tell Cole because we knew he had a bad temper, and this wouldn't go over well.

Cole ended up coming over unannounced one night when James was over. Cole flew into a rage like I'd never seen. He broke my TV and got into a fistfight with James. He threatened to kill us both.

I was absolutely terrified and called the police. They came and arrested him. However, in Cole's mind, I was the bad guy for calling the cops on him, and his violence was justified because I was dating James.

It was like Cole believed he had some divine right to keep me in his life, regardless of his actions. I joined a support group for survivors of domestic violence. When I shared what happened to me, they said it was "narcissistic rage" because it was rage due to his ego and level of entitlement.

What Makes Narcissistic Rage Different?

Unlike typical anger, narcissistic rage isn't about stress or frustration – it's about entitlement. Think of narcissists as having paper-thin emotional skin covering an enormous ego. When that fragile surface gets punctured, whether by actual criticism or merely perceived slights, the reaction can be volcanic. Narcissistic rage is an explosive display of anger that is disproportionate to the event.

These aren't merely bad tempers or anger management issues. Narcissists fundamentally believe they should be the center of the universe, wielding complete power and control. When reality challenges this belief, their reaction can escalate from 0 to 10 in mere seconds.

Two Types of Triggers: Real and Perceived Ego Injuries

Real Narcissistic Injuries

These occur when someone directly challenges the narcissist's inflated self-image. Imagine telling a self-proclaimed "king" or "queen" that they're being selfish, or entitled, or that they are wrong or can't have their way. In their mind, they're simply claiming their rightful due – how dare a mere "peasant" suggest otherwise? The resulting rage isn't just anger; it's a punishment for your insolence.

Perceived Narcissistic Injuries

More puzzling and unpredictable are the reactions to perceived slights – situations where the narcissist interprets an innocent comment or action as an attack. For example, you might ask a narcissist an innocent question, such as, "Did you take the car in for an oil change?" A question like this might be taken as an accusation of incompetence, triggering a defensive rage. In an attempt to keep the peace, you might make a mental note to never ask if they scheduled the car for an oil change ever again. And, let's say a year from now, the oil light goes on in the car while they are driving to work. They call you to pick them up, and when you get there, they are upset that you didn't remind them to schedule the car for an oil change and start accusing you of deliberately setting them up to fail.

The Two Faces of Narcissistic Rage

Narcissistic rage manifests in two distinct ways:

The Explosion

This is rage in its most obvious form – verbal attacks, physical violence, or both. It can range from verbal assaults to physical abuse and, in extreme cases, even murder. It's the narcissist's nuclear option for regaining control.

The Implosion

More subtle but equally destructive, this manifests as passive-aggressive revenge: emptying joint bank accounts, giving the silent treatment, or finding other ways to "punish" their target without obvious confrontation. These actions might not register as abuse at first, making them particularly insidious.

The Relationship Trap

Many people don't witness full-blown narcissistic rage until they're already committed, for example, after marriage, having children, or making major joint purchases. This timing isn't accidental. Narcissists often wait until they believe their target is trapped before revealing the full extent of their volatile nature.

A Critical Warning

If you're seeing signs of explosive anger or ruthless passive-aggressive behavior in someone, you're likely only seeing the tip of the iceberg. While it's natural to want to explain away their behavior by blaming it on childhood trauma or daily stress, remember that while everyone has the right to feel angry, no one has the right to be abusive.

Adult behavior should come with adult boundaries, especially around anger. No circumstance, no matter how stressful, justifies abuse. If you're walking on eggshells, constantly trying to predict and prevent the next explosion, you're not dealing with ordinary anger; you're dealing with something far more dangerous.

10 Ways a Narcissist's Anger Might Show Up in Your Life

1. **Any feedback or constructive criticism you offer is perceived to be an attack.** You mention something small they did wrong, like being late or forgetting a task. Instead of a normal response, they explode: "How dare you criticize me? I don't need this from you!" Even gentle feedback gets twisted into "disrespect."

2. **Raging over "the little things."** You forgot to put the clothes in the dryer or paid a bill late. Suddenly, they're shouting about how "stupid" and "useless" you are. The intensity is shocking; it's like dropping a nuclear bomb on an ant hill. You find yourself tiptoeing around, trying to predict what might set them off next.

3. **Lashing out when things aren't "perfect."** You have to cancel plans at the last minute because you are sick? Watch out for verbal abuse or flying objects. They might mutter about how rude and inconsiderate you are, claim that you are being manipulative, or storm out of the room. Their rage can turn physical, even if they're not touching you. For

example, they might punch a wall, slam a door, or break something.

4. **Sulking or silent treatment when you don't agree.** Disagree with them or fail to shower them with praise? Prepare for days of icy silence. They'll act like you've ceased to exist – their way of punishing you for not feeding their ego exactly how they demand.

5. **Personal insults during arguments.** Notice how arguments never stay on topic? Instead of discussing the issue, they shift the focus back to you and attack you personally: "You're a failure" or "No wonder no one likes you." Their anger is accompanied by hurtful, demeaning words designed to tear you down. If they are particularly hateful, they may even tell you to kill yourself. They're not trying to resolve anything – they're trying to destroy you or your self-worth.

6. **Blaming others for their mistakes** They miss a deadline at work, but somehow it becomes your fault. "You distracted me!" they'll claim, even if you were nowhere near the situation. They can't handle the slightest hint of failure.

7. **Making threatening or intimidating comments.** If you stand up for yourself, you might hear: "You'll regret this" or "You're lucky I'm letting this go." They use fear as their favorite tool, making you afraid to have your own opinions or boundaries.

8. **Flashes of anger when they aren't the center of attention.** Didn't praise their new shirt immediately? Failed to notice they changed their hair? Get ready for a barrage of comments accusing you of not appreciating them. They act like you've committed treason by not being their personal cheerleader.

9. **Blowing up when things don't run according to their plan.** Watch what happens when a restaurant loses your

reservation, or you have to cancel plans. They'll act like the world is out to get them. A minor inconvenience becomes, in their mind, a personal attack.

10. **Insults when you question their views.** Try pointing out a flaw in their logic or respectfully disagreeing with their opinion. They'll snap back: "I'm right, you're just too dumb to get it!" Their fragile ego can't handle even the gentlest challenge to their perceived superiority.

These outbursts aren't about you; they're about their fragile ego, desperate need for control, and constant hunger for admiration. Their anger isn't proportional because it's not really about the situation at hand. And because their intense bouts of anger have nothing to do with you, you can't fix things. I know it could seem like if you did things differently, they would be nicer to you, but with a narcissist, it doesn't work that way. You can't change yourself enough to keep them calm and happy because, again, you aren't the problem; they are. And they will treat anyone else who is in your shoes the same way. Now, it might not seem that way at first. If they get into a new relationship, they might post all about how this new person is so great. But with time, that idealization wears off, and the devaluation starts. Soon enough, the new person starts to find themselves in a living hell.

If you are experiencing any of these patterns in your relationship, please know these are important warning signs that shouldn't be ignored.

Key Takeaways

1. **Narcissistic rage isn't about ordinary anger—it's about entitlement and control.** While normal anger is proportional to the situation and can be resolved through discussion, narcissistic rage is an explosive overreaction to even minor challenges to their ego, perceived authority, or self-image. This type of rage often appears as either explosive outbursts or calculated passive-aggressive revenge,

both designed to punish you for daring to challenge their perceived superiority or control.

2. **If you're constantly walking on eggshells to avoid triggering someone's anger, you're dealing with abuse, not just a bad temper.** Pay attention to how they react when you express opinions, set boundaries, or fail to meet their expectations perfectly—their response will often be wildly disproportionate to the situation. Remember that you can't prevent their rage by changing your behavior to be more in tune with their needs because their explosions aren't actually about your behavior—they're about their need for control, and their inability to handle even minor challenges to their ego.

3. **Narcissistic rage often doesn't show its full force until you're deeply committed to the relationship through marriage, children, or shared finances.** This timing isn't accidental—it's a calculated strategy to ensure you're trapped when they finally reveal their true nature. This sudden shift in behavior can be confusing for the target, making them question what they did to cause such a reaction in their partner. The reality is the issue is with the narcissist not the target. No matter what trauma or stress someone has experienced, nothing justifies abusive behavior, and seeing these signs of explosive or passive-aggressive rage early in a relationship usually means you're only seeing the tip of the iceberg.

4. **All forms of abusive behavior get worse with time—not better.** Just because someone hasn't ever been physically abusive doesn't mean that their behavior won't escalate into physical violence. If someone is verbally abusive, they are already showing that they don't have boundaries around their anger, and they feel entitled to lash out. People like this are unpredictable and dangerous, and you would be wise to leave or have a safety plan in place.

5. **There is no excuse for abuse.** Your behavior didn't cause
   this; and changes in your behavior won't stop it either. You
   shouldn't need to be perfect to avoid being abused—and
   even if you were perfect, the abuse would still happen,
   because they'd be upset that you never make mistakes! No
   matter how upset someone gets, it is a reasonable expectation
   that they handle their anger like an adult and not take it out
   on others.

Red Flag #40: Disproportionate Emotional Responses

Henry's Story

At the last Christmas get-together, my stepmother Maya broke down about her neighbor's passing. "I just can't stop crying," she declared, dabbing at completely dry eyes. "Amara was like family to me." I shifted uncomfortably, remembering all the times Maya had complained about Amara's "annoying" Christmas decorations and how she'd actively avoided neighborhood gatherings just to steer clear of her. Now here she was, insisting she needed to take time off work to "process her grief," making elaborate social media posts about her "devastating loss," and even claiming she should be included in the family's private memorial service.

To those who knew Maya, we could tell her "grief " over Amara's death wasn't grief at all; it was a performance; and it was unsettling to watch. It was like she was using her neighbor's death for attention, and it felt so gross. It was as if she'd studied how people were "supposed" to act after a loss but it was like she studied human emotions from soap operas because the way she was acting was so over the top.

The Frozen Heart: Understanding Their Default State

In moments of crisis, this emotional void becomes particularly stark. When others are dealing with serious illness, loss, or hardship, the narcissist's annoyance at having to "deal with" these situations often leaks through their attempts at appropriate responses. They might make comments like "I guess I should visit them in the hospital" or "Now I have to send a sympathy card," revealing how they view these human moments of connection as burdensome obligations rather than natural expressions of care.

You might notice them becoming visibly agitated when attention remains on someone else's emotional needs for too long. They often employ tactics to redirect focus, either by manufacturing their crisis, changing the subject abruptly, or finding reasons to leave the situation. This behavior stems from their fundamental inability to sustain attention on others' emotional experiences.

Their indifference extends beyond just emotional situations to include others' basic human needs and experiences. They might become irritated when someone is sick and needs care, impatient when children require attention, or dismissive when partners express a need for emotional intimacy. These reactions reveal their core belief that others' emotional and physical needs are inconvenient impositions on their world.

Emotions as a Performance

Watch for the "emotional contagion test" where, in group settings, genuine emotions tend to spread naturally. When someone shares devastating news, most people instinctively feel and reflect that heaviness. The narcissist, however, often misreads the room, either overacting to match what they think is expected or failing to modulate their emotional display to fit the situation's gravity.

Pay attention to their eyes during emotional displays. Genuine emotions, especially strong ones, tend to involve involuntary muscle movements around the eyes - what psychologists call Duchenne markers. The narcissist's performances often lack these subtle but crucial indicators of authentic feeling. Their eyes might remain cold or calculating even as they act out extreme emotional states.

Their emotional performances also tend to lack the natural progression of genuine feelings. Real emotions ebb and flow, gradually shifting and evolving. The narcissist's displays often have unnatural starting and stopping points, as if they're scenes in a play rather than genuine emotional experiences. They might "turn off" their grief the moment they achieve their desired outcome or switch instantly from "devastation" to normal conversation when distracted.

Timing That is Off

These misaligned responses often become most apparent during major life events. At weddings, they might appear distracted or annoyed during the ceremony but become dramatically emotional during moments when they can command attention.

The intensity mismatch reveals itself in everyday situations, too. A minor criticism at work might trigger hours of dramatic emotional distress, while news of a close family member's serious illness receives only cursory acknowledgment. They might spend days dwelling on a perceived slight from a waiter, while completely dismissing their partner's expressions of emotional pain.

Their emotional responses often seem to operate on a completely different timeline than the situation demands. Long after others have processed and moved forward from an event, they might suddenly revive the drama, usually when attention is focused elsewhere. Conversely, they might rush to declare themselves "over" a significant loss or betrayal in an unnaturally short time frame, especially if maintaining the appropriate emotional response becomes inconvenient.

Emotions as a Strategic Display

Their emotional displays often follow predictable patterns tied to specific goals. Watch how quickly tears appear when they're caught in a lie, or how conveniently a headache or panic attack develops when they're about to face consequences for their actions. These strategic deployments of emotion serve as get-out-of-jail-free cards, instantly transforming them from perpetrator to victim.

The manipulation becomes particularly evident in their response to others' boundaries. They might respond to a simple "no" with an overwhelming display of hurt feelings, complete with accusations of cruelty and claims of devastating emotional damage. This emotional blackmail aims to make others feel guilty for maintaining healthy boundaries.

Professional settings often reveal this tactical use of emotions clearly. They might break down crying in performance reviews when receiving constructive criticism, become explosively angry when colleagues question their decisions, or display exaggerated enthusiasm when trying to win favor with superiors. Each emotional display serves a specific purpose in their professional chess game.

In romantic relationships, they weaponize emotions. They might suddenly become emotionally unavailable when their partner needs support, only to flood them with affection when they sense the partner pulling away. These calculated emotional shifts serve to keep their partners off-balance and dependent on their approval.

Key Takeaways

1. **Real emotions follow natural patterns, while narcissistic emotional displays often feel like amateur theater performances.** Watch for unnatural starts and stops to their emotional displays, as if they're scenes in a play rather than genuine feelings. Their emotions often lack the subtle physical markers of authentic feeling, and they can switch their feelings "off" instantly when they've achieved their desired outcome, or when something more interesting catches their attention.

2. **Narcissists use emotional displays strategically to achieve specific goals.** Notice how conveniently their tears appear when caught in a lie, or how quickly a panic attack develops when they're about to face consequences. These emotional performances aren't random—they're calculated tools used to transform themselves from perpetrator to victim, particularly when faced with boundaries or accountability. (If you'd like to see an extreme version of this, head to YouTube and look up videos on Nicholas Alahverdian, a man who faked his death after being accused of sexual assault and fraud. The story is absolutely wild and takes many twists and turns you'd never expect!)

Red Flag #41: Two Different Sides to Themselves

Marty's Story

The night of his sister's wedding reception, my boyfriend James was being his usual charming self. He gave a humorous and witty speech about the bride and groom, and had no shortage of thoughtful gestures, making sure every guest felt special. He even helped his elderly grandmother to her seat and humored her as she spoke for a good twenty minutes about her prized rose garden. People kept telling me how lucky I was to have such an attentive, charismatic partner. I smiled and nodded, feeling in that moment, that what James and I had was really special.

However, the moment we got into our car, everything changed. He exploded about how I had "embarrassed" him by talking too long to his college friends and that I was "holding them hostage" with stories no one cared about. The same hands that had so gently guided his grandmother were now gripping the steering wheel tightly. This type of shift in his behavior was something that I had been starting to see more of over the past six months. The contrast was jarring; just minutes before, he'd been making the entire room laugh with his toast to the happy couple, and now he was systematically tearing apart every single thing I'd said or done that evening. It was like living with two different people, never knowing which one I'd get, but always fearing that Dr. Jekyll would eventually give way to Mr. Hyde.

Understanding the Two Faces

The public persona of a narcissist is meticulously crafted; they can be charming, generous, and seemingly perfect. They're the life of every party, the colleague everyone admires, the partner others envy. This version exists primarily for an audience, carefully maintained to gather admiration and maintain social standing.

In private, they transform. The mask slips to reveal someone cold, cruel, and calculating. This isn't a mood swing or a bad day; it's a calculated shift that occurs when there's no audience to impress and no social capital to gain. The contrast between public charm and private cruelty creates a uniquely damaging form of psychological abuse.

The Sweet-Mean Cycle: A Closer Look

The sweet-mean cycle is exactly that: behavior that cycles between being sweet and then mean.

Think of it like emotional ping-pong. They serve you criticism, then comfort. Here are some examples:

- Monday: "Your parenting needs work. The kids are out of control."

- Tuesday: "You're such an amazing mother!"

- Wednesday: "You're beautiful..."

- Thursday: "You really need to lose weight and try some different makeup."

The alternations in their behavior aren't always about the same topic. They might fly into a rage because you spoke to someone they didn't like, but then they are sweet and complimentary about your cooking. ...And, sometimes the "sweet" part isn't even all that sweet. Sometimes, the sweet part of the cycle is treating you with mild indifference and acting like their mean behavior never happened.

The Sweet-Mean Cycle: Suki's Story

I never knew which version of my husband Mark I was going to get from one conversation to the next. It was like living with two completely different people who happened to share the same body.

One week, I mentioned that our credit card bill seemed high this month, Mark was the picture of reasonableness. "You're right, honey. Let's sit down tonight and go through it together. Maybe we can find some subscriptions to cancel or areas where we can cut back. We're a team on this." He even squeezed my shoulder and kissed my forehead before leaving for work.

The next week, when I brought up the same financial concerns, Mark's entire demeanor had shifted. "Well, maybe if you didn't order takeout every time you're too lazy to cook, we wouldn't have this problem," he snapped, his voice dripping with contempt. "And those Amazon packages that show up every other day? Real responsible, Suki." By the time he was done listing my failures, I was fighting back tears, wondering how the same conversation could go so differently.

A few days later brought yet another Mark—apologetic and charming. "I'm so sorry about the other day, babe. I was stressed about the Peterson account and took it out on you. That wasn't fair." He made me coffee exactly how I like it and even cracked jokes about his own bad spending habits. "Remember when I bought that exercise bike that's now a very expensive clothes hanger? We all have our moments." I found myself laughing and thinking maybe we'd turned a corner.

The next week shattered that hope completely. When I asked if he could pick up groceries on his way home, Mark sighed heavily and rolled his eyes. "Can't you handle anything yourself? I work all day and then have to do your job too? Figure it out, Suki. I'm not your personal assistant." The whiplash was dizzying—how could someone be making me laugh one day and making me feel worthless the next?

Friday brought flowers and another apology, complete with plans for a romantic dinner out. "Let me make it up to you," he said with that smile that had won me over years ago. And despite everything, I felt that familiar flutter of hope that maybe this time, the kind version of Mark would stick around for more than a day.

The Switch

The alternation between sweet and mean serves multiple purposes. By keeping their target off-balance, they maintain control through confusion. Their target begins to doubt their reality, wondering if they're imagining or exaggerating the cruel treatment.

This inconsistency creates a powerful trauma bond. Targets find themselves chasing the "good" version, trying desperately to figure out what triggers the switch to cruelty. The unpredictability becomes a form of emotional captivity.

The public persona also serves as a shield, making it harder for targets to seek help or be believed. After all, how could someone so seemingly charming or caring be abusive behind closed doors?

While the prevailing thought is that this sweet/mean cycle isn't random behavior – that it's a calculated strategy to keep the target off balance, I don't agree with that. As with all of the other behavior mentioned in this book, I truly believe that some abusive people out there say or do whatever it is that they are thinking at the moment, and there is no master strategy behind it. Regardless of how intentional or unintentional their abusive behavior is, the psychological damage to their target is the same.

Living with this dual personality is like trying to build a house on quicksand:

- You question your reality ("Was the sweet version real?")

- Your self-confidence erodes

- You start walking on eggshells

- You doubt your perceptions

- You feel constantly off-balance

Keep in mind that this behavior isn't about you – it's about them. The switch from sweet to mean isn't triggered by your actions, but by their need for control and their fragile self-image.

Holding onto hope or thinking that you can somehow appease them enough to earn consistent kindness is futile. This is because both sides are performances serving different purposes in the narcissist's quest for control and admiration.

Key Takeaways

1. **When someone shows you two drastically different personalities, they're showing you their full range of capabilities.** The kind, charming public face reveals what they're capable of when they want something, while the cruel private face shows what they're willing to do when there's no audience to impress. Both sides are equally manufactured.

2. **The switch between sweet and cruel isn't random or triggered by your behavior—it's a way to maintain control.** By keeping you off-balance and unsure of which version you'll encounter, they create a state of constant anxiety that makes you easier to manipulate. Understanding this helps you stop blaming yourself for their personality shifts.

3. **An emotionally and psychologically stable person doesn't need to maintain two separate versions of themselves.** While everyone behaves somewhat differently in public versus private, dramatic personality shifts between the two settings are a red flag. Real emotional stability shows consistency between public and private behavior, not a Jekyll-and-Hyde transformation when the audience changes.

Post-Relationship Red Flags (The Discard Phase)

When a relationship with a narcissist ends, you might expect some space to heal and move forward, but often their behavior continues to affect your life in uncomfortable ways. This is the discard phase, where you'll see how they handle the end of relationships and loss of access to you. The end of your romantic connection doesn't always mean they're ready to let go; many will find ways to stay involved in your life or make moving on difficult.

The red flags in this section show how narcissists typically respond when relationships end. They may move on to someone new remarkably quickly while simultaneously making it clear they don't want you to do the same. You might notice they avoid taking responsibility for what went wrong or keep trying to reconnect despite your boundaries. Some will cycle between seeming to accept the breakup and then reappearing in your life unexpectedly.

Pay attention to these post-relationship behaviors because they can interfere with your ability to heal and move forward. When someone moves on unusually fast but gets upset about your attempts to do the same, refuses to acknowledge their role in problems, or keeps trying to re-enter your life after you've said no, they're showing you that they struggle with accepting endings and respecting your choices. These behaviors can make it harder for you to gain closure and start fresh. Recognizing these patterns can help you set appropriate boundaries and understand that some people have difficulty accepting when relationships are truly over—especially when not on their terms.

Red Flag #42: The Speed at Which They Move On

Corbin's Story

Only three months after ending our five-year marriage, I found out through a mutual friend that my now ex-husband, Billy, had remarried. I was shocked and devastated.

Then, I made the mistake of looking at his Instagram account in hopes of getting some sort of answer or closure. What I found there made the pain so much worse.

He had pictures of his proposal to his new wife at what was once our favorite restaurant, and worse, at our favorite table! He was even wearing the Cartier watch I gave him for our last anniversary, and she was perched in what had always been my spot, their heads tilted together intimately. The caption on the picture read: "When you finally find your soulmate." I let out a deep guttural yell as I began to sob.

Just last week, he was calling me his forever person while we discussed splitting our assets. He sounded sincere at the time, but obviously he wasn't. Now I'm replaced like I never existed or mattered. I mean, I was sleeping with his sweatshirt at night, missing him terribly, and holding onto threads of hope that things could still work between us, and here he was planning his wedding!

I had started therapy and felt like I was starting to get my feet under me when this happened. So, while I was busy sorting and packing the remnants of our life together, and getting into therapy, he was already updating his relationship status and introducing the new woman to his friends and family.

I thought I would have more time to grieve, time to process, time to understand how five years could vanish so completely before either of us moved on. But that's the thing about people like Billy, they don't need time to mourn what they've lost because they never truly felt anything in the first place.

The Immediate Replacement

This pattern of immediate replacement serves multiple purposes beyond just finding a new romantic connection. For the narcissist, quickly securing a new partner proves to the world (and themselves) that they are eternally desirable. It sends a clear message that their previous partner was easily replaceable, often before that person has even processed the relationship's end.

While Billy's ex-wife was still trying to explain their divorce to their children, he was already bringing his new wife to their soccer games and posting family-style photos on social media. This immediate filling of the void happens because the narcissist's emotions don't have any depth. For them, saying "I love you" has the same depth as saying "I love pizza." It's easy to move on where the is no real attachment to begin with.

The eerie precision with which narcissists recreate their relationships often shocks their former partners. The recycling goes beyond just locations. They use the same pet names, share the same "unique" stories, and even recreate seemingly personal romantic gestures. A narcissist might give their new partner the exact same type of charm bracelet, claim your movies as "their special film," or tell inflated or false stories about their childhood to create artificial intimacy.

The Public Display

Social media becomes their primary stage for showcasing their "upgrade." Take Jessica's experience. Her ex-husband posted daily updates about his new relationship, strategically tagging mutual friends and family members to ensure maximum visibility.

These displays sometimes follow a calculated pattern. First come the vague posts about "new beginnings" and "trusting the journey." Then, mysteriously appearing couple photos that don't show their new partner's face, but instead show them holding hands or them walking down the road with their backs to the camera. The goal is to build curiosity. Finally, the grand revelation of their new relationship, usually accompanied by declarations of having found their "true soulmate" or "the love they always deserved."

The timing of these posts often coincides with significant dates or events in their former partner's life. A narcissist might choose to announce their engagement on their ex's birthday or post about their "perfect" new relationship during what would have been their anniversary. Each post is designed to wound their former partner while presenting themselves as someone who "just wants to be happy."

The Impact on the Former Partner

For former partners, the emotional whiplash can be devastating. Many former partners report symptoms of PTSD, such as experiencing debilitating sadness or anxiety when seeing happy couples or avoiding social media altogether.

The rapid replacement often leads to a crisis of self-worth. When Corbin's ex-husband remarried three weeks after their divorce, she, understandably, spent months in therapy working through feelings of worthlessness and disposability. The speed at which narcissists move on can make their former partners feel like they meant nothing, were nothing, and are easily replaceable.

Understanding the narcissist's quick transition requires a complete reframing of what you experienced. Corbin didn't lose out on a great person or a great love story; she escaped from someone incapable of authentic connection. These moments of clarity, though painful, reveal the scripted nature of the narcissist's relationships.

The very speed that feels so painful actually provides validation of the narcissist's dysfunction. His speed wasn't a reflection of his healing or her inadequacy, it was evidence of his inability to feel deep emotions.

Finding Your Own Closure

True healing often begins when you stop measuring your recovery against the narcissist's timeline. The slower pace of authentic healing brings its own gifts. Many survivors report that taking time to process allows them to rebuild stronger boundaries and clearer self-understanding. Take, for example, Mark, who spent eighteen months in therapy while his ex-wife cycled through three seemingly serious relationships, ultimately realizing that his "slower" recovery was actually building a foundation for genuine future connections.

Authentic healing can't be rushed. While the narcissist sprints from relationship to relationship, take the time you need to:

- Process your emotions without judgment

- Rebuild your sense of self

- Understand the red flags you missed

- Develop stronger boundaries

- Create a genuine support system

- Learn to trust your instincts again

Keep in mind that their rush to replace you isn't a reflection of your worth, it's their final gift to you. It's clear evidence that what you lost wasn't real love, but an illusion maintained by someone incapable of genuine connection.

Key Takeaways

1. **Being replaced quickly is not a reflection of your self-worth.** When a narcissist replaces you with seemingly impossible speed, it's not evidence of their healing or desirability. Rather, it reveals their profound dysfunction and inability to exist without constant external validation. Their speed is driven by fleeting emotions, not deep emotions.

2. **The pattern proves the performance.** The unsettling way they recreate their relationships, such as using the same pet names, vacation spots, and romantic gestures, isn't just creepy coincidence. It's concrete evidence that their "unique" connection with you was nothing more than a performance.

3. **Your slower healing is your strength.** While the narcissist races from relationship to relationship like they're playing emotional musical chairs, your slower, more difficult processing is evidence of your capacity for genuine connection. Taking time to grieve, understand, and rebuild isn't a weakness - it's a sign of emotional depth and authenticity. Think of it this way: while they're quickly repainting their empty walls, you're taking the time to repair your foundation. Your "slower" recovery is building the capacity for real, lasting love in your future.

Red Flag #43: They're Territorial and Don't Like It When You Move On

Rachel's Story

During my relationship with Marco, I was completely unaware of his extensive criminal history: check fraud, identity theft, stealing from friends, and drug possession. The truth only surfaced when he was arrested for soliciting a sex worker. Horrified, I immediately ended our relationship and told him never to contact me again. During his six-month jail term, he repeatedly tried calling me, which I ignored.

Upon his release, he contacted me through a fake number and demanded we meet so he could retrieve his belongings. When I informed him I'd already mailed his things to his mother, he insisted I "owed him" a meeting. Despite my firm statements about moving on, he persisted, trying to manipulate me by claiming what we had was "special" and pleading for just a conversation. After repeatedly refusing and enduring his continued pressure, I finally hung up on him.

For six months, he relentlessly stalked me. When I blocked his number, he'd call and text from different ones. I had to delete my social media accounts and create new ones under a different name, and, yet, somehow, he still finds them and continues his harassment.

His messages swing wildly between professing to miss me and hurling vicious insults. Recently, he texted that he'd driven by my house and saw another car in my driveway. He went from texting me that I was "trash" for moving on to claiming it wasn't fair that I was seeing someone new because he "was there first." His entire attitude revealed he didn't see me as a person, but, instead, a possession that he had a disturbing sense of ownership over.

The Territorial Tactics

Digital Stalking and Surveillance

Jonah's monitoring started subtly but grew increasingly invasive. He created fake Instagram accounts to watch my stories after I blocked him. He'd make new email addresses to bypass my filters, sending messages like "Just checking you're being treated right" at 3am. When I posted my first photo with Juan, he immediately texted mutual friends asking if they'd "vetted" this new guy. He did this despite living with his new girlfriend for months.

"Coincidental" Run-Ins

His physical presence became calculated, but still erratic enough that, to others, it made me seem paranoid for thinking his presence was anything more than a coincidence. He'd periodically show up at my regular grocery store during my usual Sunday shopping time. He switched his gym schedule to match mine. He even started taking his morning jog past my best friend's house, something he'd never done during our marriage. What was even creepier is that it seemed he planned his jogs right when she was leaving for work. It was like he wanted her to see him, as he knew she'd tell me and that we'd end up talking about him.

Love-Bombing and Hoovering

The harassment alternated between intimidation and attempts to remind me of "our love." He'd send lengthy emails about how he was "just trying to protect me" and "no one will ever understand you like I do." One day I'd receive threatening messages, the next day he'd send funny video clips. He'd switch between warning me that my new partner "seemed like a loser" to sending screenshots of our old text exchanges with messages like "remember how good we were?"

Triangulation Tactics

Deon masterfully manipulated our social circle to maintain control. He told my friends he was "worried about my mental health" since dating Aaron. He contacted my family members claiming "concern" about my "hasty" new relationship. Aaron and I would periodically see him at gatherings involving the kids, like birthdays and soccer practice, and Deon would loudly tell stories about our marriage, always within Aaron's earshot: "Remember that time in Cabo when she..." or "That's the perfume I always bought her." Meanwhile, his own girlfriend stood uncomfortably by his side.

His tactics eventually escalated to direct attempts at sabotage. He'd send Aaron messages warning him about my "emotional instability." When I planned a weekend trip with some mutual friends and Aaron, Deon mysteriously needed our mutual friends' help with an "emergency" that same weekend.

The Double Standard

Public Perception vs. Private Control

Narcissists often maintain two contradictory narratives simultaneously: publicly presenting themselves as blissfully moved on while privately refusing to allow their ex-partner the same freedom. They'll showcase their new relationship on social media, share elaborate stories about finding their "true soulmate," and present themselves as completely devoted to their new partner. However, behind this carefully curated image, they actively work to prevent their former partner from establishing new relationships.

The Contradiction in Action

This double standard manifests in specific, observable patterns. The narcissist might move in with a new partner within weeks of ending their previous relationship, yet express "concern" about their ex dating someone new. They'll plan elaborate public displays of affection with their new partner while simultaneously sending warning messages to their ex's potential romantic interests. Some might even begin planning a wedding with their new partner while attempting to sabotage their ex's dating life through mutual friends or social media.

The Hidden Agenda

The underlying purpose of these control tactics extends beyond simple jealousy or attachment. Narcissists strategically maintain access to multiple sources of narcissistic supply, keeping former partners accessible for future attention while simultaneously cultivating new relationships.

Their image management operates parallel to their control tactics. They carefully cultivate a public persona of being caring and concerned while privately engaging in manipulation and harassment. This dual approach allows them to maintain their reputation while exercising control, often leaving targets struggling to prove the abuse due to the narcissist's carefully maintained public image.

The power dynamics at play reveal the true nature of their agenda. By maintaining psychological dominance over former partners while pursuing new relationships, they create a web of dependency and control; and their control extends to multiple people simultaneously.

The Breaking Point

The control system typically reaches a crisis point when traditional methods of manipulation begin to fail. This often coincides with their ex-partner entering a serious new relationship, making public announcements about moving on, or successfully establishing firm boundaries. The narcissist's response to these triggers usually involves escalating their control tactics, often to the point where their carefully maintained facade begins to crack.

These crisis points frequently lead to increased harassment, intensified smear campaigns, and more direct interference in their ex's new relationships. The narcissist's behavior may become more erratic and obvious as their subtle control methods prove ineffective.

Resolution typically only comes through decisive action, such as legal intervention or complete social circle separation. Documentation becomes crucial at this stage, as the narcissist's escalating behavior often finally provides concrete evidence of their behavior. The establishment of strict no-contact boundaries, while challenging to maintain, usually proves necessary for breaking free from their control.

Key Takeaways

1. **Control through contradiction.** The narcissist's control system operates on a sophisticated pattern of contradictions. While publicly presenting themselves as happily moved on, often in a new relationship, they simultaneously maintain an intricate web of surveillance and control over their ex-partner.

2. **The systematic nature of their control.** What appears as random acts of harassment, or coincidental encounters, is actually part of their controlling nature. The narcissist's tactics aren't emotional reactions, but rather calculated moves in a larger strategy of maintaining access to multiple sources of attention and validation.

3. **Moving forward requires understanding their mindset.** Breaking free from narcissistic control tactics requires more than just blocking their number or avoiding mutual friends. It demands a comprehensive understanding of their entire control system: how they manipulate social circles, maintain their public image, and create plausible deniability for their actions. Only by recognizing these patterns can targets effectively counter them. This might mean documenting seemingly minor incidents; maintaining firm boundaries even when this might seem excessive to others; and accepting that the narcissist's apparent "happiness" in a new relationship doesn't mean they'll stop their control tactics. Protection comes through understanding that their control system is persistent, purposeful, and won't end simply because they've found someone new.

Red Flag #44: Never *Sincerely* Apologizes

Marie's Story

Daniel's second affair in our 18-year marriage forced me to confront an impossible choice: stay for our two children, or leave to preserve my sanity and self-respect. Having watched my own mother repeatedly forgive my father's infidelities, I was horrified to find myself in the same pattern. When I discovered Daniel's first affair, he initially denied everything, calling me paranoid until his mistress contacted me directly. His subsequent remorse seemed genuine. He went to therapy and cut contact with her as promised, leading me to believe our relationship had recovered.

Seven years later, I discovered he was having an affair with his co-worker. I was devastated and entered therapy immediately. Daniel apologized profusely about his affair and promised to do anything and everything to save our marriage. I asked him to give me space, as I needed to think, but he wouldn't do that. Instead, I received a barrage of flower arrangements and letters promising his devotion and telling me how much he loved me and what a fool he was for having another affair.

I wanted so desperately to believe him, however, during my time with my therapist, I began recognizing disturbing patterns in our relationship. I realized that I was in a cycle with Daniel; that he'd do something destructive or hurtful and then promise me he'd change but then continue doing whatever hurtful thing he swore he'd never do again. The only real difference is that he'd get better at hiding it.

I finally realized that Daniel wasn't sorry for hurting me; he was only sorry he got caught. His apologies were manipulation tactics, and not genuine remorse. And while he would press me into taking him back and keeping our family together, I realized that he, not I, had destroyed our family through his repeated betrayals.

The Narcissist's Mindset

To understand why narcissists never sincerely apologize, you have to first understand their mindset. Dayna Craig's poem, "The Narcissist's Prayer," captures the narcissist's mindset perfectly:

That didn't happen.

And if it did, it wasn't that bad.

And if it was, that's not a big deal.

And if it is, that's not my fault.

And if it was, I didn't mean it.

And if I did, you deserved it.

In a narcissist's mind, they are always right. This belief stems from their overwhelming sense of entitlement, which leads them to think they have the right to do whatever they want, regardless of whether it goes against moral standards, logic, or even laws. They feel justified in their actions and, as a result, are rarely, if ever, sorry.

Additionally, narcissists lack empathy and remorse, meaning they don't understand or share other people's emotions. They only feel their own emotions, so they have little awareness of how their actions affect others. Instead of offering a genuine apology, they might say things like, "I'm sorry you feel that way" or "I'm sorry for my part in things." However, many people who interact with narcissists never even receive these half-hearted apologies. In some cases, narcissists will place all the blame on others, refusing to take responsibility for their behavior.

Instead of apologizing, narcissists tend to use the following five manipulative tactics to avoid taking responsibility for their actions:

1. **Denial:** When confronted with their bad behavior, narcissists will usually deny it ever happened, even when presented with clear evidence. If they admit anything, it's

often the bare minimum, known as "trickle truthing." They will downplay the severity of their actions or the extent to which they occurred, causing the target to question their own perception of events. Narcissists are expert manipulators, and they create confusion to the point where the target might start doubting their own reality.

2. **Pity:** Narcissists know that if they can get you to feel sorry for them, you'll shift your focus from their bad behavior to their supposed trauma or personal struggles. They might try to make you feel sorry for them by bringing up their difficult childhood, stress at work, issues with alcohol, a bad breakup, or even exaggerated claims of illness. Their stories are often exaggerated or entirely fabricated, but their goal is to manipulate your emotions and distract you from their actions.

3. **Guilt:** Narcissists often turn the tables and make their targets feel guilty for the narcissist's behavior. They might claim that the target's actions, such as not spending enough time with them or not meeting some other arbitrary standard, somehow justify the narcissist's cheating, lying, or other harmful behavior. This is the classic "Look what you made me do" manipulation.

   The target may begin to believe that they somehow caused the narcissist's actions, even when the narcissist is fully to blame. For example, if the target forgets to buy something at the store, the narcissist may lash out them which, clearly, would be a disproportionate response to the situation. If the target gets upset and points out the disproportionate response, the narcissist won't apologize and, instead, will claim it wouldn't have happened if the target had only remembered to buy the item. The result is that the target feels that they are to blame for being abused.

4. **Intimidation:** Narcissists may use threats—either subtle or direct—to intimidate their targets. This doesn't always

involve physical threats; it could be threatening to ruin their reputation, take away their children, or attack their financial security. They might even engage in physical intimidation, such as breaking things or hurting objects around you, to create fear and gain control.

5. **Hope:** Narcissists are skilled at convincing their targets that they will change. They put on an emotionally convincing act that keeps the target hoping things will get better. This hope is what often leads targets to stay in toxic situations, believing the narcissist's promises of change. Even those outside the relationship—such as family members, friends, or even professionals—might continue to believe the narcissist's promises. A narcissist I once knew told me, "Hope dies last," when explaining why targets come back to their abusive partners despite the cycle of manipulation. And he was right. Hope does die last, but it can die much sooner if we can see a problematic situation for what it is.

Here are some examples of how narcissists avoid genuine apologies:

1. **The Non-Apology Apology:**

    1. "I'm sorry you feel that way" (blaming your feelings)

    2. "I'm sorry if you got hurt" (using "if" to avoid responsibility)

    3. "I'm sorry but you made me do it" (blame-shifting)

    4. "I'm sorry you misunderstood me" (making it your fault)

2. **Deflection Tactics:**

    1. Brings up things you've done wrong in the past instead of addressing their behavior

    2. "Well, what about when YOU did xyz?"

    3. "You're being too sensitive, it wasn't even a big deal"

    4. Changes the subject and gets angry if you try to return to it to the original topic

3. **Playing Victim:**

    1. "I guess I'm just the worst person ever then" (sarcasm, or seeking pity)

    2. "Nothing I ever do is good enough for you"

    3. "Everyone's always against me"

    4. Starts crying when confronted and makes it about their pain

4. **Gaslighting Instead of Apologizing:**

    1. "That never happened"

    2. "You're remembering it wrong"

    3. "I would never do something like that"

    4. "You're making things up again"

5. **Minimizing:**

    • "It wasn't that bad"

    • "Other people have it worse"

    • "You're making a mountain out of a molehill"

    • "Why are you still talking about this?"

And if a narcissist is forced to apologize expect them to do the following:

1. Give an obviously insincere apology then expect immediate forgiveness

2. Use the apology to extract favors or sympathy

3. Bring up the apology later as proof of their goodness

4. Get angry if you don't immediately act like everything is fine after their "apology"

You might be wondering if there is a way to tell if they are truly sorry and that this time will be different. The short answer to both is no. Just like with anyone else, you'll have to wait and see if there is a lasting change in their behavior. Anyone can act their best for a short period, but with manipulative people, even if their deceitful behavior stops temporarily, you can never be sure if they've truly changed or just gotten better at hiding what they're up to. For that reason alone, it's enough to leave, because if you stay you'll be constantly anxious and distrusting of them (for good reason).

If a narcissist's bad behavior finally catches up with them, you might see what looks like genuine remorse. But don't be fooled. Their expressions of regret are often exaggerated or fake. They may sob without tears; or act overly dramatic, yet strangely emotionless, while claiming their innocence. Make no mistake: narcissists aren't sorry for what they've done—they're sorry they got caught and now have to face the consequences. And for a narcissist, consequences don't lead to personal growth; they just enrage them.

Key Takeaways

1. **A narcissist's apology is typically a manipulation tactic, not a genuine expression of remorse.** This is evident through their use of specific patterns like non-apology apologies.

2. **Narcissists follow a predictable pattern moving from denial to minimization to blame-shifting.** When confronted with their behavior, they systematically work through stages of avoiding responsibility: first claiming it didn't happen, then downplaying its significance, and finally blaming others for deserving it.

3. **The key indicator of a narcissist's false apology is the lack of behavioral change following their expressions of remorse.** While they may put on a convincing show of regret, especially when caught, their primary concern is avoiding consequences rather than genuine personal growth or understanding the harm they've caused others.

4. **Hope dies last.** If you decide to give someone a second chance, get clear on what kinds of changes you need to see and in what timeframe. This way you won't endlessly hold onto hope; you'll know when it's time to walk away.

Red Flag #45: They Keep Coming Back

Carlos' Story

I stared at my phone screen in disbelief, my heart pounding. It was another text from Jasmine. "I think I might have cancer, can you talk?" I hadn't heard from her in six months, not since our devastating breakup, but she kept finding ways to come back into my life.

It started on my birthday, a simple "Happy Birthday" text that I stared at for hours, unsure how to respond. I felt rude ignoring her, but I knew I couldn't risk falling back into her web of manipulation. Then came the random likes on my social media posts, little reminders that she was still watching.

Two weeks ago, she called me in the middle of the night, claiming she had dialed the wrong number. My stomach twisted into knots at the sound of her voice. I didn't believe for a second it was a mistake. Jasmine never did anything unintentionally.

Now this: a text declaring she might have cancer. Part of me wondered if it was just another one of her games, a ploy for pity and attention, and another way for her to try and reenter my life. But what if it was true? The thought of Jasmine facing a terrifying illness alone made my heart ache, even after everything she had put me through. The thought of not responding made me feel like a heartless monster, but the thought of responding left me full of dread.

The Narcissist's Toxic Game

Dealing with a narcissist is like playing an endless, soul-crushing game that you can never win. No matter how hard you try to walk away, they always seem to find a way to slither back into your life. It's called "hoovering;" a term appropriately named after the vacuum cleaner, because that's what a narcissist does: they try to suck you back into their toxic web.

At first, it might seem like they've changed. They put on a convincing act, pretending to be the good person you once knew or hoped they could be. But don't be fooled. This is just another manipulation tactic in their twisted playbook.

Empty Promises and Dramatic Displays

When a narcissist reaches out, they often make grandiose promises of change. They may beg, plead, cry, or even show up at your doorstep unannounced. These dramatic displays of devotion can be incredibly convincing, but the reality is that if a narcissist lacks the ability to form deep emotional bonds with others, then they are also incapable of true love. They're only doing this to reel you back in and continue using you for their narcissistic supply.

So don't mistake their attempts to reconnect with you as a sign that they care, because this isn't what's going on. More likely, it's because their latest victim wised up to their games and now they need someone else to feed off. Relationships with narcissists are not about mutual love; they're just a game that the narcissist controls. And it's only over when they decide it's over.

Recognizing the Patterns

Narcissists have a predictable bag of tricks they use when trying to hoover you back in. They may feign concern, act like nothing happened, or use special occasions as an excuse to reach out. If you have kids, they might try to use them as a pawn in their game.

They also love to stir up jealousy, guilt, or pity. They might send you messages meant for their current partner "by accident" just to make you feel bad. Or they'll spin tales of bogus family crises or health issues to tug at your heartstrings.

These are all textbook manipulation tactics. Don't fall for it. If the relationship has involved abuse, chronic lying, cheating, or stealing, you are not in a healthy partnership. You're in a manipulationship.

Staying Strong and Moving On

The key to breaking free from a narcissist's grip is to be brutally honest with yourself about your dealbreakers. A narcissist will always return when they need something from you. And when they don't, they'll vanish without a trace. Recognize these patterns for what they are: a toxic game and nothing more.

It's not easy to walk away from someone you once loved, even if that love was never truly reciprocated. But you deserve so much better than to be a pawn in a narcissist's never-ending game. Stay strong, keep your distance, and don't look back. True happiness and peace are waiting for you on the other side.

Key Takeaways

1. **Getting a narcissist out of your life is a lot like trying to scrape gum off the bottom of your shoe.** Narcissists often try to "hoover" their targets back into the relationship after a breakup, using manipulative tactics like faking illness, exploiting important dates, or manufacturing "accidental" contact. It's crucial to recognize these for what they are: attempts to regain control.

2. **Even when you logically know the narcissist is toxic, their hoovering attempts can stir up immense emotional turmoil and self-doubt.** You may feel cruel ignoring them or agonize over whether their latest crisis is real. Remember that your wellbeing must come first. You don't owe them your care after they've repeatedly hurt you.

Breaking trauma bonds with a narcissist is incredibly difficult, but it is possible and necessary for your peace and healing. It takes tremendous strength to leave the past behind when they keep showing up in your present. But with time, boundaries, and belief in your worth, you can reclaim your life and heart from their grip. Never stop choosing you.

Red Flag #46: Future Faking

Rose's Story

Brian and I had been on and off for about five years. I didn't realize our relationship had a cycle to it until about a year after it was over, and a friend told me about the cycle of narcissistic abuse. I had always figured our highs and lows and the makeups and breakups our relationship went through were fairly normal; but now I realize they weren't.

This last time around, Brian had gone so far as to give me an engagement ring three months after we got back together. I really thought our relationship had turned a corner and I excitedly began planning what I thought would be the next stage of our lives together. We had decided to move in together shortly we got in engaged. He found us a great apartment in an even greater location. I had moved over my first carload of things to the apartment, and he said he'd meet me there to help me unload it. But Brian was nowhere to be found.

All of my calls went straight to voicemail. I kept thinking that surely, he had a good explanation for not being there. Then a creeping realization came over me. The lease was only in my name; the engagement ring was a "starter" ring—some cheap trinket that was a placeholder until we could properly go ring shopping together, he told me. I realized that he had nothing to lose, and that I was now the one who was left with a one-year lease on an apartment that I couldn't afford alone.

This was the fourth time I'd believed him when he said things would be different. Each time we'd broken up, each time I'd sworn I was done, he'd come back with promises that were somehow even more elaborate than before. And he was right; things were always different. They were worse.

The first time we got back together, he'd promised we'd communicate better. The second time, he swore he'd go to therapy.

The third time, he'd shown up at my door crying, saying he'd finally realized what he'd lost and would do anything to make it right. Each reunion started with such seemingly sincere promises that this time would be different. So much so, that I'd forget why I'd left in the first place. This latest round had been the most convincing, devastating, and costly one yet. I'd like to think that his promises and all of our reconnections were real, and that things ended because he couldn't handle the commitment. But I think it was more than that. I think all of this was some kind of weird or sick game for him. Maybe he enjoyed seeing if he could continue to reel me in or to see how much I would put up with. I don't know. I do know that now I see the cycle for what it is, I'm done.

The Narcissist's False Paradise

Future faking is one of the most devastating tactics a narcissist uses, and it is rarely used alone. It typically comes packaged with love bombing—overwhelming displays of affection and attention—and rushed intimacy that makes you feel like you've found your soulmate in record time. This powerful combination creates an intoxicating cocktail that's designed to bypass your natural defenses and create an intense emotional bond quickly.

Future faking is the practice of making promises (usually elaborate ones) about a shared future that they have no intention of fulfilling. They paint vivid, enticing pictures of the life you'll build together, knowing exactly what you want to hear and dangling it just out of reach.

This manipulation tactic serves multiple purposes for the narcissist. If the future faking happens early in the relationship, it creates an intense emotional bond quickly, bypassing the natural skepticism that comes with getting to know someone slowly. When someone promises you everything you've ever wanted while showering you with affection and pushing for deep emotional connection, it's intoxicating. Second, it keeps you invested in the relationship even when red flags appear or when the relationship has ended, because you're not just having a relationship with them—you're having a relationship with the fantasy they've created.

The Mirage of Commitment

Future faking doesn't always involve grand romantic gestures—sometimes it's much more subtle and targeted. While it can include elaborate promises like planning dream vacations you'll never take or talking about marriage on the first date, it often focuses on exactly what you've been longing for. If you've been wanting a baby, they'll suddenly start talking about starting a family. If you've begged for couples therapy, they'll promise to make the appointment. If you've expressed feeling disconnected, they'll talk about the life you'll build together once things settle down.

The narcissist becomes a master at identifying your specific emotional needs and promising to fulfill them. They're expert storytellers, weaving tales of your future together with such targeted precision that you can't help but believe them—because they're promising you exactly what your heart has been crying out for.

A twist to this is that a narcissist might re-enter your life and talk about the future you could have together, but only if you change! And because oftentimes what they may claim you need to change can have nuggets of truth to them, it can be difficult to see this manipulative behavior and their skewed perspective of you and of the relationship. Here's an example:

A narcissist might say something like, "I can see us having this amazing life together, traveling the world, building our dream home, and maybe even starting a family, but you really need to work on yourself first. I mean, your anxiety is exhausting to deal with, and the way you get emotional when we argue just shows you're not ready for a serious relationship. If you could just learn to be less needy and stop questioning everything I do, we could be so happy. I've been thinking about proposing next year, but honestly, I need to see some real changes from you before I can commit to that."

"You have so much potential. We have so much potential. I want us to be the best versions of ourselves so we can have the best relationship possible, but you have to meet me halfway. Once you fix these issues and become more trusting, I know we'll have an amazing relationship. I'm willing to wait, but I don't know for how much longer. You are 'my person' and I can't imagine a life without you, but things between us are so toxic. Let's get into couple's counseling and try to save what we have. We owe it to ourselves to do that."

This example shows classic future faking - dangling exciting possibilities like marriage and shared dreams - while simultaneously tearing down the target's self-worth and making the fantasy conditional on them "fixing" themselves. The narcissist positions themselves as generous and patient while implying the target is fundamentally flawed and lucky to have someone willing to "work with them."

But here's the cruel reality: narcissists don't actually experience deep, lasting love the way healthy people do. They can't genuinely envision a future with you because they're incapable of the emotional investment that requires. Instead, they're using your hopes and dreams as bait to hook you emotionally.

The promises become tools of control. When you start to question their behavior or pull away, they'll remind you of all the wonderful plans you've made together and make it seem as though you are the manipulative one doing all the future faking!

The Revolving Door of False Promises

What makes future faking particularly insidious is that it doesn't just happen at the beginning of the relationship—*it's a cornerstone of the entire cycle of narcissistic abuse.* Each time the relationship implodes, and you try to leave, each time you crack the door open just a sliver, the narcissist returns with the full arsenal: renewed love bombing, rushed intimacy, and a fresh batch of sweet talk about your future together.

The narcissist doesn't just use future faking to hook you initially; they use it to re-hook you every time you try to break free. They've learned from the last round. They know exactly which dreams of yours they crushed, and they'll promise to make them come true this time, often while overwhelming you with affection and pushing for immediate emotional reconnection.

"I know I messed up before, but I've changed," they'll say, painting an even more enticing picture of the life you could have together while showering you with the kind of attention that made you fall for them in the first place. They'll tell you how special you are, how they want to make things work, and paint the picture of a good life with them, all the while pushing to skip past the rebuilding phase and jump straight back into intimacy.

This is when future faking becomes particularly dangerous, because it's packaged with behaviors that feel like genuine connection, interest, love, or remorse. What's tragic is when someone says and does all the right things, it can feel like the two of you have this amazing chemistry. And of course you do, because they are intentionally buttering you up. None of this is real. It's a manipulative person reeling you back in.

And while you've been broken up, you've been grieving not just the loss of them, but the loss of the future you thought you'd have together. When they return offering to resurrect that dream while love bombing you with attention and faking this deep connection, it feels like being offered water in the desert.

But here's the pattern: the promises get bigger and more elaborate each time they try to win you back, while their actual follow-through gets smaller and more short-lived. The love bombing becomes more intense, the push for intimacy more urgent, and the future faking more targeted, especially if they know what worked before.

Key Takeaways

1. **Future faking, love bombing, and rushed intimacy work together as a powerful manipulation package.** When someone makes elaborate promises about your shared future while overwhelming you with attention and pushing for deep emotional connection very quickly, be especially cautious. This combination is designed to bypass your natural skepticism and create intense emotional bonds that cloud your judgment. These behaviors are red flags whether they're happening in a new relationship or during reconciliation attempts after a breakup.

2. **Pay attention to the gap between promises and actions, especially during reconciliation attempts.** A narcissist's words will be beautiful, but their actions will tell a different story. This becomes especially important when they return after a breakup with even grander promises than before. If someone talks constantly about your future together but consistently fails to follow through on smaller commitments, they're showing you their true character. Notice if the promises get bigger each time they try to win you back while their actual follow-through gets smaller.

3. **Your dreams and desires should never be used as weapons against you.** In a healthy relationship, your partner supports your goals and works with you to achieve them. A narcissist will learn your dreams only to dangle them in front of you as a way to maintain control.

4. **The stronger the chemistry, the slower you need to go.** I can't stress this point enough. The whirlwind that lovebombing, future faking, mirroring, rushing intimacy, and making you feel like the two of you have this intense chemistry or connection can be intoxicating—if you don't see it for what it is. Meaning, you don't see it as the idealization stage of the cycle of abuse.

The path to healing from future faking involves grieving not just the relationship, but the beautiful future that was never going to happen. It takes time to rebuild trust in your own judgment and in others' promises. But remember: someone who truly loves you will show you through consistent actions, not just pretty words about tomorrow.

I intentionally ended the red flags section with future faking because it represents a crucial turning point in the cycle. After enduring all the pain from the previous red flags and the brutal behaviors of the discard phase, future faking signals that your relationship is cycling back around to the idealization phase. This merry-go-round from hell ends when you decide enough is enough.

Part 3: Putting it All Together

CHAPTER 6

Understanding the Cycle of Narcissistic Abuse

The individual red flags we've discussed don't exist in isolation; they form part of a cyclical pattern known as "The Cycle of Narcissistic Abuse." This cycle involves three distinct phases: idealization, devaluation, and discard. Understanding what all is involved in each phase of the cycle as well as there being a cycle in general, is more than just eye-opening, it can be absolutely illuminating.

Understanding this cycle helps to explain why abusive relationships are so confusing and damaging, as each phase of the cycle leaves the target disoriented and emotionally depleted. And the more times the target goes around this cycle, the more disoriented and depleted they become.

However, it's important to note that *not every target experiences all of these phases, or in this exact order.*

I say this because before a person (or their support system) is aware that there is a cycle and that this cycle has phases, and that certain behaviors come with each phase, they don't view their experience as anything other than a relationship with highs and lows. Viewing an abusive relationship in terms of highs and lows, only further adds to the confusion, as all relationships have highs and lows. So, for the person experiencing these highs and lows, they don't readily realize that what they are experiencing isn't "normal." Which, of course, begs the question of "What's normal?"

However, for the sake of simplicity, I divided the red flags we previously explored into these three phases (idealize, devalue, and discard) to help you see the larger picture of how problematic behaviors fit into the overall picture. The reason being, as so many of you know, when you are in a manipulative relationship you don't see the overall picture. You don't realize that your relationship has a cycle. You might think about your relationship in terms of "the good times being really good, and the bad times being really bad" but because you, like the rest of us, live your life on a day-to-day basis, you only experience the high or the low as they're happening. For this reason, it can be difficult to zoom out and see a pattern.

So, while the cycle of narcissistic abuse is: "Idealize, Devalue, Discard," this only describes the narcissist's behavior. I find it helpful to also describe what the target feels during each of these phases, which is along the lines of "Relief, Fear, and Devastation." What this looks like in motion is that when the narcissist is idealizing the target, the target experiences excitement or relief. When the narcissist devalues them by putting them down or ghosting them, the target feels fearful that they might lose this relationship. When the narcissist discards the target, the target feels devastated.

Simply put here are the two cycles:

Narcissist: Idealize

Target: Excitement or Relief

Narcissist: Devalue:

Target: Fear of losing the relationship

Narcissist: Discard

Target: Devastation

Understanding these cycles provides crucial context for recognizing how individual red flags connect to form a comprehensive system of control and manipulation.

Let's take a moment to back out a bit and explore each of the phases of narcissistic abuse as a whole.

During the idealization phase, also known as "love bombing," or "the honeymoon stage" in more traditional models of abuse, the abuser creates an illusion of the perfect relationship. They may give the target excessive flattery, constant attention, say all the right things, give gifts, and shower the target with seemingly endless affection. This overwhelming display of admiration creates a powerful emotional dependency, as the victim feels uniquely understood and valued.

The red flags in this phase, such as moving fast, boundary violations disguised as romance, and declarations of being soulmates, can be difficult to see as problematic because they're camouflaged as positive attention. This phase effectively establishes the foundation for future manipulation by setting an unrealistically high standard that the victim will later desperately try to recapture.

The devaluation phase begins subtly but escalates over time. The abuser employs various tactics, including gaslighting (making the victim question their reality), triangulation (introducing rivals for attention or for stirring the pot), silent treatment, ghosting, put downs and name calling, and intermittent reinforcement (unpredictable positive responses), to name a few. The red flags we identified in this category, including criticism, jealousy, emotional withholding, and comparison to others, become more prominent as the narcissist gradually reveals their true nature.

These behaviors deliberately undermine the victim's self-worth and confidence. The victim often becomes increasingly isolated from support networks during this phase, as the abuser may actively work to damage external relationships or convince the victim that others cannot be trusted.

The discard phase represents the most overt rejection, though it may not always mean a complete end to the relationship. The narcissistic abuser might suddenly abandon the victim emotionally or physically, potentially replacing them with a new person, or merely threatening abandonment as a control tactic. The red flags associated with this phase: sudden coldness, cruel comments, explicit rejection, and replacement, all create profound trauma for the victim, who is left to process feelings of rejection alongside confusion about what went wrong.

Importantly, narcissistic abusers often return after discarding, a pattern known as "hoovering," (or an attempt to suck the victim back in like a hoover vacuum cleaner) reinitiating contact with renewed idealization to draw the target back into the cycle.

While this cyclical model provides a valuable framework for understanding narcissistic abuse, it's essential to remember that abuse rarely follows perfectly neat patterns in reality. The phases may overlap, skip ahead, or manifest differently based on the specific relationship dynamics and context. In non-intimate relationships, such as with parents, colleagues, or friends, abuse patterns often manifest differently. Power dynamics in these relationships are structured differently, and the cyclical nature may be less obvious. The unpredictability of abuse often serves as another control mechanism, keeping targets in a constant state of hypervigilance and uncertainty, regardless of whether the abuse follows a recognizable pattern.

CHAPTER 7

Frequently Asked Questions Regarding Whether or Not Narcissists Can Change

Here are some frequently asked questions I get when it comes to whether a narcissist (or anyone else) can change. If you have any lingering confusion about your relationship with a problematic person, hopefully this section can help clear things up.

1. How do I know for sure that they are a narcissist, sociopath, or psychopath?

The truth is, you don't need to figure out whether someone is, in fact, a clinically certifiable narcissist, sociopath, or psychopath. You really don't, and I say this for two reasons: 1. Mental health diagnoses change over time, and 2. While a diagnosis gives a name to a cluster of problematic behavior, *that problematic behavior exists regardless of whether there is a diagnosis.* Let me explain.

The Diagnostic and Statistical Manual of Mental Disorders (DSM-5) is, at least in the United States, the official book where mental health diagnoses live and die. And, as with all books, each edition comes with revisions. The DSM is currently in its 5th edition and has seen numerous changes. Some "disorders" have changed names, while others have changed diagnostic criteria. Some diagnoses have even been removed altogether.

The best use of mental health labels is to view them as pointers to concerning behavior. While having an official diagnosis can feel validating, that, yes, what you experienced is indeed outside of the realm of "normal" problematic behavior, problematic behavior is just that: problematic, and you truly don't need a diagnosis to validate your situation.

So, I encourage you to focus on observable actions rather than diagnostic categories: Does this person consistently disregard your boundaries? Do they feel justified in how they mistreat you or others? Do they struggle to express empathy in ways that you need them to express it? Do they lie, cheat, and steal? How staunch are their morals when they think they won't get caught? These are the things that matter. Your well-being doesn't depend on confirming a specific personality disorder. It depends on recognizing unhealthy relationship dynamics and making choices that protect your mental health.

2. What if I (or their therapist) am Wrong and They Aren't a Narcissist?

I've found that when people ask this question, it's because they are thinking that if a person isn't a narcissist, then they can change/the relationship can be saved, but if they are a narcissist, then they can't and they need to walk away. For anyone caught up in this thinking, I encourage you to put aside the label of "narcissist" and look at the behavior. Does this person have problematic behavior that crosses into your deal-breaker territory? Is this person sincerely remorseful?

Does their behavior show that they are sincerely remorseful, or did they say enough of what you needed to hear to keep them in your life? Because if their behavior hasn't changed much, if any, then they haven't changed. If they seemed like they changed, but then you caught them doing something else along the same lines, then they haven't changed; they just got better at hiding what they're up to.

Regardless, even if that person is seemingly remorseful and all of their actions line up with them being sincerely remorseful, this doesn't mean that you need to give them a second or a twenty-second chance. It's okay to walk away if someone's behavior has crossed over into deal-breaker territory and you are done.

3. What If They Say Their Therapist Says They Aren't Narcissist, Sociopath, or Psychopath?

Clinical diagnoses have significant limitations, especially for personality disorders. Many mental health professionals do or don't diagnose clients for a variety of reasons: stigma, insurance coverage issues, the clinician's concerns about giving a client a certain diagnosis and the learned helplessness it can create, and, not to mention, clients present drastically different in therapy than they do in an intimate relationship.

In general, a clinician will not inform a client that they have the diagnosis of NPD or ASPD. The reason being that as a mental health clinician, if you have a highly manipulative and exploitative client who is in therapy because their life isn't working, the one thing you don't do is tell them they have a diagnosis that unintentionally gives them more of a reason to stay stuck where they are. Instead, you work directly on identifying problematic behaviors regarding awareness, acceptance, accountability, and sustained behavior change.

4. They Said Their Therapist Doesn't Think They Are a Narcissist, Sociopath, Psychopath—Or Even Manipulative or Abusive, So Now What Do I Do?

First off, what someone *says* that their therapist said and what their therapist *actually* said are often two very different things. Not to mention, if they are incredibly manipulative, there's a good chance they aren't even in therapy and there is no therapist!

However, even if their therapist tells you to your face that they don't think this person has NPD or ASPD, this doesn't mean that the behavior you are experiencing isn't a problem.

Even if you were to meet with the therapist in person, and they were to tell you that they see nothing problematic about this person's thought process or behavior, remember that what the clinician is being told by the problematic person comes from the problematic person's viewpoint, which will be radically different than yours.

What I mean by this is that problematic people, especially the intelligent and highly manipulative ones, are highly skilled at presenting well in controlled environments such as therapy sessions. It often takes a clinician multiple sessions to have an inkling that certain things don't align. So, rather than being swayed by secondhand reports of what a therapist supposedly said, stay grounded in where your boundaries, standards, and deal breakers are for the people in your life. These three things: your boundaries, standards, and deal breakers are the fundamental criteria to use when making a decision.

5. Their Therapist Thinks I Am the Problem. Could This Be the Case?

Be wary of accepting blame based on secondhand reports from someone with a skewed sense of reality and a pattern of deflecting responsibility. A healthier approach would be to explore your concerns with your therapist, who hears your direct experience. Remember that in truly abusive dynamics, a common behavioral pattern for abusive people is to convince the victim (and others) that the victim is actually the abuser. Trust your lived experience and the assessments of professionals who have actually worked with you directly.

6. They Seem to Be Showing Signs of Changing. Does This Mean Change Is Possible?

Temporary behavioral improvements are often part of the idealize or honeymoon stage of abuse. Included in this is "love bombing" where professions of love and promises to change are common when someone fears losing their relationship or "source of supply". These surface-level changes typically follow a threat to the relationship and disappear once the perceived threat passes. True change follows a different pattern: it's consistent, sustained even when there's no immediate benefit, acknowledges past harmful behavior, is accountable for the harm they caused, and doesn't expect excessive praise or immediate forgiveness.

Instead of focusing on whether or not change is possible, ask yourself the following:

- What changes do I need to see happen and in what timeframe?

- Does this person understand that what they did is a problem and why? Or do they continue to minimize or justify their behavior?

- Do I believe this person is truly remorseful, accountable, and is willing to do the work to change?

- How will I know a person's behavior has truly changed, and they just haven't gotten better at hiding things?

- How long am I willing to wait to see if they can or will change?

- What and where are my deal breakers when it comes to this relationship?

Once you have clarity as to these questions, you'll have a lot more clarity with how to move forward.

7. I've Heard That Narcissists Won't Go to Therapy Because They Don't Think They're the Problem, but the Person I Think Is a Narcissist Is Now Going to Therapy...So What Does This Mean?

Attending therapy doesn't automatically indicate a genuine desire for change. Additionally, just because a person is in therapy doesn't mean that they are going to therapy to discuss the issues you have with them. They might be in therapy to discuss issues with their mother and not speak a word about their dynamic with you. And even if they did speak about their dynamic with you, it will come from their perspective, which will be very different from yours. A narcissist might get into therapy to heal from the relationship, but because their perspective is so skewed, they might sincerely view themselves as the victim and you as the abuser!

People with narcissistic traits often enter therapy for strategic reasons: to appease a partner threatening to leave or to improve their image. However, whether it's intentional or not, during their time in therapy, people with problematic personalities gain therapeutic language they can weaponize later. I've come across numerous manipulative people who can talk at great length about all of this insight and awareness they have about themselves and, yet, still have major blind spots when it comes to their behavior.

Some problematic people may genuinely believe they need help, but their focus is on everything other than developing sincere accountability for healthy relationships. What matters isn't whether they attend therapy, but how they engage with it.

A person can sit in a therapist's office for years without meaningful change if they aren't willing to do the actual work of changing. Do they seem to present a sanitized version of events, where they are either the victim or the hero? Do they use therapy insights to deflect responsibility ("my trauma made me do it") rather than take accountability? Do they expect praise just for being in therapy? Watch for how they apply therapeutic concepts in daily life—true engagement with therapy creates humble, consistent, lasting changes in behavior, not just new vocabulary to justify the same patterns.

8. They've Changed Some Behaviors but Not Others. What Does This Mean?

Partial change often reveals someone's true priorities and capabilities. If a person is making changes but these changes aren't enough, then it means they aren't ready, willing, or able to make the changes you need to have happen. So, then the question becomes, "now what?" You are the only one with that answer. How much time, and energy, and potentially money are you willing to invest to see if this person can change in the ways that you need for the relationship to work before you walk away?

9. They Say They'll Change but Need My Help to Do It. Is This Reasonable?

When someone imposes responsibility for their change on you, they reveal a fundamental misunderstanding of how personal growth works. Healthy change comes from within and is self-motivated. Being cast as someone's change manager, reminder system, or emotional regulator keeps you trapped in an exhausting parent-child dynamic rather than an equal partnership.

While having supportive people is always nice, there's a crucial difference between support and responsibility. Support looks like acknowledging their independent efforts, while responsibility involves you tracking, reminding, or managing their behavior. If their change requires your constant vigilance or falls apart when you're not actively maintaining it, it's not real change. Sustainable transformation continues whether you're watching or not, because it's driven by their internal values, not your external oversight.

10. How Can I Tell the Difference Between Manipulation and Genuine Efforts to Change?

Genuine change and manipulative performance share surface similarities but differ in fundamental ways. Manipulative "change" is typically dramatic, announced rather than demonstrated, and timed strategically when the relationship is threatened. It often includes grand gestures that demand recognition but lack consistency. There's usually an expectation of immediate forgiveness and restoration of trust, with impatience or anger if this isn't granted.

Authentic change, by contrast, tends to be slower, steadier, and less performative. The person acknowledges that rebuilding trust takes time, accepts consequences without resentment, and continues their efforts towards improvement regardless of whether the relationship is salvaged. They show curiosity about how their behavior has affected you rather than defensiveness, and they don't keep score of their improvements or use them as leverage.

11. If They Were Different in the Past, Couldn't They Return to That Person Again?

The idealized "good version" we remember from early in a relationship often reflects a carefully crafted persona rather than authentic character. Most people show their best selves early on while temporarily suppressing their problematic behaviors.

Think of it this way: When a person is on a job interview or recently hired, they are on their best behavior. Once they settle in, they start to become more comfortable with being themselves. When that happens, a different side of them starts to surface—and that new side of them can be surprising! If this person gets in trouble at work, what do they usually do? They start acting on their best behavior again…until they slide back into getting comfortable. So, rather than hoping for a return to a largely performative initial persona, focus on who they've shown themselves to be over time—because that's who they really are.

12. What's the Difference Between Giving Someone Another Chance and Staying Stuck in Wishful Thinking?

Giving someone another chance based on evidence of change looks fundamentally different from remaining in a relationship based on wishful thinking. A thoughtful second chance is extended after seeing consistent preliminary evidence of transformation, includes clear boundaries and consequences, and maintains a realistic perspective on reverting to old patterns. You remain vigilant without hypervigilance, hoping for the best while prepared for setbacks, and knowing where your boundaries, standards, and deal breakers are.

Wishful thinking, by contrast, relies on potential rather than evidence, conflates promises with action, and dismisses patterns in favor of exceptions. It often involves moving goalposts ("at least they didn't do X this time") and creating elaborate explanations for continued problematic behavior. One key distinction: when giving a reasoned second chance, you feel clear-eyed and empowered regardless of the outcome; with wishful thinking, you feel anxious, confused, and dependent on the other person's change for your emotional well-being. True second chances are given from a position of strength and boundaries, not desperate hope.

CHAPTER 8

Recognizing Boundary Issues

Adam's Story

For decades, I didn't realize there was a problem with my boundaries. I thought I was strong and emotionally mature by continuously forgiving others who treated me poorly. I also saw my acceptance of their justifications for their bad behavior as me being understanding, and my patiently explaining, time and again, how their behavior was hurting me, as being compassionate. And, I thought anyone who didn't treat others like this was unempathic, uncaring, and emotionally immature.

I used to think being endlessly tolerant was admirable." Look how much I can take," my actions said. "Look how I never give up on people." I genuinely believed that by continuing to give chances to someone who repeatedly hurt me, I was doing the right thing. After all, isn't that what good people do? Stay? Try to understand? Give others the benefit of the doubt?

Each time the narcissist in my life crossed a line with me, I would sit them down for another heart-to-heart. I'd carefully explain my feelings, often through tears, detailing exactly how their actions impacted me. They would seem to listen intently, sometimes even cry with me, and promise to do better.

I thought these conversations were evidence of my emotional maturity and our shared commitment to growth. The truth was that I was teaching them exactly how to hurt me more effectively. The more I opened up about what upset me, the more they knew exactly how to get to me. Always giving second chances wasn't fixing anything; it was just making things worse.

I finally realized that what I called compassion was actually just fear. I was fearful of being abandoned, so I stayed even when things got bad. I feared conflict, so I kept forgiving instead of standing up for myself. I feared that setting boundaries would make me seem mean or selfish, so I kept accepting poor treatment. I feared being alone, so I convinced myself that trying harder would fix things.

I kept trying to explain myself over and over, not because I was emotionally mature, but because I desperately wanted someone to understand me who never would. Refusing to walk away wasn't brave—I was just too afraid to face the unknown of being on my own. I learned that real compassion means setting limits, even when it's uncomfortable. True strength isn't *about how much hurt you can absorb; it's about how consistently you can protect your right to be treated with respect.*

Boundaries

Boundaries are the invisible lines we draw to protect our emotional, mental, and physical well-being. Much like a fence around a house, boundaries define where we end, and others begin. When they are functional, they allow us to maintain our authentic selves when interacting with others. Boundaries aren't meant to be barriers that isolate us; they serve as the bodyguards of our standards.

Another way to think of boundaries, is that they are your personal constitution: a living document that evolves as you grow in self-awareness and self-love. Without them, we risk becoming emotional chameleons, shifting and bending to meet others' needs while losing touch with ourselves. Clear boundaries protect us from manipulation and emotional exhaustion while creating the space necessary for genuine connection and mutual respect.

The journey to developing healthy boundaries often begins with the recognition of their absence. Unfortunately, that awareness only comes from painful experiences. Most of us weren't taught boundary-setting in school, nor did we see it modeled at home. Instead, we've pieced together our understanding through a variety of influences: family, friends, religion, movies, and media being the main ones.

Our perception of "normal" in relationships is profoundly shaped by our lived experiences, making it challenging to recognize problematic patterns in our own behavior or even in the behavior of others. When it comes to understanding red flags and discussing "our part in things," it's vital to give ourselves understanding and grace.

This is not to say we share a part in our victimization. We don't. There is no excuse for abuse.

While knowing better helps us do better, self-awareness and recognizing the red flags can only protect us so much. Predators prey on the vulnerabilities of others, and because we are human, we will always have vulnerabilities. Having vulnerabilities isn't a bad thing, they help us develop compassion and connection to others. So, if you get caught up with a manipulative or exploitative person, or even several of them (like I have), this is not your fault; however, you might have some weak boundaries that you aren't aware of.

The Pattern We Don't See

Sure, we might have noticed we had a pattern of hurtful people or one-sided relationships in our lives, or that we were continually giving to the point of exhaustion. But because we thought the issue was with the other person, once that relationship ended, we breathed a sigh of relief, thinking our worries were over. Little did we know that these dynamics weren't isolated events, but patterns in how we interacted with others.

Again, this is not to blame you for being in an abusive relationship. It is not your fault. Manipulators are skilled at eroding people's boundaries, especially if we, or those around us, repeatedly dismiss or minimize their actions. These boundary erosions are incremental and gradual, you might have been manipulated or abused for years thinking you were somehow to blame for how they treated you before you even realized what was happening.

Learning the Hard Way

And because healthy boundaries aren't taught, we might not have noticed that there was an issue. Or, if we did notice an issue, we might have thought it was the other person who had the problem. As a therapist, I hear phrases such as, "If only my mother would stop lying," "Our relationship would be great if my boyfriend would stop drinking," "My friend is always late, and it's so inconsiderate!" or "My boss is so condescending. I dread going into work."

On the surface, is seems as though the solution is simple: the other person needs to change. One person's mother needs to stop lying, the other partner needs to stop drinking, the friend needs to be on time, and the boss needs to learn basic respect. However, we don't have control over anyone else's behavior, let alone whether they will change. And staying in a relationship or dynamic based on hoping the other person will change when they've shown no sincere interest in or consistent action to change, will take its toll on your mental and physical health.

When our only strategies for dealing with difficult people are to hope they'll change, use niceness to try and get on their good side, vent to others, or get better at walking on eggshells or enduring the unendurable, there is a problem. The problem is that we unknowingly have given away our power to rely on someone else to improve our lives. In short, we've put our keys to happiness in someone else's pocket. The reality is that you only have control over yourself, and your happiness is your responsibility.

Your Feelings Are Valid

If someone crosses your boundaries, they don't get to decide that they didn't—and they don't get to decide how you feel about what they did. If you have a problem with how you're being treated, then it's a problem. All any of us can do is to make our boundary violations known to those who cross them. If they care about us, they won't cross that boundary again. If they continue hurting you, they're not respecting your boundaries; and if they don't respect your boundaries, they don't respect you. At that point, you have some decisions to make when it comes to having that person in your life or to what degree.

Recognizing Boundary Issues

Whether we realize it or not, we are continually defining and redefining our boundaries based on our subconscious standard for how we think we should be treated. The exciting thing is that once we start aligning with who we are and how we *really* feel, we can become more assertive and raise our standards—and then (and only then) do our lives begin to radically change.

Paying attention to how you feel is a good way to tell if your boundaries need work. If you feel irritated, frustrated, angry, or resentful during or after an interaction, it's usually because a boundary has been crossed. If that boundary continues to be crossed, you may feel like a doormat and wonder why you seem to attract people who take advantage of you.

Our bodies often recognize boundary violations before our minds do. You might notice a tightness in your chest when certain people call, or a knot in your stomach when you see their name on your phone. Perhaps you feel exhausted before meeting with certain people, knowing they'll dump all their problems on you without ever asking about your life. These physical reactions aren't random—they're your internal alarm system trying to alert you to boundary issues.

Think about the last time you agreed to something you didn't want to do. Maybe you stayed late at work again because saying "no" felt impossible, or you loaned money to a friend who never pays you back but makes you feel guilty for mentioning it. Notice how these situations often leave you feeling drained, anxious, or resentful. These feelings aren't character flaws or signs of being "too sensitive"—they're indicators that your boundaries are being crossed.

Pay attention to patterns in your relationships. Do you often find yourself making excuses for others' behavior? "She didn't mean to forget my birthday again, she probably got busy" or "He's just going through a rough time, that's why he keeps borrowing money." If you frequently downplay or justify others' disrespect of your time, energy, or resources, you're likely dealing with weak or non-existent boundaries. The people in your life have learned they can count on you to put their needs first, even at the expense of your own well-being.

Your calendar can also reveal boundary issues. Look at how you spend your time and energy. Are you constantly rearranging your schedule to accommodate others while your own priorities get pushed aside? Do you find yourself saying yes to commitments you dread, then feeling trapped by obligations you never wanted? These patterns often indicate that your boundaries around time and energy need strengthening. Remember: every time you say yes to something you don't want to do, you're saying no to something you might actually want to pursue.

Understanding Healthy Boundaries

Boundaries are lines that are continually redrawn as we align with our wants and needs. The more we know ourselves, the less inclined we are to spend time around people and things that drain us of our energy. What we might have tolerated in our twenties or thirties becomes completely unacceptable in our forties and fifties, not because we've become more rigid, but because we've developed a clearer sense of our worth and what we need to thrive.

This evolution is healthy and natural - it signals that we're becoming more attuned to our authentic selves and more confident in honoring our own truth. And once we quit living to please others and start prioritizing ourselves, we're less likely to be sucked into, or stay in, drama and one-sided relationships.

The ripple effects of strong boundaries extend far beyond our immediate relationships - they transform our entire way of being in the world. When we consistently honor our boundaries, we develop an internal compass that helps us navigate decisions large and small. This might mean turning down social invitations that don't align with our values, stepping away from friendships that no longer serve our growth, or even making major life decisions like changing careers or ending long-term relationships. The clarity that comes from knowing and respecting our boundaries helps us make these decisions with confidence rather than doubt or guilt.

Most profoundly, maintaining healthy boundaries creates a positive feedback loop in our lives. As we become more selective about where we invest our energy, we naturally attract people and opportunities that respect and reinforce our boundaries. This self-reinforcing cycle leads to increasingly authentic relationships and experiences that truly resonate with who we are. The drama and chaos that once seemed unavoidable begin to fade away, not because we're actively avoiding it, but because our healthy boundaries naturally filter out situations and relationships that don't align with our well-being. This creates space for genuine connections and meaningful experiences that energize rather than deplete us.

The Pushback

When you begin establishing boundaries with people accustomed to having free rein, their resistance often manifests in predictable yet challenging ways. They may attempt to make you feel guilty, label you as mean, insensitive, or cruel - classic manipulation tactics designed to make you question your perfectly reasonable limits.

The emotional impact can be significant, leaving you upset and frustrated, wondering why others can't understand and respect you without you insisting that they do. But it's crucial to recognize that this reaction is more about their discomfort with losing control than any actual wrongdoing on your part.

The process of maintaining boundaries is particularly difficult because many of us are conditioned from an early age to prioritize others' comfort over our own well-being. We're taught to be nice, accommodating, and avoid conflict at all costs. This societal programming can make it especially challenging when we finally decide to stand firm in our boundaries. The reason being is we're fighting against others' resistance and our own ingrained beliefs about what it means to be a good person. However, it's essential to understand that setting boundaries is not an act of aggression or selfishness - it's an act of self-respect and, ultimately, respect for our relationships.

The truth is that empathetic individuals must learn to be strong fighters for their wellbeing since they tend to draw others who will exploit their compassionate nature. By setting and holding healthy boundaries, compassionate individuals aren't being mean - they're simply demonstrating healthier relationship dynamics that are more respectful of everyone involved, even if others don't necessarily realize it at the time. That uncomfortable process is what enables mutually respectful, long-term relationships that can truly flourish down the road to become possible.

The Cost of Not Setting Boundaries

If you aren't comfortable saying no, then you'll have to get comfortable with the consequences of always saying yes. This means sacrificing yourself to save relationships, and no relationship is worth that sacrifice.

The pattern of always saying yes often stems from deeply ingrained beliefs about unworthiness and feelings that we are difficult to love. Many chronic people-pleasers grew up believing their value was tied to their usefulness to others, or that love had to be earned through constant sacrifice and availability.

This conditioning creates a vicious cycle where the more you give, the more others come to expect, and the harder it becomes to break free from the role of perpetual caregiver. What starts as occasional favors can quickly escalate into an unsustainable situation where you become the go-to person for everyone's problems, emotional support, or financial needs.

Perhaps most insidiously, this dynamic actually prevents the formation of genuine, balanced relationships. When you're known as the person who never says no, you attract people looking for someone to take advantage of rather than those seeking an authentic connection.

True friends want to know your real thoughts, feelings, and limits - they want to engage with you as a whole person, not just as a source of endless support and resources. By learning to say no, you protect yourself and create space for more meaningful relationships based on mutual respect and genuine care rather than dependency and obligation.

Common Mistakes in Boundary Setting

Many "over-givers" initially confuse being aggressive (screaming, yelling, or threatening consequences) with being assertive and setting boundaries. This often happens because they aren't okay with what's going on but don't want to leave. They stay stuck in a pattern of threatening or trying to "set others straight" rather than establishing and maintaining real boundaries.

This confusion often stems from a deeper misunderstanding about boundaries. True boundaries aren't about controlling others or forcing them to change—they're about clearly communicating our own limits and then taking appropriate action to protect those limits.

In short, our boundaries are to protect us, not to punish others.

When we resort to emotional outbursts or manipulation tactics, we actually engage in the same boundary-violating behavior we're trying to prevent. This creates a toxic cycle where both parties feel increasingly frustrated and unheard, leading to escalating conflicts rather than resolution.

Another common pitfall is the tendency to announce boundaries as ultimatums during moments of high emotion, rather than thoughtfully establishing them from a place of self-awareness and calm. For instance, someone might snap, "If you ever do that again, I'm never speaking to you!" in the heat of anger, rather than calmly expressing, "I'm not comfortable with how you spoke to me. I don't like to be treated that way, so please don't do that again." The first approach is reactive, whereas the second one is responsive. The reactive approach often leads to boundaries that are either too rigid or impossible to maintain, undermining our credibility and making it harder for others to take our boundaries seriously in the future.

Sometimes the Best Boundary is Distance

Manipulators often use a sneaky trick where they cross your boundaries on purpose just so they can punish you for getting upset about it. They do this to stay in control while making you look like the bad guy. When they push you until you finally snap or get angry, they can then point to your reaction and say, "See how crazy you're being?" This shifts attention away from what they did wrong and puts it on how you responded. Over time, this makes you second-guess yourself and walk on eggshells around them.

This behavior messes with your head because it makes you doubt what's really happening. Someone will keep crossing lines they know bother you, then act surprised or hurt when you get upset. They'll say things like "I was just kidding" or "You're overreacting" even though they knew exactly what they were doing. This kind of mind game makes you start questioning whether your feelings are valid or if you're just being "too sensitive." Slowly, you lose confidence in your ability to tell when someone is treating you badly.

What makes this pattern so harmful is that it teaches you to ignore your gut instincts about protecting yourself. Eventually, you might stop setting any boundaries at all because you're afraid of how they'll react or punish you for it. The manipulator wins because they get more control while you put up less resistance. Breaking free from this cycle means understanding that your reactions to boundary violations are completely normal and that they're the ones creating the problem, not you.

Sometimes the healthiest boundary you can set is going no contact - completely cutting off communication and walking away. You don't need to announce this decision, have a big confrontation, or try to fix things first. You don't owe anyone an explanation for protecting yourself. Sometimes the only solution is to quietly remove yourself from the situation entirely. This isn't giving up or being weak - it's recognizing that some people can't be reasoned with, and your peace of mind is worth more than trying to make them understand.

Your Boundaries, Your Choice

Remember that your boundaries are an extension of who you are, so they are deeply personal. You, and you alone, decide where your boundaries lie. If you are afraid to set boundaries because you fear certain people might leave, then, please know that if people only want you in their lives based on what they can take from you, or what you're willing to overlook, then there's no real relationship to preserve.

The process of discovering and defining your boundaries often requires deep self-reflection and a willingness to honor your own experiences and intuition. What feels completely acceptable to one person might cross a fundamental line for you, and that's perfectly valid.

For instance, one person might be comfortable lending money to friends, while another considers it a firm boundary never to mix finances with friendships. Neither position is inherently right or wrong - they simply reflect different personal values, life experiences, and comfort levels. *The key is recognizing that you don't need to justify or explain your boundaries to anyone, even if they differ from what others consider "normal" or "reasonable."*

When you begin to view relationships through the lens of mutual respect rather than obligation or transaction, it becomes clearer which connections are worth nurturing and which ones may need to be released. *Healthy relationships naturally evolve and strengthen when both parties respect each other's boundaries, even if they don't fully understand them.*

In contrast, relationships built on conditions - "I'll only accept you if you let me cross this line" or "I'll only stay close if you keep giving beyond your comfort zone" – function much like a spinning top—with time they will become inherently imbalanced and topple over. While potentially painful, this realization can be incredibly liberating as it frees you to invest your emotional energy in connections that truly honor and celebrate who you are, rather than trying to contort yourself to maintain relationships that fundamentally disregard your needs and limits.

Part 4: Moving Forward

Breaking Free

The process of healing from narcissistic abuse is like waking up from a long, disorienting nightmare where everything you thought you knew about yourself, love, and reality, has been warped and twisted into something altogether unfamiliar. You question everything: your memories, your perception of reality, your judgment, even your sanity.

But here's what you need to know: this confusion, this pain, this feeling of being lost – it's not a weakness. These unpleasant feelings are the tools that will help you the most when it comes to your healing. While you might feel broken right now, please trust me when I say this—you can turn those feelings of brokenness into a breakthrough that can radically change your life for the better.

All that confusion and pain is your inner wisdom finally breaking through the fog of manipulations, telling you something isn't, and wasn't, right. And just as the narcissist's manipulation worked gradually to break you down, healing happens gradually too, one small act of self-reclamation at a time.

7 Stages of Healing After Narcissistic Abuse

Stage 1: Acknowledge What Happened

Narcissists excel at making you doubt your perceptions, question your judgment, and blame yourself for their behavior. But recognition that there is a problem, and that it might not be you, is the first crack in their carefully constructed illusion.

This crack begins with confusion, and is followed by an uncomfortable feeling that something isn't quite right. You start talking to others in hopes of gaining clarity as to what's going on and if you're to blame. You start googling phrases like "toxic relationships," "what is gaslighting," "trauma bonds," or "why does my partner make me feel crazy?" Your search for answers marks the beginning of understanding, even if you can't yet name what's wrong.

During this stage, many survivors experience their first taste of validation as they discover terms like "narcissistic abuse" or "manipulation." Suddenly, what felt like a collection of confusing experiences has a name. The relief of knowing you're not alone, not crazy, not imagining things, not making a big deal out of nothing—and that it's not you—can be overwhelming.

The hardest part can be the creeping realization that the person you loved may never have truly existed. The charming, loving persona they showed you was a mask, carefully crafted to win your trust. This realization can feel like grieving someone who's still alive.

Stage 2: Uncertainty and Doubt

The first stage involves becoming aware that there is, indeed, a problem—and that problem isn't you. The second stage involves swinging between certainty and confusion; this stage brings intense waves of self-doubt. One day you're sure about what you've experienced, and the next day not so much. This emotional ping-pong is exhausting but normal.

In stage one, you are on a search for answers. In stage two, you have some of those answers. Now you are looking for validation from others, either hoping they'll tell you things aren't so bad (so you can stay) or confirm that, yes, what you're experiencing is abuse (so you can leave). The tricky part is that most people in your life won't understand the subtle nature of manipulation, offering well-meaning but potentially harmful advice like "every relationship has problems" or "no one is perfect."

During this time, many survivors start seeing problematic behavior everywhere, sometimes feeling paranoid or hypervigilant. But here's the truth: you're not being paranoid – you're developing awareness. It's like getting a new pair of glasses; suddenly, what was once blurry is now clear.

Stage 3: The Dawn of Acceptance

Acceptance doesn't arrive in the form of a lightning bolt – it seeps in gradually, after exhausting every other avenue first. It's the moment when "what if" turns to "what is," and fantasy no longer fights reality. It isn't the stage where you accept the fact of your situation.

With acceptance, there is sorrow – deep, tremendous sorrow for the relationship you believed in, the future you envisioned, and sometimes even the person you once were. You may grieve your lost innocence regarding people and the world. This sorrow, as painful as it is, is healing and essential.

A lot of survivors grapple with shame at this stage – shame for staying, for not realizing sooner, for letting the abuse go on. However, manipulation is insidious precisely because it's difficult to detect and even more difficult to leave. You have absolutely no reason to be ashamed or embarrassed about what happened to you; you're human. If anything, they should be ashamed and embarrassed by how they treated you. You were manipulated and got sucked into an emotional meat grinder that was originally presented to you as love. Not one bit of this is your fault.

Stage 4: Learning to Trust Your Instincts

Like a sailor learning to navigate by the stars, this stage is one of reclaiming your inner navigational system. You begin to trust your own instincts once again. The need for constant external validation starts to lose its grip.

You may find yourself becoming more self-protective, such as being more cautious about trusting people, or taking longer to get to know people before you let them into your inner circle. Some of these adjustments may feel like walls and not boundaries initially—and that's okay. Learning that it's okay and necessary to have defenses and when to use them is a large part in defending yourself. With time and practice, those walls won't need to be so high, as you'll become more comfortable with the other ways you can keep yourself safe (your intuition, standards, and deal breakers).

Practice is your best teacher. You will continue to encounter toxic people, but you will become aware of their behavior sooner and distance yourself faster. The fantasy of "what could be" with these types of people no longer has the power to overrule your instincts about "what is."

Stage 5: The Great Awakening

This is when the larger pattern comes into focus. That one traumatic relationship that started your healing path might have been the earthquake, but now you're noticing the aftershocks. This is the ripple effect where you begin to see other toxic relationships you were involved in that you didn't recognize before, perhaps stretching back to childhood.

Anger often surfaces here – anger at lost time, at missed opportunities, at the unfairness of it all. This anger, while uncomfortable, is both natural and necessary. It's the fuel that helps forge stronger boundaries and a clearer sense of self.

Support becomes crucial during this phase, and getting support becomes easier as now you're now better equipped to recognize who's emotionally safe to lean on. Your radar for authenticity in others is improving, and while your inner circle might become smaller, it is significantly more nurturing.

Stage 6: Rebuilding From the Ground Up

This is where rebuilding starts. You realize that you are the architect of your life, and that you need to rebuild it from the ground up. You begin to inspect your core beliefs, your boundaries, your standards. You find that some of those qualities you assumed were virtues, such as boundless patience, bottomless forgiveness, continual understanding, and giving without end are unhealthy, and require moderation that can only be found when healthy boundaries are in place.

Your communication with others and with yourself begins to transform in this stage. You are learning how to be assertive without being aggressive, compassionate but not compromising, and more authentic without apologizing.

Your relationships with others start to change as you set new boundaries. Some will resist the changes—and this is normal. Going from weak boundaries to stronger boundaries is confusing for others. Any relationship between two people is like a choreographed dance in that each person has their role and knows their steps.

When we start setting different boundaries, for the others person, this is akin to changing the dance. It's confusing and can be upsetting for them, but they'll learn if they want to keep dancing with you, they'll have to adjust—and many of them will. After all, dancing with you is still enjoyable, even with some different steps. In fact, some of these people might, with time, enjoy the dance *even more* because of these new steps.

While certain people are willing to learn and abide by your boundaries, others will just fall away. This clearing, sometimes painful, creates space for healthier relationships. Additionally, the way you view trust starts to change. *You shift from relying on others not to hurt you, to knowing you'll handle it appropriately if they do.* This shift is subtle but profound – it's the difference between being a leaf in the wind and being the tree itself, firmly rooted regardless of weather.

Stage 7: Emerging Stronger

In this last stage, you find that not only have you recovered – you've changed. Like a phoenix rising from the ashes, you're wiser for having passed through fire. Your relationships are more genuine, your boundaries more effortless, and your sense of self is more solid.

You find yourself naturally gravitating toward healthier people and situations, no longer needing to constantly analyze or second-guess. You take comfort in that you know how to protect yourself.

What once felt like hypervigilance has matured into healthy discernment. You can spot red flags without feeling the need to continually assess or analyze them.

The past loses its power to define you. While you don't forget the lessons, they no longer consume you. Instead, they inform your wisdom and strengthen your compassion for yourself, and for others going through similar transformations.

Navigating Trust After Narcissistic Abuse

My Story

When I was around three or four years old, I took swimming lessons. The last day of class was a graduation of sorts, with all the parents watching. The final challenge was to dive and retrieve a lollipop from beneath the swim instructor's foot.

When my turn came, I dove in and something went wrong: I didn't hold my breath correctly, or I was unprepared to jump. I don't remember exactly what went wrong, only that I inhaled a bunch of water.

I was about two feet from the bottom of the pool and tried to resurface immediately. However, the instructor, seeing or feeling me rise back up, lifted one of his legs and placed it onto of me, basically stomping me down to the bottom of the pool, forcing me to get the lollipop under his other foot.

Being stomped on pushed out whatever air I had in my lungs and water rushed into my nose and mouth. I truly thought I was going to drown. I still remember this event with great clarity, even forty-something years later.

When I finally resurfaced, I remember coughing, burping, and throwing up water, and feeling my sinuses burn from all the chlorine. No one seemed to have seen what happened, and, instead, everyone was clapping. I was confused and traumatized.

Even when I did tell people what happened, they minimized it and told me that I was fine. But I wasn't fine. I'm 47 now, and I've never been able to dive off the side of a pool or even go underwater without holding my nose. I have tried. I still have a very visceral fear of inhaling water.

When I have tried diving, my body won't cooperate, and I end up doing a belly flop of sorts. My hand also instinctively moves to my face and pinches my nose shut. Even a simple bob underwater requires me to pinch my nose.

I've made peace with these limitations. I'm okay with not diving and having to hold my nose when I go underwater. It took me a while to feel safe in a pool after that experience, but with practice and honoring my boundaries—moving at my own pace— eventually, the trauma no longer prevented me from enjoying being in the water completely.

In fact, my favorite thing to do is to spend time on a body of water. I can still swim in a pool, and I love to snorkel in the ocean.

Dating after narcissistic abuse feels remarkably similar. You might want to dive back into the dating "pool," but you're frozen by fear. Your mind knows that the water itself is relatively safe, but it's the other people in the pool that you worry about.

And your body... your body remembers the trauma.

Just as I learned to return to the water on my terms, healing from narcissistic abuse isn't about forcing ourselves to "get over it," "just do it," or "move on" in ways that feel unsafe. It's important that we acknowledge our trauma, respect our boundaries, and find our own way to wade back into the waters—if we decide we even want to try again.

Because it's okay not to date (or be near water) again. Sometimes the trauma is too much, and that's understandable. You don't need to be in a relationship to have a fulfilling life.

If you do want to date again, then it's okay to move at a pace you are comfortable with. It's okay to change your approach in a way that makes you feel safer, stay in the shallow end until you're ready, and most importantly, move at a pace that feels right for you.

Because if you try and throw yourself back in before you are ready, you don't magically overcome your fear, you increase it and can hurt yourself in the process.

If you jump in before you are ready, meaning, without reconnecting with your instincts, boundaries, standards, and deal breakers, then you will let the other person set the pace of how fast things move. When this happens, odds are you will feel like an anxious and unhinged mess the whole time—because you are looking to others to keep you safe, instead of relying on yourself to do that.

What Healing Really Means

The path to healing isn't what most people think it is. It's not about getting over your ex, finding others attractive again, or even wanting to date. These surface-level markers are actually poor indicators of true healing.

True healing is not about becoming who you were before the abuse. This is impossible, as we are changed by each experience we have in life. However, this isn't necessarily a bad thing—or at least it doesn't have to remain being a bad thing. You can squeeze out everything you can from every experience, no matter how painful, and become even "better" and stronger than before.

Healing means developing a new kind of relationship with yourself. In large part, *it means knowing your worth isn't determined by whether someone else sees it*. It means understanding that loneliness, while uncomfortable, isn't an emergency that requires rushing into another relationship.

True healing is about developing the ability to validate yourself. It's reaching a place where you can say, "This doesn't feel right to me," and standing firm in that knowledge even if everyone around you disagrees. It's about trusting yourself enough to walk away from something that feels wrong, even if you can't fully articulate why.

Most importantly, healing means understanding that a healthy relationship isn't built on chemistry alone, but on consistent respectful behavior, clear communication, and compatibility. It's about recognizing that love shouldn't cost you your peace, your friendships, or your sense of self.

The Truth About Trust: Debunking the Myths

Contrary to popular belief, being cautious about trust after abuse isn't a sign of damage – it's a sign of wisdom. The myth that trust should be automatic and freely given is particularly dangerous. Trust isn't a gift to be handed out indiscriminately; it's something that is earned through consistent, reliable behavior over time. Your hesitation to trust immediately isn't a problem ; it's your internal security system working precisely as it should. Additionally, trust exists on a spectrum. You don't have to either fully trust or completely distrust someone. It's healthy to trust different people with different things, to different degrees, based on their proven reliability in specific areas.

The Elements of Healthy Trust

Think of trust like building a house. You wouldn't start with the roof – you'd begin with a solid foundation. In relationships, this means understanding that consistent actions, not words, are the building blocks of trust. Promises and grand gestures mean nothing without consistent, reliable behavior to back them up.

Each healthy boundary you set becomes a load-bearing wall in this new structure. These aren't barriers to intimacy; they're the framework that makes genuine closeness possible. When someone respects your boundaries consistently, they're helping to create a space where trust can safely grow.

The goal isn't to learn to trust *everyone* again. The goal is to trust yourself so completely that you can allow *certain people* to earn their way into your life at a pace that feels safe for you. Your healing journey hasn't made you less capable of love – it's made you *more* capable of loving wisely, authentically, and safely.

Trust isn't about being perfect or finding someone who never makes mistakes. It's about finding someone who owns their mistakes, makes genuine efforts to repair damage, and shows through consistent behavior that they're worthy of increasing levels of trust. It also means that whatever information you share about yourself is handled in an appropriate way. Meaning, they aren't gossiping about you to others or using it against you when they get upset.

Also, appropriate trust is situational. You might trust someone completely in a professional context while maintaining healthy reservations about emotional intimacy. This kind of discernment isn't "trust issues;" it's emotional intelligence in action.

These are the elements needed to develop well-placed trust. When we have a healthy trust in others and in ourselves, we realize that love doesn't require us to abandon our boundaries, ignore our instincts, or rush past our comfort zones. Once you learn to trust your reality as well as yourself to honor those perceptions, you're not just surviving anymore; you're learning to thrive on your own terms.

Healthy vs. Unhealthy Relationships

Learning to love or trust after being hurt by a narcissist isn't easy, and it takes time. Many times, a person tries to find a "good" partner, thinking that a good person treats them well. And on the surface, this line of thinking makes sense. However, finding a "good" partner is only one aspect of what makes for a healthy relationship.

A healthy relationship is something that grows moment-by-moment between two people. It's essential to separate a "good man" (or woman) from a "healthy relationship" because a person can be good in all the ways that you list, but they will still have moments where they cross your boundaries. And when this happens, the relationship becomes unstable—much like a spinning top that is slightly bumped. At first, the wobble is small, almost imperceptible. However, if left unaddressed, the spinning top will topple over. If you want to keep your relationship spinning, you need to know how to correct the wobble.

However, before I get into the elements of a healthy relationship, I feel it's important to acknowledge that the term "healthy relationship" is often misunderstood. This leads people to feel defensive or to dismiss the concept altogether, thinking that a "healthy relationship" is an idealized concept that doesn't exist in real life. If this is you, try instead substituting the word "healthy" with the words "nourishing" or "functional." Doing so can help you to see the concept more clearly.

A healthy relationship is similar to a healthy plant. We can tell when a plant is healthy because it has a good root base, it's growing, periodically has new blooms, and is thriving where it is. An unhealthy plant has any number of issues going on that are preventing it from growing. There might be moldy soil, the soil is lacking in nutrients, the pot is too big or too small, the roots are rotting, the leaves are turning yellow or developing spots, or the plant is wilting due to too much or too little sun or water.

To avoid having an unhealthy plant, we need to know the requirements necessary for it to be healthy. A plant has five main requirements for growth: a certain amount of light, the appropriate-sized pot, the right amount of water, the soil changed regularly, and the maintenance of a certain temperature.

If just one of the five elements is missing, there is an imbalance and the plant struggles to survive. In this way, a relationship also has specific, non-negotiable criteria essential for growth.

Some of those criteria are: open, honest, sincere, and solutions-oriented communication, accountability, respect, good chemistry (meaning, you actually like the person you are in love with), and compatibility, meaning, the desire to move through life in the same direction.

Relationships, just like plants, are limited by toxic elements. For example, just as no healthy plant could survive being watered with gasoline, no otherwise healthy relationship can thrive with pathological lying. In other words, a relationship can only be as healthy as the unhealthiest behavior in it.

In short, a functional relationship is one that is not only healthy but also thriving. Whereas a dysfunctional relationship is one that isn't healthy; it's struggling, dying, or even dead—but you are in denial and don't want to "bury" it, in case it magically comes back to life.

People often think of dysfunctional relationships only in the context of extreme, deal breaker behavior, such as addiction, physical abuse, or adultery. When, in reality, many less extreme factors can lead to a relationship not working (becoming dysfunctional). Sometimes what makes a relationship dysfunctional isn't even something that's necessarily problematic with the other person—it's only problematic for you. For example, they want children, and you don't. Or, your sex drives don't align, or, perhaps, you each grow and change in different directions and now your lives together are no longer as satisfying as they once were and both of you feel lonely in this relationship.

When a relationship is healthy, the dynamics run smoothly because:

- Both people feel they are being true to themselves or, being their "authentic selves."

- Both people recognize that conflict arises from time-to-time in a healthy relationship, and work to address it.

- Both people realize that being passive, passive-aggressive, or aggressive doesn't solve anything, and doesn't help the relationship to grow.

- Both people use assertive communication the vast majority of the time. Meaning, they are open, honest, sincere, and solutions-oriented. While doing so can be painful at times, both know that in the end, they will become closer because of it.

- Each partner maintains healthy boundaries and is responsible for their feelings. Meaning, they aren't blaming the other for making them feel a certain way. (No one can make us feel a certain way. They might try to guilt trip you, for example, but their actions are only successful if we allow them to be.)

- Each partner is responsible for their self-esteem. Each person's self-esteem comes from within; they don't continually look to the other to make them feel loved or good about themselves.

- Both people feel safe, secure, validated, respected, and appreciated, because they have proven themselves to be a safe person.

- Anxiety and resentment about the relationship or towards each other are minimal or non-existent.

- Both partners are comfortable sharing their thoughts, feelings, wants, and needs with each other. Even where there is disagreement, respect is still present.

For a dynamic to be healthy, these elements must be true for *both* partners.

Remember, a healthy relationship isn't about perfection – it's about growth, mutual respect, and the willingness of both partners to work through challenges constructively. Just as a gardener doesn't expect their plants to bloom perfectly every day, partners in a healthy relationship understand there will be seasons of growth and seasons of stagnation or even regression.

What matters most is having the foundational elements in place: open communication, emotional safety, mutual respect, and connection. When these core elements are present, the relationship can weather difficulties and emerge stronger, creating a sustainable dynamic where both partners can flourish.

Conclusion: The Next Chapter in Your Life

You are the author of your life story, and, as with any good story, it's not just what happens, it's what the main character (you) chooses to do with what happens, and who they become because of it. There is a lot of energy in hurt and anger, and for this reason, I encourage you not to waste it. Give your pain a positive purpose. Use the energy in these feelings as fuel to use towards your highest and greatest good. You can heal from this, and you can move forward into living a good life.

The journey doesn't end here. Each day brings new opportunities to practice these skills, to deepen your self-trust, and to choose what truly nourishes your soul. But now you're navigating from a place of power rather than fear. You're not just surviving anymore; you're consciously thriving. Every step forward, no matter how small, is a victory. When you do this, you are creating a life reflecting your truest, strongest self. And that's something no one can ever take away from you.

About the Author

Dana Morningstar is a Licensed Professional Counselor (LPC) and dedicates her practice to guiding survivors through healing from abuse. Her work centers on building awareness and helping survivors rebuild their lives with renewed confidence and strength. Through her comprehensive approach, she empowers survivors to reclaim their power, establish healthy boundaries, and rediscover their authentic selves.

As the founder of "Thrive After Abuse," Dana reaches survivors through multiple channels, including her written work, website, podcast, and YouTube channel. She also facilitates several online support groups, creating safe spaces for healing and connection. In her free time, Dana finds peace and renewal in aerial yoga, gardening, listening to audiobooks, and spending time on the nearest body of water.

To learn more, visit: www.thriveafterabuse.com

www.ingramcontent.com/pod-product-compliance
Lightning Source LLC
Chambersburg PA
CBHW061135120626
46546CB00005B/1794